EARLY AVIATION AT FARNBOROUGH

Volume I. Balloons, Kites, and Airships

Early Aviation at Farnborough

The History of the Royal Aircraft Establishment

VOLUME I · BALLOONS, KITES, AND AIRSHIPS

Percy B. Walker

C.B.E., M.A., Ph.D., F.R.Ae.S.

Former Head of the Aircraft Structures Department
and Special Consultant to the Director of the
Royal Aircraft Establishment

Foreword by Lord Kings Norton

MACDONALD · LONDON

First published in 1971 by
Macdonald & Co. (Publishers) Ltd.
St Giles House, 49 Poland St,
London W1

Made and printed in Great Britain
by Hazell Watson & Viney Ltd, Aylesbury, Bucks

SBN 356 03520 4

Contents

Contents

Contents

List of Illustrations

Acknowledgements for Illustrations

I am grateful to the following for providing material for the illustrations: Admiralty Library; Air Ministry Library; *Automotor Journal*; Mr L. Cody; the late Miss C. T. Copland; *The Graphic*; the late Mrs Ursula Goold; *Illustrated London News;* May's Collection; *Navy and Army Illustrated*; Mrs Edith Previté; The Public Record Office; Royal Aeronautical Society; Royal Aircraft Establishment; Royal Engineer Committee; *Royal Engineers Journal*; School of Military Engineering, Chatham; Science Museum, South Kensington; *The Sphere*; Sir Gerald Templer; *Transvaal War Album*; War Office Library; The Rt. Hon. Lord Ventry.

Foreword *by Lord Kings Norton*

I have known the author of this book for forty-four years and the great establishment about which he writes for forty-one. The former has the qualities of a first-class historian, his subject the characteristics of a first-class theme. It is a privilege to write a few words about each of them.

In 1926, when I was one of the youthful team* calculating the external loads of the airship *R-101* and the stresses in its novel structure, we were joined for a short time† at Cardington by a burly and brilliant Cambridge graduate. He had a gigantic fountain pen and enormous handwriting and an intellectual sturdiness which matched them. The first two have diminished with the years, but the intellectual force has not: the grasp of essentials and the passion for clarity and accuracy which characterized Dr Walker's work in those distant days are manifest in this book now. I felt in reading it what I felt in 1926 – the utter dependableness of the man. Where admiration and criticism are expressed in the following pages I feel that they are just – not exaggerated by partisanship nor distorted by prejudice.

This is the kind of dispassionateness which we all hope for in historians but which, when we get it, is often dull. But enthusiasm for his subject, and the deep insight which comes from having the analytical mind of a scientist as well as the vision of an historian, ensure that Dr Walker is never dull.

Certainly, Farnborough is an inspiring theme. The story of the growth of a great organization is always absorbing, but when that growth is contemporaneous with the entire growth of modern aviation and is an important part of it, the attractiveness of its story is irresistible to anyone interested in the development of flight.

Farnborough is one of the great aeronautical establishments of the world.

* Mr T. S. D. Collins, Mr (now Sir John) Baker, Miss Hilda Lyon and Dr Roxbee Cox (myself).
† We should like to have kept him, but he had to return to Cambridge to take up the Busk Aeronautical Research Studentship which he had been awarded during his sojourn with us.

Perhaps those of us who know it and love it may be forgiven for thinking it the greatest. It has nurtured great aeronautical scientists, theoreticians and experimenters. At one time it produced great aircraft designers who left it to succeed in the aircraft industry. Great names punctuate its history. It has had the good fortune to be guided by a series of outstanding directors, starting with the great Colonel Templer who is the hero of the early part of this history. For the author of this book, and for me, it was and is a place for research and development in the problems of aeroplanes. But this first volume of Dr Walker's history is not about them. It is about balloons and kites and airships – all Farnborough activities which ended long ago but which now are fortunately and faithfully recorded. To read about Farnborough's early aeroplanes we shall have to wait for Volume II.

The research which has gone into the making of this book is impressive. None of us, even those with an interest in Farnborough's past, knew more than a very little of the fascinating story which Dr Walker tells. Its heroes are Colonel Templer, Colonel Capper and Mr Cody, fascinating and gifted people. At the end of the book other giants appear briefly on the stage – O'Gorman, Green and de Havilland.

It is sad that Templer never received the honour that was clearly his due. Neither, for that matter, did O'Gorman or Green, as I am sure we shall decide when the epic story is complete. This is too often the fate of people who are ahead of contemporary values. Perhaps poor Cody would have won formal recognition if he had lived longer. He is the most extraordinary of them all. This history shows how talented this illiterate man was, and – news I think to most of us – what a major contribution he made in the lighter-than-air field as well as in the heavier-than-air field on which his fame rests.

I am proud to think that I knew some of the people in this book – McWade who was with us at the Royal Airship Works, Cardington; Vivian Cody whom I knew at the R.A.E. in the early thirties when he was still making kites, I think for use by submarines; and Mr Crosson, whose testimony has helped Dr Walker in his researches. And I am privileged to have known too those great men O'Gorman and Green, whose work shines out in the Farnborough story.

Here is a record of happenings in another age, when in the golden Edwardian afternoon balloons and kites and airships enhanced the Farnborough scene as superbly as have the Concorde and the Harrier – and, like the latter, demonstrated the merits of vertical take-off.

Preface

When Professor James Lighthill F.R.S., then the Director, first suggested that I should write a history of the Royal Aircraft Establishment I never dreamt that some seven years must elapse before the first volume could be completed. The task seemed easy and straightforward, but I was soon disillusioned. A preliminary review of published information convinced me that the history of early aviation at Farnborough had been gravely distorted and was rapidly degenerating into myth and legend. Here, however, was a challenge – to produce a story with its primary structure created entirely from authentic documents and contemporary accounts.

The present volume is the first product of five years research involving much travel, interviews with many people, and the reading of thousands of documents. It has been suggested that some account of the investigation should also be recorded as distinct from the history itself, and so I have included a description of my main sources in the Introduction.

It should also be recorded that this work would have been impossible without the enthusiastic help of many people. I am indeed most grateful to those who have given direct testimony in interviews and correspondence, and to those who have generously placed at my disposal their private store of ancient relics, documents and photographs. I am grateful also to many libraries and museums throughout Britain who have helped in various ways, and would especially like to thank the members of the staffs of the following: the Library and Museum of the Royal Engineers at Chatham; the old War Office Library, now in the Ministry of Defence; the Public Record Office in London; the Science Museum in South Kensington; and the Library of the Royal Aeronautical Society. Lastly, for the Royal Aircraft Establishment itself, I must record an immeasurable debt to my friends in the R.A.E. Library and equally to my friends in the Printing and Photographic Department.

Special thanks are due to four people who have contributed directly to my researches. Mr C. H. Gibbs-Smith, the aviation historian, has not only provided much authentic information but has painstakingly read the original manuscript. Mr D. W. King, Chief Librarian to the Ministry of Defence, has been a continuous source of reference on the British Army in general as well as upon the special responsibilities of the Royal Engineers. Mr L. G. Seed, of the Public Record Office, has given invaluable help in the search for elusive but vital documents. Finally, I am happy to include Mr A. T. E. Bray, of the R.A.E., who has generously provided me with some useful historic material from his own researches.

Introduction

In a geographical sense, Farnborough is a small town in Hampshire, just outside Surrey and close to the border of Berkshire. It has become known the world over, however, through having given a name and a home to the Royal Aircraft Establishment, or the R.A.E., as it is more frequently called. Many people now speak of Farnborough when they refer to the R.A.E., so closely has the town become identified with the Establishment.

The Royal Aircraft Establishment is essentially a place for research and experiment, and primarily dedicated to aviation. But in the study of flight so many branches of science and technology are called upon that the Establishment has become a huge scientific laboratory that is almost unique in its breadth of interest.*

There are probably few places in Britain that have been so suitable for aeronautical experiments as Farnborough. The present R.A.E. (excluding its many outstations in different parts of Britain) now covers about eleven hundred acres of mostly level ground, which includes the famous Laffan's Plain. Like most nationally-controlled establishments in the leading countries of the world, the R.A.E. was at one time a predominantly military organization. The military background must not be given undue emphasis, however, lest we should fail to do justice to the R.A.E.'s early contributions to the fundamentals of flight, and fail to recognize its tremendous potential as a research organization which has existed from the earliest times.

Farnborough's place in aviation was aptly expressed by the late Air Chief Marshal Sir Philip Joubert when he referred to Farnborough as 'the cradle of British aviation'. He had in mind, no doubt, the Royal Air Force as much as the Royal Aircraft Establishment. Both share a common ancestry and owe

* The Establishment became part of the newly formed Ministry of Aviation Supply on 20 October 1970. In the past it has been controlled by a long chain of Government Departments: the War Department; Air Ministry; Ministry of Aircraft Production; Ministry of Supply; Ministry of Aviation and Ministry of Technology.

their origin to the Royal Engineers, with ballooning associations going back not only to Farnborough, but to Aldershot, Chatham and Woolwich, and having a long history of military balloon operations, including especially those of the South African War. Although Farnborough once housed the Headquarters of the Royal Flying Corps, however, its direct descendant, the Royal Air Force, has long since been dispersed over Britain. The Royal Aircraft Establishment now monopolizes Farnborough, and is essentially a civilian organization, though there are always to be seen members of the three fighting Services working alongside the scientists and engineers.

The present volume of history describes events at Farnborough in the Establishment's most formative years – roughly the first decade of the present century. Although the R.A.E. was then known as the Balloon Factory, its responsibilities covered design, experiment and research, as well as manufacture. Furthermore, as is well-known, its work was not long restricted to balloons but came to comprehend also man-lifting kites, airships and aeroplanes.*

Also at Farnborough was the body of Royal Engineers that came to be known successively as the 'Balloon Sections', the 'Balloon Companies', and then the 'Balloon School'. This essentially military organization was mainly responsible for operational flying, both for training and for taking part in Army manoeuvres. Historians of the Royal Air Force may therefore rightly claim the Balloon School as its ancestor. For the period of Farnborough history here under consideration, however, the Balloon School and the Balloon Factory have in certain matters to be treated as one. Irrespective of whether they were under separate leaders or under a single leader, the two organizations worked together and both were involved in research and experiment. The Balloon School, in fact, undertook duties not dissimilar to those performed today by the Experimental Flying Department; and this Department, although operated by Service flying personnel under command of a Serving Officer, is an integral part of the R.A.E. itself.

It was not until about the year 1905 that the Balloon Factory came to make the present Farnborough site its headquarters; and the Balloon School joined them there at about the same time. Both had previously been stationed at or near Balloon Square, which was situated inside the Royal Engineers Establishment at Aldershot, south of the Basingstoke Canal.

The story of Farnborough as told here, however, begins in 1899 when Britain went to war in South Africa. It was largely the success of balloons in South Africa that made the British Government begin to accept the captive observation balloon as an essential piece of military equipment. Thus it came

* The Balloon Factory's early work on aeroplanes is reserved for Volume II of this History.

about that, when the active phase of the war was over, the decision was made to expand Britain's interests in military ballooning in all its aspects. In particular, plans were made for creating an entirely new factory and experimental station to be erected at Farnborough, the forerunner of the R.A.E. we know today.

As things turned out, of course, there was not much of a future for balloons for military use. From the broader standpoint of history, however, this was a matter of no great moment: balloons were merely the first step into the wider and ever-expanding realm of aviation. Balloons got men up into the air, and familiar with the notion of looking down upon the men below. Furthermore, the whole organization for design, construction and operation of balloons moved smoothly onwards to comprehend first man-lifting kites, then airships, and finally aeroplanes.

In some ways the most striking feature of this first decade of the new aviation is the variety of aerial machines that existed more or less simultaneously and in competition with each other. At the beginning of this century the observation balloon had pride of place in the military world, being virtually without any realistic competitor. The practical man-lifting kite, on the other hand, was born, reached maturity, and virtually died – all within the one decade. In this same period the airship, which at the beginning was no more than an ingenious toy, came to be regarded as the main aerial weapon of the future; but, as the decade ended, the aeroplane was coming along fast and eventually destined to surpass them all.

Farnborough was, of course, involved in all this, and in many ways the early history at Farnborough is a typical slice of world history in aviation. It is salutory to remember, however, that, while Britain led the world in observation balloons and man-lifting kites, in the realm of airships and aeroplanes she held no such place in the period covered by this volume. The early history of Farnborough is not all pleasant reading: mechanical ingenuity and creative thought were to a great extent frustrated by political considerations; by a reluctance to accept the changes which aerial inventions were bound to impose; and, above all, by a national policy of stringent economy for anything suggestive of preparation for a possible war. In actual fact it took a war, and one infinitely more serious than that in South Africa, namely, the Great War of 1914–18, to bring Britain back into line with the leading nations in world aviation, and even to surpass them.

From the historical point of view, the great problem has been to discover precisely what happened at Farnborough and Aldershot in these early years. Everything possible seems to have operated against obtaining the full story. To begin with, it is unlikely that any person directly concerned at the time really understood the situation; could foresee the future of aerial inventions, or the political reactions of the men in control. In the ordinary way we should in such circumstances collect together all the relevant documents and judge the situation with the superior vision that hindsight gives us; but it is here that the difficulty arises. In the first place, there is firm evidence that many of the more important technical decisions were never properly recorded, and it is equally certain that instructions were rarely committed to paper whenever they could easily be passed on by word of mouth. In the second place, there are indications that a large proportion of the documents that did once exist have been destroyed, long before their historical interest was appreciated. Finally, those documents that remain are not at all easy to locate, are often virtually inaccessible, and in not a few cases are not readily identifiable for what they are, so that discovery is often accidental.

In what now follows, a brief review is given of some of the main sources of information that have been used in compiling the present history. No single source has anything approaching completeness in itself. Taken together, how-ever, the various sources equal much more than is obtained by mere addition; for, as a general rule, they fit each other like pieces of an intricate jigsaw puzzle and lead, there is every reason to believe, to something very near the truth.

Surprisingly, the most likely source of original information – the R.A.E. it-self – is the most disappointing. In 1919, that is just after the end of the 1914–18 war, a large mass of original correspondence and other documents was sent to the historical section of the recently formed Air Ministry. So far as is known the documents were never returned, and most of them are believed to have been destroyed.

R.A.E.'s photographic records of early work at Farnborough seem to have met with a similar fate, though in a different way. There is evidence that in 1942, or thereabouts, all R.A.E.'s historic negatives, which in those days were made of glass, were laid out on the tarmac and a steam-roller run over them. It was probably not long after this that the cross marking the place where Cody struck the ground, when he fell to his death in 1913, was plough-ed up and pulverized so that all trace was lost. These destructive tendencies were, perhaps, a normal symptom during the Second World War of 1939–45, when concern with the present and the future suppressed all thoughts of the past.

In the circumstances it is appropriate to mention that in recent years the R.A.E. has taken great care of its surviving historic relics. Furthermore, a certain amount of new historical material has been collected in the last twen-ty years or so and carefully preserved. Most of it relates to events happening

4

from 1910 onwards, however, and so is no great help for the period under consideration, but there is at least one important exception in the *May's Collection* of photographic negatives.

The firm of William May & Co. Ltd, photographers and printers of Aldershot, acquired in the early years of aviation at Farnborough over five hundred photographic negatives covering the Balloon Factory's aeronautical activities for a period extending roughly from 1906 to 1912. When the firm relinquished its photographic work in 1946 the whole collection was sent to R.A.E., where it has been preserved.* In themselves the photographs have only limited value since most of them have neither a date nor a title for proper identification. Used in conjunction with information from other sources, however, several of them have a unique value historically; and in the course of the last few years I have been able to identify practically all the important ones.

A rather different story is to be told about the Library and Museum of the Corps of Royal Engineers at Chatham, which are closely associated with the School of Military Engineering. From the year 1882 until the move to Aldershot in 1891–2, Chatham was the home of military ballooning in Britain; and the Library and Museum have maintained an interest in aeronautics up to the time (1912) when the Royal Flying Corps was formed and the Royal Engineers ceased to have control of military aeronautics. Not being strictly an official body, the library has few original items of correspondence, but it has a unique collection of articles and pictures dealing with contemporary aeronautics that appeared in the better quality news-magazines of the early years. In addition there are complete series of copies of the *Royal Engineers Journal* and of the *Professional Papers of the Royal Engineers*. All the articles and papers dealing with early aeronautics were systematically listed and indexed; and the entire collection was placed at my disposal for the present history.

A more direct and official source of documentary information was found in four boxes of ancient War Office files that I was allowed to examine in the old War Office Library, now part of the Ministry of Defence. In these boxes were forty-two files of early correspondence and internal minutes; and, despite difficulties in deciphering handwriting in places where the typewriter had not been used, I perused well over a thousand foolscap pages.

An interesting feature of these files is that in the main they are financial, that is to say they deal primarily with expenditure. This is the reason why

* The story so far as R.A.E.'s records go is little more than legend; but I have been able to obtain factual information from Mr S. H. May, the only surviving brother of the original William of William May & Co. Ltd.

they have survived: papers of scientific or wider historical interest may pass on to the incinerator, but in Britain finance is near to being sacred! Financial records were only destroyed with the greatest diffidence since at any time for years afterwards a financial query might be raised. Thus several files and other records dealing with financial transactions often survived long enough to become recognizable as historic relics and worth preserving indefinitely.

Financial records have the great merit of accuracy and precision. Accurate accounting, of course, is to be expected but this is unimportant historically compared with the fact that it is usually accompanied by equal precision in the recording of dates – a vital consideration in any kind of historical investigation. Furthermore, whenever money was spent in any quantity a case had to be made, and this usually provides a fund of information that may not be obtainable from any other source. A good example of this is found in the case of Colonel Templer. For nearly thirty years he reigned as virtual king of military ballooning; then, towards the end, arguments arose about his pay, the possibility of a special award, his retirement, and his pension. The records of these arguments provide more information about Templer and his work than all the other surviving documents put together.

Genuine history also got entangled at times with finance in another rather different way. A file would be opened for some technical project, and the trend of discussion later take a financial turn, thereby leading eventually to the preservation of the whole file. It is ironical, for example, that the official account of the first aeroplane flight in Britain, by S. F. Cody in October 1908, would probably not have been preserved if the file had not later dealt with Cody's discharge from the Service and the financial conditions laid down for lending him an engine.

Apart from the four boxes already mentioned, the old War Office Library proved to be a mine of information on official aeronautical affairs, much of it preserved in a tidy and printed form. It is not practicable to go into details about the multiplicity of references that have been made; but one particular source requires special mention. This is the long series of printed volumes of *Extracts from the Proceedings of the Royal Engineer Committee*, which give the official account of much that happened at the Balloon Factory up to the year 1909.

From the Army we pass naturally to the Navy. As is to be expected, there is in the Admiralty's records only a limited amount of material dealing with the early period under consideration. There is, however, the most complete account of man-lifting kites in existence. How this came about has a simple explanation: on two separate occasions, namely in 1903 and 1908, the Admiralty decided to investigate man-lifting kites for Naval use. In the event they decided against them, but the evidence of genuine trials was retained as a record. The two or three hundred pages are somewhat untidy and disarranged, but the account they give is sound and comprehensive, and it is accompanied by a unique collection of photographs. The outcome of examination of these Naval records is a much clearer understanding of what the kites were like and how they were operated.

The last official source for consideration is the Public Record Office in London. The War Office and Admiralty records already mentioned are now held there, but there is also a considerable amount of miscellaneous aeronautical material, some of it properly titled and some of it not, some of it valuable and some of it almost worthless. No criticism of the staff is here implied: the Public Record Office have inherited all kinds of papers and there are economic limitations to the amount of sorting and editing that can be done. For the purpose of this History, however, it is desirable to record that with generous help from the staff I have examined all the documents that seemed likely to be of interest; and from my notes these are estimated to comprise about fifty files.

Passing out of official circles, there is next to be considered the daily newspapers and the illustrated news magazines. It is perhaps not generally recognized how valuable this source of information can be. The regular reporting of events provides something unobtainable in any other way. Dates are automatically precise and the reaction to the news is usually spontaneous. For the years under consideration, moreover, there is evidence of careful and accurate reporting in the great majority of cases. Some of the magazines, such as the *Illustrated London News* and the now defunct *Navy and Army Illustrated* have also provided some remarkable photographs and original drawings.

The technical press naturally falls into a somewhat different category, and usually has some additional advantages. One of the most useful publications has been the *Automotor Journal*. As its name implies, it was intended primarily for motorists; and by modern standards it had great antiquity, having started life in the previous century. It seems, however, to have shown interest in aeronautics from its inception; and a weekly review of aeronautics became a regular feature. Most important from the standpoint of the present History is the constant watch that was kept on what was happening at Farnborough, and which was duly reported upon.

The main technical periodicals in Britain that were exclusively aeronautical did not, unfortunately, begin publication until rather late in the period under consideration. Thus *Aeronautics* first came out in December 1907 and *The Aero* in May 1909. There were also, of course, technical publications abroad, such as *l'Aérophile* in France; and papers in the United States, such as *Aeronautics* (which should not be confused with the British publication of the same name). These provided aeronautical news of great interest but, in general, can scarcely be regarded as primary sources for local news of Farnborough.

The *Aeronautical Journal*, the official organ of the Aeronautical Society of Great Britain, tends to stand on its own as a source of information for the present history, and it was in circulation throughout the entire period under consideration. Apart from some valuable early papers and articles on kites, its main contribution to the Farnborough story derives from the reports of lectures and extempore speeches by the three main protagonists of the Balloon Factory – Colonel Templer, Colonel Capper and S. F. Cody; all of whom were members of the Society. With the Journal there is naturally to be associated the Society itself (now the *Royal* Aeronautical Society) as a source of information; and from its archives some further useful historical material has been obtained.

There remains for consideration the direct testimony of those who lived in those early days and acquired first-hand knowledge of what went on at Farnborough and Aldershot. Some thirty or forty people have been interviewed in person, and several others have entered into correspondence with me. It is remarkable how many people remember Cody, who was killed in 1913; but the number who remember events before 1910 is limited, and some have died since I first consulted them about writing this book.

It is in some ways regrettable that the most striking impression from all this interviewing is how fallible the human memory is when unassisted by original notes and documents. Events seem to re-arrange themselves in order of time and sometimes two or more events, by a kind of mental magic, coalesce into a single one. Not infrequently, moreover, a person interviewed has got a fact completely wrong. A good example of this immediately comes to mind. As is well known, S. F. Cody was killed in 1913 while flying his *biplane*, yet two witnesses, entirely unknown to each other, testified that he was killed in his *monoplane*. The two men were exceptionally good witnesses as a general rule, of high intelligence and integrity, and extremely cautious in giving their testimony in their desire not to mislead. Both had expert knowledge of aviation, moreover, and were of reasonably mature age at the relevant time, and knew Cody well. Yet despite all these things they were convinced that Cody met his death in the monoplane. In actual fact there was an element of underlying truth in their story, though grotesquely distorted. Cody did wreck his monoplane – in 1912, by collision with a cow on Cove Common. The accident, moreover, was indeed a fatal one, but it was the cow that was killed, not Cody!

8

In the present history, the testimony of people relying entirely on memory is rarely if ever used without certain and independent confirmation. This does not mean that direct testimony is useless: often the truth can be brought out in discussion or by what some might describe in stronger terms as cross-examination. Conflict of testimony is always a challenge, moreover, and it is nearly always worthwhile to find out the origin of a mistaken fact. Pure invention, though not unknown, is rare; and there is nearly always an explanation.

So far as the present History is concerned, there is one special aspect of the direct testimony that needs to be mentioned. Many of the witnesses have given not only of their memories but also of their treasured relics and mementoes – newspaper cuttings, letters, post-cards, personal notes, all kinds of odds-and-ends and, perhaps most important of all, photographs. Historic material has been showered upon me with a generosity rivalled only by a surprising enthusiasm for aviation history. Many of these contributors think that some wonderful things happened in Farnborough and Aldershot in the early pioneering days, and they want the world to know about them.

Most of this kind of evidence is priceless in the preparation of a history. A few items, of course, are mere relics having only sentimental value, but they are appreciated by me none the less. I have, for example, a piece of goldbeater's skin from the envelope of a balloon, and the keys of the first airship shed. But my most treasured possession is a steel spanner, five-eighths inch Whitworth at one end, and half inch at the other; and on it is engraved the legend: 'STOLEN FROM S. F. CODY'.

1 The War in South Africa 1899-1902

1   British military ballooning in 1899

When war broke out in South Africa in October 1899, Lieutenant-Colonel James Lethbridge Brooke Templer was Superintendent of Her Majesty's Balloon Factory at Aldershot.* He had officially held this post since his formal appointment in 1887 at a salary of £700 per annum, but for all practical purposes he had been head of the Balloon Factory, with various titles, for over twenty years: since 1878 in fact. He had also been effectively, over this same period, the Chief Instructor in ballooning to the Royal Engineers, and the Chief Designer of army balloons. The various titles that were used over the years tend to be confusing, but he can certainly be described as the driving-force behind military ballooning in Britain and the inspiration of all the more enterprising people concerned with it.

The year 1878 is given as the beginning of his official career because in that year the Government allocated £150 for Captain Templer, as he was then, to make the first British military balloon, appropriately named the *Pioneer*. Perhaps even more significant was the official undertaking to pay him ten shillings per day (but only on flying days) for training Royal Engineer officers in ballooning. Templer was at that time a skilled balloonist, and one of the conditions was that he should use his own private balloon *Crusader* for training the engineers until *Pioneer* was completed.

At the beginning of the South African War neither Templer nor anyone else could have foreseen that the success of balloons in that war would revolution-

* See the contemporary portrait at Fig. 1.

10

ize military ballooning in Britain. When the war was ended, public opinion, impressed by this one of the few bright spots in a dismal and disappointing expedition, demanded a re-appraisal of military ballooning. As will be seen, this led to an expansion of all aspects of balloon work in the military field, and to the abandonment of the cramped quarters at Aldershot for the more open terrain at Farnborough.

It is now seen to be ironical that, while so much thought was being given to balloons, they were doomed to extinction as primary weapons; and when the Balloon Factory did reach Farnborough about the year 1905 they were already on the way out to give place to airships, which in turn were to give place to aeroplanes. This does not seem to have dismayed the men of the Factory, however, for Templer had created a new way of life in scientific engineering. Mechanics and fitters, woodworkers and smiths, as well as designers and scientists, had all been brought up to expect impossible demands from their revered leader. Novelty and originalty were the expected and the normal. In design, construction, research and experiment, therefore, the eventual change-over from balloons to airships was to be accomplished without any noticeable disturbance. This versatility in skills and flexibility in outlook are the two characteristics of which the R.A.E. is still proud today.

It is in some ways unfortunate that so many derogatory things have been written about early British military aviation. In order to understand the early history as here presented it is necessary to recognize and appreciate that in the critical year of 1899 the balloon contingent of the British Army was unequalled anywhere in the world. It would be wrong to imagine, of course, that the French and the Germans were inferior in *all* respects. They may, for example, have been more scientific in their methods, though this was not necessarily so. Both countries, however, were ahead in their work on airships, although many years were to elapse before airships became of any use at all.

The essential thing is that, on the realistic basis of potential efficiency in war, Britain was supreme in the field of captive balloons for reconnaissance and observation. The British organization was compact and ship-shape, and essentially practical in a typically British way, and above all it was ready for action at a moment's notice. There was, moreover, an understanding, even comradeship, between those who made the balloons and those who flew them, of a kind unlikely to be found under the more inflexible military systems on the European continent.

This general state of efficiency, achieved at small cost to the nation, was largely attributable to the genius of Templer and the ability of two or three Royal Engineer officers who from time to time served with him – whether over him or under him did not seem to matter at all, such was the enthusiasm generated for ballooning.

Success would hardly have been attainable to anything like the same degree, however, had it not been for a curious quirk in the administrative system, coupled with the astuteness of the Royal Engineers in playing it advantageously. Templer never was a Royal Engineer, but a member of the militia: specifically, the King's Royal Rifles. As a militia-man, therefore, he could on occasion be treated as a civilian. His salary, for example, was a matter for negotiation, as also was any specific appointment. He could not be pushed around at the whim of the War Office, or moved somewhere else in the real or supposed interests of his career like a professional soldier. Thus, while Royal Engineer officers came and went at intervals, he always remained to maintain continuity and to gain more and more experience as the years went by.

On the other hand, Templer could become a true soldier when the situation demanded, and on one occasion he actually commanded a combat unit, though this was exceptional. On formal parades he would appear as a soldier in uniform, and the general public did not know the difference. At such times he was no obvious civilian dressed up for the day, but a magnificent figure dominating all around him.

Another important contribution to Britain's status in military ballooning was some actual experience in real military operations. A British expeditionary force was sent to Egypt in 1882. In this case the balloon unit was never engaged in combat but a valuable lesson was learned: there was delay in getting the men and balloons out there owing to indecision at home, and the war was over before they arrived. Subsequent study of the military action that had taken place, however, indicated that balloons would have been of greatest value in revealing hidden strength in the enemy's preparations, which could easily have been seen from the air.

There appears to have been no delay in the next expedition, when a fighting force was sent to Bechuanaland in 1884. A balloon detachment was dispatched as quickly as possible to Mafeking, via Cape Town, and stayed in Bechuanaland until well into 1885. The amount of actual fighting, however, seems to have been small, but it has been seriously suggested that the mere sight of the balloon was sufficient to ensure peace.

Meanwhile much more serious events were happening in the Sudan. On 26 January 1885, General Gordon was killed at Khartoum, and another expeditionary force had to be sent to the Sudan. Men and balloons were required for this operation also, which put the remnants of Britain's balloon organization at home in a quandary. A scratch team of men and balloons was successfully collected, however, no one quite knew how; and Templer himself was given the command, with a young Royal Engineer officer under him. He embarked with his men for Suakin on 15 February 1885, to accomplish the most successful ballooning operation then on record.

The direct military importance of these operations was perhaps minor, but the experience transformed British military ballooning from a vague concept to a practical reality. Equipment was modified to meet circumstances *known to exist*, and the whole organization acquired a feeling of confidence that was to prove invaluable in the South African War of 1899–1902.

In parallel with developments in the technique of balloon operation and its military application, there had also been many developments in design of balloons and their essential equipment. In twenty years Templer had introduced many changes, most of which were necessary if successful military operations had to be undertaken. There seems always to have been a practical purpose in these developments, and yet there was always in the background some good scientific principles, for Templer got on well with scientists, who all appreciated his vigorous and flexible mind.

Three developments were particularly outstanding. The first was the use of goldbeater's skin, in superposed thicknesses, for the balloon envelope. In this the Balloon Factory was far ahead of any rivals. The earlier balloons when Templer came into the field were made of silk or other fabric and varnished in a number of different ways to prevent leakage of the hydrogen. Now, hydrogen is the most elusive of all substances and in time can penetrate almost anything. In Templer's view the leakage rate for any of the various varnished fabrics was far too high to be acceptable for a military balloon. Goldbeater's skin, on the other hand, is the most impenetrable of all flexible materials, and just about the lightest and strongest also. It is made from the caecum or blind gut of an ox, each animal providing about one and a half square feet (1400 square cm).* Templer evolved procedures for collecting, cleaning, and treating the material, and finally a joining process for producing a near-spherical envelope. The standard British military balloon of the year 1899 had a capacity of about 10,000 cubic feet (285 cubic metres), and was the most compact balloon in existence for its lifting power. An interesting illustration is reproduced in Fig. 2, where the balloon is seen to be carrying two men.†

* The caecum, a *cul-de-sac* in the intestines, is disproportionately large in ruminants or cud-chewing animals.
† While calling for skilful handling and organization on an industrial scale, the basic principles of manufacture were not – as has often been supposed – either complicated or particularly secret. Adhesion of overlapping pieces of goldbeater's skin was achieved by gentle pressing together while clean and wet. In due time the tissues 'grew' together to produce a permanent

The second major development was the steel cylinders for carrying hydrogen compressed about a hundred times. Such cylinders now seem a commonplace affair, but when Templer began they were largely a novelty, and successful only after much research and experiment. With the cylinders went the design of a compact wagon for transport (usually known as a tube-wagon) and an ingenious system of pipes and valves for rapid filling of the balloon. Three or four wagons went with one balloon, and each required at least four good horses, though six were better. A special wagon had also to be provided for the folded balloon and the winding-in winch. Fig. 3 shows a tube-wagon and a balloon that is being filled, with the winch wagon in the background.

Finally, there was the manufacture of the hydrogen itself. There are countless ways of making hydrogen, at least as a laboratory process, but it took some years to produce a practical method for ordinary use under field conditions. That eventually evolved was based on the action of sulphuric acid upon zinc. In Templer's view, however, the zinc-acid process had limitations, and in particular was likely to lead to slight corrosion of the balloon envelopes through minute traces of acid passing through the system. Templer therefore developed the alternative method of electrolysis of water for balloon hydrogen. This gave a gas of greater purity and, in particular, free from acid traces. In 1899 an electrolysis plant had been working at the Balloon Factory for some time. As often happens in such cases, however, both methods were used when war came along: the electrolytic process for hydrogen made in England and shipped to South Africa, and the zinc-acid process for operation at sub-bases erected in Cape Town and Durban.

2   Steam traction engines

The war in South Africa provided an opportunity such as occurs once in a lifetime for Templer to make use of his vast experience of military ballooning. At that time there was probably no one in the world who could measure

gas-tight joint. The Templer balloons and early Farnborough airships had envelopes made entirely of goldbeater's skin in many layers, about seven being normal for a balloon. A method developed much later had only one or two layers, attached as an internal hydrogen-holding lining to fabric material. This second method was used for the interior gas-bags of the airship *R-101*, which met with disaster at Beauvais, France, on 5 October 1930.

up to him. Yet the War Office made what at first sight must seem an incredible decision – to take Templer away from ballooning altogether and to appoint him Director of Steam Road Transport, South Africa.

The decision appears to have been made without delay or hesitation. The South African War effectively began on 12 October 1899, when General Joubert* crossed the border into Natal, and Templer's appointment was officially confirmed and promulgated on 28 October. So far as is known, Templer raised no objection, and it is certain that he began his new task with his usual enthusiasm. He did, indeed, ask for an increase in salary, but only to put forward a reasoned case. His request was, in fact, granted in principle, and he was awarded £1,200 per annum, instead of £700, while overseas. The letter in which he makes his request has survived. It was written on 28 November 1899, just before he left for South Africa, and he says that he is due to leave on the *Denton Grange* 'next Saturday', which makes it 2 December. The related correspondence has interest because it gives us an authoritative assessment of Templer's abilities, made by men at the War Office, without any of the natural exuberance of writers for the press. The following is a good example: 'I look upon Lt-Col Templer as quite phenomenal for energy and for his power of putting through matters in his own line.'

The connection between balloons and traction engines, the lightest and heaviest of vehicles, seems at first sight to be very remote, yet both were the concern of Templer and the Balloon Factory. The tube-wagons developed by the Factory were very heavy when loaded, but a complete train of wagons was still an easy day's work for a steam traction engine. According to Brigadier-General R. B. D. Blakeney, who comes up later as the commander of a balloon section, one traction engine could do the work of twenty or thirty horses. The use of steam traction engines was in considerable measure encouraged, moreover, by a general shortage of horses whenever any large operation was undertaken. In 1889, for example, the balloon detachment at Lidsing, near Chatham, had found itself engaged for major cross-country manoeuvres without any horses at all, so that steam traction was the only way.

It was probably on this occasion in 1889 that traction engines became recognized as providing a practical alternative means of towing a balloon train. The matter did not rest here, however, since Templer's activities became known far and wide, and he was soon using traction engines for army purposes in all their diversity. With him were the men of the Balloon Factory, which became a kind of research and experimental establishment for traction engines as well as for balloons. The photograph in Fig. 4 shows

* General Petrus Jacobus Joubert (1834–1900) nominal leader of the Boer Forces in 1899.

Templer and some of his men with a 'steam sapper' at the Balloon Factory in Aldershot.*

Templer's work on steam traction engines had aroused much public interest, and as a personal interest of his own they obviously came second only to balloons. There are people alive today who have nostalgic memories of Templer tearing around Aldershot and Farnborough on one of his traction engines. It is said that he used to take Mrs Templer shopping in Aldershot in a trailer pulled by one of them. Colonel Templer became, in fact, almost a legendary figure; and this alone has rendered necessary some careful sifting of evidence to get the historical truth.

While many would not agree with the War Office in taking Templer away from balloons, their action clearly cannot be dismissed out-of-hand as being ill-considered. Steam road-transport had for some years been a responsibility of the Royal Engineers, but the war in South Africa found them without any definite organization for dealing with it, if we except Templer's somewhat irregular activities.† The War Office therefore had to create a new organization, and on two counts the appointment of Templer as Director must have appeared to be a master-stroke. In the first place, Templer was unquestionably the most knowledgeable person on steam traction engines who could be relied upon to work with the Royal Engineers. In the second place, Templer was widely known to the public at large for his work on traction engines, and this was important at a time when public opinion mattered a great deal to the War Office.

The formation of a regular Royal Engineer unit followed almost immediately after Templer's formal appointment as Director. The 45th Company of the Royal Engineers was created for steam road-transport on 1 November 1899, and Captain G. P. Scholfield R.E. was put in command.

Templer was probably told of his own appointment some time before it was officially promulgated. He seems to have spent much of October and November (1899) touring the country in search of traction engines. Among firms that he visited was Fowler's of Leeds who had made the first practical traction engine in 1857. His responsibilities for balloon work were handed over in November to his temporary successor Brevet Lieutenant-Colonel

---

* The term 'Steam Sapper' was not applied to a particular engine, as some have supposed, but to them all. 'Steam Sapper' was abandoned *officially* in 1894 and replaced by 'Traction Engine'.
† Both the Royal Engineers and the War Office have been adversely criticized for alleged neglect in this field. Outright condemnation is not necessarily justified, however, and certainly not on the evidence collected for the present History. According to the official Royal Engineers History (Vol. IV, by Brig.-Gen. W. Baker Brown, 1952), the R.E.s obtained their first steam traction engine in 1868, from Aveling and Porter of Rochester.

J. P. L. Macdonald R.E., who thus became Acting-Superintendent of the Balloon Factory.

Templer embarked at Southampton for Cape Town on the *Denton Grange*, not on 2 December as expected, but on 5 December (1899). From this point the story disagrees radically from the majority of accepted histories. For some reason the adventures of Templer, and especially the circumstances of the loss of the *Denton Grange*, seem to have been largely suppressed; though possibly they were merely overlooked in the near-chaos of the war in the early stages. From odd pieces of information that have come to light, however, and above all from an official report written by Captain Scholfield himself,* it has been possible to ascertain most of the essential facts.

The *Denton Grange* had on board nine traction engines, four-winding engines,† and forty-three trucks, in the way of equipment. There were also, in the way of personnel, eleven artificers and a professional engineer referred to as 'Mr Templer', who is believed to have been Colonel Templer's brother.

The ship safely reached Las Palmas, the capital of the Grand Canary Island, on 11 December 1899. When manoeuvring outside the harbour there, however, the stern of the ship fouled the bottom and stuck. *H.M.S. Furious* next morning tried to pull her off, but without success. No lives were lost but much of the material on board was either lost or ruined. Two engines carried as deck cargo were saved and, with twenty-eight trucks, were sent on to Cape Town in the steamship *Yoruba*. Templer himself left Las Palmas in the hospital ship *Maine* on 3 January 1900.

The loss of the *Denton Grange* is mentioned only casually in the official history of the war,‡ in a statistical review of ships lost during the war, and nothing is said about what was being transported or when the ship had left Southampton. For reasons that will probably never be accurately known now, the whole story was suppressed at the time. This dearth of factual information has led to much invention. It has hitherto been generally accepted that the ship ran ashore in a storm, and Templer was supposed to have been marooned on the island with no means of escape. This is nonsense, of course, since Las Palmas was a regular port of call, and there were other ships there at the time. One newspaper described how Templer had to plead with Lady

* Captain Scholfield's full report was found for me by Mr D. W. King, originally the War Office Librarian and now the Chief Librarian to the Ministry of Defence. The report is dated 1903 and has a War Office reference A825. Captain Scholfield was not only the original officer-in-charge of the 45th R.E. Company for steam road-transport but later took over from Templer as Director for South Africa.

† Presumably two pairs of ploughing engines with cable drums.

‡ *History of the War in South Africa, 1899–1902,* by Major-General Sir Frederick Maurice, Vol. I, 1906; Vol. II, 1907.

Randolph Churchill* to be taken aboard the *Maine* in order to escape at all. This may well have been a typically distorted story having some measure of truth, since the *Maine* was a hospital ship provided by American well-wishers, and Lady Randolph Churchill was president of the hospital committee running it. His status as a combatant, therefore, might have prejudiced his position. Several of Templer's men followed later on 7 January 1900 in the *Siberian*.

Suppression of the facts about the loss of the *Denton Grange*, probably a legitimate war-time measure, was a minor matter compared with the neglect and distortion of facts concerning Templer's activities after his arrival in South Africa. Major-General J. E. Capper, in his obituary for Templer in 1924† implied that Templer's work with traction engines in South Africa was almost negligible, since virtually all the engines had been lost in the shipwreck. Obituary notices are notoriously unreliable, and this more so than most, but Capper was only repeating a widely accepted story.

In point of fact, the *Denton Grange* was only one of *two* ships sent with traction engines to South Africa, and actually the second to leave Southampton. The first ship, *Bulawayo*, left Southampton on 3 November 1899 with eleven engines and thirty-five trucks on board, and also a considerable store of ancillary equipment. The ship arrived at Cape Town without the captain knowing where he was supposed to go or what he was supposed to do. Eventually he was directed or misdirected to proceed to Durban, a thousand miles away, and his cargo was unloaded there. This was the wrong decision as it happened; and Templer when he arrived had to collect the whole outfit, which had been dispersed over Natal. He then had them loaded at Durban on the *Urmston Grange*, and brought to Port Elizabeth for use in Cape Colony and later in the Orange Free State.

The traction engines did much useful work in South Africa, and were of great value in hauling heavy loads from the ports. In advanced positions they were less useful owing to their ravenous appetite for fuel and water, and a tendency to sink into soft ground. They were rarely used for balloon trains. The engines with their wagons eventually provided a kind of subsidiary railway service, and were especially useful in the Kimberley district.

The work of Templer's engines was much appreciated by the British public. Following Britain's inglorious war record, the enterprise of Templer appealed to the imagination, and war correspondents made the most of it. One artist with his 'traction-mounted infantry' (see Fig. A) fancifully antici-

---

* Lady Randolph Churchill was the American-born mother of the late Sir Winston Churchill.
† 'Colonel J. L. B. Templer', by Major-General Sir John E. Capper, *Journal of the Royal Engineers*, Vol. 38, March 1924.

(A) 'The traction-mounted infantry':

Templer's fame as an expert in steam traction spread far and wide. In the South African War he had to leave his balloons to become Director of Steam Road Transport for South Africa. In the picture, an artist gives a futuristic impression of a traction engine as an offensive combat weapon

pated the tank of the First World War. Another picture that has survived (Fig. 5) shows one of 'Templer's babies', as his engines were called, taking refugee children for an outing.

One of the greatest tributes to the Royal Engineers' organization under Templer's leadership is a passage in the *Times History*:*

So great was the volume of freight put ashore from the ships that it exceeded the powers of the land transport contractors and the Army Service Corps to deal with it. By the beginning of 1900 the docks were so seriously congested with baggage and stores

* *'The Times' History of the War in South Africa 1899–1902*, by L. S. Amery. Vol. I, 1900; Vol. II, 1902; Vol. III, 1905; Vol. IV, 1906; Vol. V, 1907; Vol. VI, 1909.

that a deadlock might have resulted. At this point Colonel Templer, with his steam traction engines and trailers, came to the rescue, and the docks were cleared within a week. Henceforward the use of steam transport enabled the work of discharging cargo to go forward without difficulty.

At the end of October 1900 Templer was informed of his pending release from the post of Director of Steam Road Transport. The war was then thought – mistakenly as things turned out – to be virtually over, and the Commander-in-Chief himself, Lord Roberts, had already been told of his own recall. In any event, Templer had completed his task of creating a new and original organization. The rest was primarily a job for the Royal Engineers. Captain Scholfield became Director and the unit went from strength to strength as the war continued.

3   Balloons in combat
     1899–1900

The part played by balloons in the war in South Africa gave conclusive proof of the value of twenty-one years' dedicated service by Templer and his colleagues at the Balloon Factory. The scale of balloon operations went far beyond anything that has occurred before or since, the nearest approach being that of General McClellan's Federal Army in the American Civil War of 1861–5. Unfortunately, for a number of reasons, the work of the balloon sections in South Africa has never been adequately recorded or sufficient credit given to the men responsible. Official historians, in particular, have shown little enthusiasm for what must have appeared to them a mere sideline in a most complicated war. It is only when the fullest story now possible is obtained that the suspicion arises that balloons must have had a much bigger influence on the war than has ever been realized.

To understand the work of the balloons in South Africa it is necessary to have at least a rudimentary picture of the broad strategy behind the war. The terrain is shown in the map of Fig. B. In the extreme south was the large British-held Cape Colony with its important capital and seaport of Cape Town. North of this was the Orange Free State, and still further north lay the Transvaal, both of which were to fight Britain in the forthcoming war. On

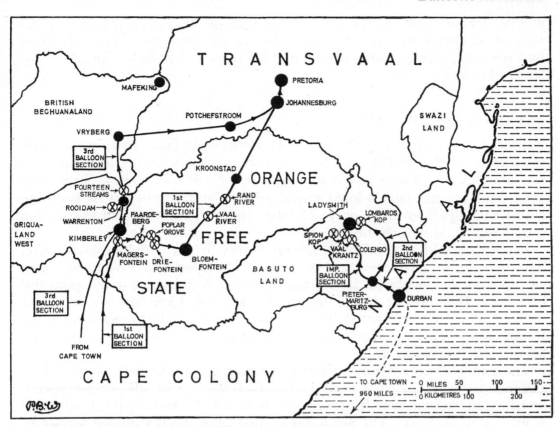

(B) Balloon operations in South Africa (1899 and 1900)

the eastern side of the Free State was the British province of Natal with its capital and seaport of Durban. On the west side of the Free State lay Griqualand West and Bechuanaland, both under British control.

Hostilities with the Transvaal were expected, but up to the very last there was uncertainty whether the Orange Free State (which had no particular quarrel with Britain) would participate, though in the event it did so. During the first year of the war, which covered the whole period of balloon operations, there were virtually two separate conflicts. One British army was defending Natal against the invading Boer armies. Another British army had to fight its way through the north of Cape Colony, further northwards through the Orange Free State, and finally into the Transvaal. Both armies made use of balloons.

Preparations for the almost inevitable war began in England in the summer of 1899. The single balloon section at Aldershot was split into two parts,

21

which became known as the 1st and 2nd Balloon Sections respectively; and these were then built up individually to full strength. Apparently Templer had provided a large enough reserve of balloons and balloon equipment for this to be done.

2ND BALLOON SECTION

For some unknown reason the first balloon section to leave Britain and enter the war was designated the *2nd Balloon Section*. This embarked at Southampton for Durban (Natal) in the steamship *Kinfauns Castle* on 30 September 1899, that is some days before General Joubert started the war by invading Natal with his Boer army on 12 October 1899. In command of the section was Major G. M. Heath R.E.*

While the 2nd Balloon Section was on its way by sea a deplorable situation developed in Natal. For political reasons and in response to pressure at home, an attempt was made to defend the whole of Natal against the powerful invaders. This proved to be impracticable, and Lieutenant-General Sir George White V.C. retreated into Ladysmith with a large portion of the British army. This was the prelude to the historic siege of Ladysmith which began on 2 November 1899.

The 2nd Balloon Section arrived at Durban on 26 October 1899, and its advance party seems to have dashed to Ladysmith with all possible speed, just in time to take part in the preparations for the last battle, Lombard's Kop† (see map, p. 21). The Section is said to have given valuable service in locating Boer movements for two or three days before fighting broke out. Then, during the battle of Lombard's Kop itself, on 30 October 1899, it was able to direct the fire of the British artillery. As is all too well-known, the battle was lost; and the 2nd Balloon Section was trapped in Ladysmith with the rest of Sir George White's forces.

Inside Ladysmith the conditions were most favourable for effective balloon operations, with both friend and foe well anchored down, apart from the limited movements of the Boer army on the periphery. These movements were closely watched from the Section's only balloon, a photograph of which is reproduced in Fig. 6. It was found possible, moreover, to produce useful sketch maps of the country round Ladysmith, some covering terrain as far as the town of Colenso, twenty miles away. Gun fire was again directed from the air whenever possible, particularly for the naval Long Toms, which had

* Later Major-General Sir Gerard M. Heath.
† *Kop* = hill (head). Other local terms used fairly consistently are: *krantz* = cliff; *drift* = ford; *fontein* = spring or stream (fountain).

arrived at Ladysmith from Durban with a contingent of the Royal Navy just before the gates were closed. Communication with the British relieving force under General Buller was mainly by heliograph, and for this method of signalling the balloon was unique as a station for both transmitting and receiving.

Unfortunately, the train of the 2nd Balloon Section, in its rapid approach to Ladysmith, had had its tail cut off by the besieging army. Left outside was not only much of the ancillary equipment but also the tube-wagons bringing the precious hydrogen. A hydrogen factory (described later) had been set up in Durban, but there was no way of getting through. Thus it came about that, after one month's valuable work inside the besieged Ladysmith, the 2nd Balloon Section ceased to operate through lack of hydrogen. It was never revived again in South Africa, and the men took on other work as Royal Engineers to face starvation with the rest.

THE BALLOON IRREGULARS

It might well have been expected that this was the end of military ballooning in Natal. The initiative of one Captain G. E. Phillips R.E., however, changed the whole situation. In the attempt to relieve Ladysmith from the siege which was to last nearly four months, General Buller's army soon realized the need for balloons. With an enterprising spirit rivalled only by that of Colonel R. S. S. Baden-Powell at Mafeking, Captain Phillips scraped together a balloon section. He found some of the lost stores of the 2nd Balloon Section in the town of Pietermaritzburg, which lies between Durban and Ladysmith. By some means or other he was also able to get men and materials from the hydrogen factory and balloon depot at Cape Town. Much of what Captain Phillips did, however, was never properly recorded and probably will never be known. What is certain is that he produced a band of irregulars that proved to be just about the finest military balloonists that have ever existed.

The *Improvised Balloon Section*, for so it must be described, since it never had a proper name or number, took part in three major battles south of Ladysmith. These are represented diagrammatically as crosses in the map on page 21 and comprise: Colenso on 15 December 1899; Spion Kop on 24 January 1900; and Vaal Krantz on 5 February 1900. In all these, the improvised section reported enemy movements and directed gun fire. The work of the section, however, cannot be expressed entirely in terms of actual battles, since much of the work was observing for several days preceding and following a battle. For some weeks, in fact, the balloons were up and watching the enemy practically every day.

Among the most important contributors to the history of the Improvised Balloon Section, as well as to the history of the other balloon sections, were the war correspondents of British newspapers and magazines. The *Transvaal War Album* had a most interesting photograph (Fig. 7) showing a balloon belonging to the Improvised Balloon Section at Zwarts Kop.* Part of the caption, which is most informative, reads:

It will be remembered that the Sappers' balloons were of utmost service to Sir Redvers Buller's columns, and that it was by balloon that the trap was discovered which the Boers had prepared when the attack was made on Vaal Krantz. The balloon here represented was photographed for ascent near Potgeiter's Drift.

Zwarts Kop was a hill two miles south of Vaal Krantz, which the Boers were defending. Vaal Krantz was bombarded by heavy British guns mounted on Zwarts Kop, with a balloon taking observations. Potgeiter's Drift, mentioned in the caption, was in a valley close by Zwarts Kop. The location of a particular balloon varied at different times, so that different reports do not always agree exactly, but for the changes in position there was a definite reason. The Boers wasted much ammunition firing at balloons, at a cost entirely disproportionate to the damage and inconvenience produced. The firing was most effective or, more correctly, *least ineffective*, when the balloon was just leaving the ground. It was desirable, therefore, for a balloon to bob up quickly from its place of concealment, like a cork in water, and from a location unsuspected and unpredictable.

There was a long line of Boer defences running roughly east to west from the heights of Spion Kop to Vaal Krantz, and usually identified as Brakfontein. A balloon seems to have made a daily practice of observing up and down the line like a general inspecting troops on parade, to the manifest vexation of the Boer soldiers.

The same caption in the *Transvaal War Album* also gives an interesting description of the ballooning equipment:

A ballooning section of the engineers carries its balloons upon a cart, but it has four other carts for gas-tubes and various gear, each drawn by four horses, in addition to two baggage and store carts. The gas is stored in a compressed state, the equipment is complete, and the winding apparatus very strong and efficient.

The end of the siege, which was also the end of the Improvised Balloon Section, is almost an anticlimax. General Buller's persistence was rewarded by a comparatively easy victory in the Battle of Pieter's Hill on 22 February

* The *Transvaal War Album* was edited by Commander C. N. Robinson R.N. and published by Newnes in 1899–1900. 'Zwarts' could probably have been more correctly written as 'Zwart', meaning 'black'. Other alternative spellings sometimes used are 'Swart' and 'Swaartz'.

1900, and the town was relieved on the following day. The Improvised Balloon Section, which had done so well, was disbanded. Thereafter balloons were not used in Natal since the terrain passed through by the retreating Boers was too mountainous and their movements too speedy.

THE 1ST BALLOON SECTION

Meanwhile balloons had also been active in the western area of combat, in the Orange Free State. The 1st Balloon Section embarked at Southampton for Cape Town in the *Kildonian Castle* on 4 November 1899. Captain H B. Jones R.E. was in command. The section reached Cape Town on 22 November 1889, and proceeded northwards to join Lord Methuen's army near Modder River on the western border of the Orange Free State, on 9 December.

This was just before the Battle of Magersfontein, which took place on 11 December 1899. From the moment of arrival the balloons were continuously observing the enemy and directing gunfire. During the actual battle great damage was done to the enemy by British howitzers working to directions supplied by one of the balloons. The immediate objective was a breakthrough to relieve the besieged town of Kimberley, but in this the British were not immediately successful. Desultory warfare continued until the middle of February, with the balloons making frequent ascents despite severe dust storms.

The situation began to change when Lord Roberts, the new Commander-in-Chief for South Africa, arrived bringing with him not only the master-brain (his own) of the war on the British side, but also considerable military reinforcement. Kimberley was relieved on 15 February 1900 by Lieutenant-General J. D. F. French* with a balloon watching every move and reporting the Boer evacuation. Next day General Cronje† with his Boer Army moved eastwards out of Magersfontein, and shortly afterwards Lord Roberts began the first really successful British operation of the war, namely the Investment of Paardeberg, which was to lead to the capture of Cronje's entire force. From 22 February, Lieutenant A. W. H. Grubb R.E., second in command of the 1st Balloon Section, personally watched the Boer movements from the air, making useful sketches of Boer positions and directing the British Artillery.

* Later Sir John French, Commander-in-Chief of the British Expeditionary Force in France 1914–15, and still later Earl of Ypres. He appears again in this History as C.-in-C. Aldershot Command.
† General Piet Arnoldus Cronje (1835?–1911), Commander of the Western Army of the South African Republics.

Then came the final Battle of Paardeberg on 26 February 1900, and to this the balloon section appears to have made the biggest contribution to victory ever recorded for a balloon operation. Even the Official History,* always reluctant to give credit to the balloon sections, pays special tribute:

The officer in the balloon reported that the enemy's main position consisted of a series of entrenchments parallel to the right bank [of the river Modder] and covered by a short flanking trench which ran northwards from the river for thirty-five yards. Between this flanking trench and the north-east end of the trench excavated by the 19th Brigade the ground was open, and when once this space was crossed and the Boer flanking trench had been captured, the enemy's main position could also be enfiladed at close range. After inspecting the British works, Lieut-General Colvile . . . obtained leave from Lord Roberts to make on the flanking trench a night attack, the orders for which were issued in the course of the afternoon.

The attack took place that night 26/27 February, and early next morning General Cronje surrendered unconditionally. The day of surrender was also the day of General Buller's victory at Pieter's Hill, and on the following day came news of the relief of Ladysmith.

Lord Roberts's next objective was the capture of Bloemfontein, the capital of the Orange Free State, but two battles had to be fought on the way: Poplar Grove on 7 March 1900, and Driefontein on 10 March (see map, p. 21). At both of these battles the balloon section fulfilled what now had become a normal role, and then it kept watch all the way to Bloemfontein, which surrendered on 13 March 1900.

Then followed the long trek to Pretoria, the capital of Transvaal. Resistance was encountered at various places, notably Vet River (5 May) and Zand River (10 May). Kroonstad Town was occupied on 12 May 1900 and there is an interesting picture of a balloon train passing through this region taken from a copy of *The Graphic* (Fig. 8). The wagons are being pulled by oxen under conditions of great difficulty in wild desolate country, with both heat and high ground to contend with. Despite the difficulties, the balloon section continued to be the eyes of the Army until Pretoria came into view. Then it again prepared the way by preliminary reconnoitring of the Boer defences, and the town was taken without much difficulty on 5 June 1900.

The section did not do much more after this. It had been the intention to move on to Eastern Transvaal but this came to nothing. The valuable oxen were handed over to the artillery and the section disbanded. It had had the longest life of all the balloon sections, and after watching the marginal defeat

* *History of the War in South Africa, 1899–1902,* by Major-General Sir Frederick Maurice. Vol. I, 1906; Vol. II, 1907.

at Magersfontein it had witnessed a succession of victories almost unequalled in history.

3RD BALLOON SECTION

Shortly after the victory at Paardeberg, another balloon section was sent out from England. This was the 3rd Balloon Section under the command of Lieutenant (temporary Major) R. D. B. Blakeney R.E. Unlike the 1st and 2nd sections, it had been created *ab initio* and the men had been specially trained. The Section embarked on 7 March 1900 and arrived at Cape Town on 30 March.

From Cape Town it moved north to Kimberley, now in British hands; and then on to Warrenton where it arrived on 23 April 1900. Here it joined Lord Methuen's division on the left flank of Lord Roberts's army. Though a late arrival, the 3rd Balloon Section had now the benefit of acquired experience of balloons in actual warfare. Its first task was to reconnoitre the Boer positions at Rooidam and Fourteen Streams (see map, p. 21), the Boers being driven out of Rooidam on 5 May and being compelled to evacuate Fourteen Streams on 7 May. At Fourteen Streams, especially, the balloon section played an important part by locating the strength of the hidden enemy and directing the British gun fire. A 6-in. gun brought up by rail from Kimberley had a devastating effect when working in conjunction with the balloon. The Boers stated afterwards that it was the balloon which made them decide to evacuate Fourteen Streams.

This victory at Fourteen Streams was one of the factors which made the relief of Mafeking possible on 17 May 1900, after the famous siege and defence by Colonel R. S. S. Baden-Powell. After its effective action at Rooidam and Fourteen Streams, however, the end of the 3rd Balloon Section was somewhat inglorious. Contradictory orders were given to it at the time and there have been conflicting stories about what happened since. The plain fact is that the rapidly advancing army did not need this balloon section any more. The section moved slowly north to Vyberg, Potchefstroom and Johannesburg, and there it was disbanded in much the same way as its forerunner the 1st Balloon Section.

4   The Balloon Factory in wartime

1899–1900

The war in South Africa put a heavy load on the Balloon Factory. Its effort was directed mainly towards straightforward manufacture of balloons and ballooning equipment. The forward thinking of the kind associated with Templer in the past seems to have been absent, and there does not appear to have been anything equivalent to the operational research by which practical experience in war is used to improve design and extend scientific knowledge. Against this it must be remembered that, although the war lasted over two and a half years, balloons were in operation for only about one year.

At the time when war seemed almost inevitable, in the summer of 1899, the Balloon Factory was situated in Alison's Road, Aldershot, on a site that came to be known as 'Balloon Square'.* Territorially it was part of the Royal Engineers Establishment, which covered an extensive area southwards from the Basingstoke Canal (see map, Fig. C).

As an organization the Balloon Factory was by this time well established. It had been created in a rudimentary form at Woolwich as early as 1878, had been moved to Chatham four years later, and then moved again to Aldershot in 1892. There had grown up alongside it a corresponding operational unit of the Royal Engineers. This also was devoted to military ballooning, and had had a very similar history. Templer had been connected with both organizations, being responsible for design and manufacture of balloons on the one hand, and responsible for training the men who flew them, on the other.

Up to the year 1897, however, precise responsibilities and terms of reference had not been clearly defined; but amidst all the vagueness and uncertainty two things stand out that were to prove crucial when war broke out. One was that, over the years, many Royal Engineer Officers of the highest intelligence had passed through Templer's ballooning course in a tour of official duty. The other was that they all regarded Templer as a great leader and the grand master of the ballooning art.

* Demolished for re-building in 1963, as described in the epilogue to Section 5 of Chapter 2.
   In *The War in the Air*, Volume I (1922), Sir Walter Raleigh wrongly states that the Balloon Factory was in South Farnborough, instead of Aldershot, a mistake that has regrettably passed into many histories.

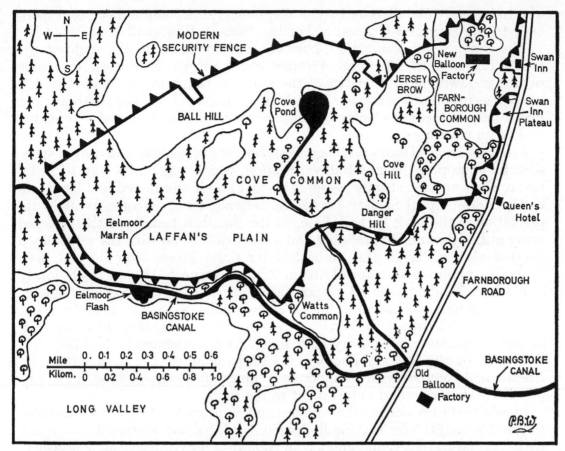

(C) The R.A.E. terrain in the first decade of the twentieth century. This was originally common land covered by trees and scrub, with clearings made for Army camping and manoeuvres

Much of the organizational uncertainty disappeared in 1897, i.e. about two years before war broke out, when an attempt was made to rationalize British military ballooning. On 1 April 1897 the Balloon Factory was officially recognized as existing in its own right, and no longer as something vaguely attached to a military unit; and Lieutenant-Colonel Templer was formally appointed to the newly-created post of 'Superintendent of the Balloon Factory'. At the same time a properly-established Balloon Section was created under an Officer Commanding who was a Royal Engineer. This Balloon Section, essentially an operational unit, was to remain under Aldershot Command; but – and this was the remarkable innovation – the Balloon Factory

29

was to be controlled directly by the War Office, and Templer became responsible to the Inspector-General of Fortifications in Whitehall.

The changes in organization, however, did not affect in the slightest the good will that existed between Templer and the Royal Engineers. The value of this goodwill and the merits of the re-organization made themselves felt as soon as mobilization for war began. The changeover from peace to war ran like a perfect piece of clockwork despite the fact that Templer, the leader, had to go elsewhere.

From evidence of dates it is clear that Templer himself was mainly responsible for equipping the 2nd Balloon Section, which was on its way to Natal before the war had actually begun. This he himself mentioned in a later talk to the Aeronautical Society,* when he referred to Sir George White's appreciation of the work he had done, to the manifest benefit of the besieged army in Ladysmith. He probably had a great deal to do with the 1st Balloon Section also, although this embarked for Cape Town after he had been formally appointed Director of Steam Road Transport. There was obviously a gradual handing-over of responsibility to the Acting-Superintendent, Brevet Lieutenant-Colonel J. P. L. Macdonald R.E., while Templer went chasing around Britain in search of traction engines. Macdonald was a man of great experience in military ballooning. As a lieutenant he had been left in charge of the Balloon Factory at Chatham in 1884–5 when Major H. Elsdale had gone out with a balloon detachment to Bechuanaland, and Templer had taken a second detachment to the Sudan.

In addition to providing the balloons and equipment, the Factory had also to provide facilities for making hydrogen. Each balloon section was sent out with a generous reserve of cylinders of compressed hydrogen, made in Aldershot by the electrolytic plant. It was considered desirable, however, to be able to renew further supplies nearer the field of operations. In consequence hydrogen factories were set up in Cape Town and Durban, for the 1st and 2nd Balloon Sections respectively. Electrolysis was not practical for these places, and the zinc-acid process was used. Strong sulphuric acid was sent out in mild-steel containers for the two factories.† Compression equipment was also required for the factories for replenishing the hydrogen cylinders.

The policy of installing hydrogen factories in South Africa and sending acid by sea seems now to have been much open to question. It would probably have been better just to send the hydrogen from England. The issue

---

* 'Balloons in the South African War' (talk to the Aeronautical Society, 15 July 1901), by Lieutenant-Colonel J. L. B. Templer, *The Aeronautical Journal*, October 1901.
† Acid over 70 per cent strength does not attack iron or mild steel. The acid used would probably be well over 90 per cent pure.

was raised in a somewhat indirect way when the 3rd Balloon Section went to Cape Town. Proposals were made to have one big hydrogen factory in Cape Town, combined with a single repair and service depot, for all the balloon sections. The few papers that have survived concerning this matter make depressing reading, for some of the people at the War Office helping to make decisions seem to have known virtually nothing about balloons. The need for a Templer to advise was never more obvious. In the event, amalgamation was avoided and the 3rd Balloon Section had its own factory and depot.

Throughout the war, the actual balloons were made in Aldershot and dispatched by sea. This was by far the best procedure since the treatment of goldbeater's skin was a specialized process, and shipping was easy because the Boer States had no navy with which to interfere. The practical way in which the various engineering problems were dealt with seems remarkable even by present-day standards. A good example is the method of packing the goldbeater's-skin envelopes in soldered airtight tins whose contents seem to have reached the operational units in perfect condition. It is on record that Captain Phillips of the Improvised Balloon Section returned one balloon for repair. It had many bullet holes collected in a three-day exploration of the Boer lines at Brakfontein in January 1900. Generally, however, it appears to have been best to replace balloons, damaged beyond field-repair, by new ones.

A further load was placed on the Balloon Factory when the Boxer rebellion broke out in China in May 1900. A complete section was created which became the 4th Balloon Section. It did not, however, embark until 11 August 1900, by which time the balloon war in South Africa was virtually over. The Factory had also to provide a leader for the expedition in the person of the Acting-Superintendent himself, Lieutenant-Colonel J. R. L. Macdonald. He was succeeded as Acting-Superintendent by Major F. C. Trollope, another experienced balloonist who had actually been second-in-command in the 1884–5 Bechuanaland expedition.*

The most critical issue of the war in South Africa from the balloon standpoint was the rate at which new balloons could be manufactured. The normal peacetime rate of production appears to have been about one per month. This was increased to two per month during the war, and seems to have been adequate. The balloons were mostly of 10,000 cubic feet capacity (284 cubic metres) and about 28 feet (8½ metres) in diameter, though a few are on record as having been somewhat larger.

* The 4th Balloon Section was never called upon to fight in China, since the war there was over when it arrived. The Section was transferred to India where it served for some years.

5   The final appraisal

The war naturally provided much practical information about the design and use of military balloons. It also brought out the special difficulties of operating in South Africa. The effect of the high ground was particularly noticeable, since the rarified atmosphere reduced the lifting power considerably. The normal height of the ground in level country could be anything from 3,000 feet to 6,000 feet, with another thousand or more for local hills and mountains. The adverse effect of height alone was aggravated by high air temperature which rarified the atmosphere still more.* Such conditions had scarcely been allowed for in the original design of the balloons. In practice, however, compensation was obtained by sending up only one man instead of the more usual two as in England. It is probable that, apart from training and dual instruction, this was no serious handicap since two men tended to get in each other's way. As already mentioned, moreover, there were one or two balloons in use that were somewhat larger than the standard balloon of 10,000 cubic feet capacity. These would have, of course, greater lifting power.

The balloon sections were handicapped also by the difficulties of cross-country travel. They had never held their proper complement of horses, and steam transport was not practical in remote places. Reliance had to be placed on mules or oxen, which were scarce and often in demand for the artillery. Oxen, which appear to have been used most in the northerly advance to Pretoria (see Fig. 8), were not only slow but could only work in the cool of the morning and evening. Often, therefore, the balloons lagged too far behind for reconnaissance ahead, and they were undoubtedly much more effective when watching manoeuvres that were restricted to more-or-less prepared positions.

In two respects, however, the balloons proved better than the most optimistic expectations. First, there was their comparative invulnerability to enemy fire despite the unchallengeable skill of the Boer gunners. This invulnerability was a rather complex affair, with three distinctive elements. In the first place, the balloons were difficult to hit; and it is probably true to say

* Aeroplanes suffer from similar disadvantages. Some years ago, for example, when an aeroplane was being designed for operation from South African airfields, it was necessary to assume an equivalent ground level height of 9,000 feet. This was for the purpose of calculating the take-off run, and the 9,000 feet represented the combined effect of true height and air temperature.

that the ammunition wasted by the Boers would alone have paid the bill for the balloon sections. Next, as a general rule, a balloon had to be hit not once but many times in order to bring it down. Finally, if a balloon was indeed brought down, it usually descended fairly gently, with the balloonist unhurt and the balloon needing only minor repairs.

The second meritorious feature of the balloons was the remarkable serviceability of the goldbeater's-skin envelope. Despite the adverse conditions of war manoeuvres and climate, the leakage rate for hydrogen was exceptionally low. It was common practice, in fact, for a balloon to go up daily for ten days or a fortnight without hydrogen replenishment. Mechanically, also, the material stood up to the unavoidably harsh treatment, and very few complaints were recorded.

These technical considerations were naturally important from the standpoint of the Balloon Factory, but from the broader military aspect the overriding consideration was the contribution that the balloons made to military success. Unfortunately a full military appraisal has been rendered more difficult than it need have been by the Army's general prejudice against balloons as used in South Africa, and a reluctance to give credit where credit was due.

The more cynical writers have been disposed towards suggesting that the Army's attitude was merely resistance to new ideas and unwillingness to accept new inventions. There is not, however, any substantial evidence that this was so. The most probable explanation is more complex, and perhaps rather difficult to appreciate by anyone who has not studied the curious psychology of the Boer War as revealed on both sides.

The Boer soldiers put up such a tremendous resistance because they believed they were fighting a just war and defending their homesteads against an invader. The fact that there were strong arguments to justify the British actions is irrelevant to the particular issue: it is what the Boers thought and believed that mattered. Even more important, however, was the fact that the British soldier, while not going the whole way with them, was in considerable measure sympathetic.* The British Army were willing to fight the enemy, but they were going to fight in a way they considered fair; and to a great many soldiers the use of balloons against burghers and farmers was not fair. Analogies with sport and games were prevalent in those days, and balloon warfare in South Africa would have been described as 'not cricket' or 'hitting below the belt'.†

* The real warriors on the British side were the people in England, who fought their vicarious battles at home over their newspapers.
† The concept of war as a kind of sport, applied specifically to the war in South Africa, has been developed at some length in *Handbook of the Boer War*, published by Gale and Polden in 1910.

It hardly seems credible nowadays that the future, not only of the Royal Aircraft Establishment, but also of the Royal Air Force, should have depended upon such emotional and psychological considerations. The transition from balloons to aeroplanes when it came about was smooth and natural; but if balloons had faded out after the Boer War then the difficulties of starting afresh would have been tremendous. Fortunately there were army leaders who recognized what balloons had done and what they might do in the future. The greatest of them all, Lord Roberts, is reputed to have said: 'The captive balloon gave great assistance by keeping us informed of the dispositions and movements of the enemy.'

The attitude of the Boers themselves has been clearly defined: they detested them. They even regarded them at times with almost superstitious awe. At the outbreak of war they believed that Britain would bomb Pretoria from balloons as soon as Natal was invaded. The Balloon Factory did indeed work out a general scheme for bombing from free balloons, but this was only an exercise and no one ever seriously contemplated using it.

Apart from these exaggerated fears, the Boers felt they were always at a disadvantage when manoeuvring in sight of a balloon, and that the balloon nullified their own exceptional and instinctive skill at melting away into the South African countryside. The Boer leader, General Cronje, who, it will be remembered, surrendered at Paardeberg, wrote in an official despatch: 'The British were greatly assisted by balloons.'

The last word in this appraisal, however, must go to one of the most colourful characters in history: Colonel Arthur Lynch. How he came to be involved in the Boer War is described in one of his books, *My Life Story*, published in 1924. He was born in the town of Smythesdale near Ballarat in Australia. His father was Irish and his mother Scottish. He was educated in Melbourne, Berlin, Paris and London; and among his many qualifications was that of physician and surgeon from St Mary's Hospital, London.

When war broke out in South Africa he went as a correspondent for some English periodicals. Once there, however, he became sympathetic to the Boers, and by sheer nerve and effrontery persuaded President Kruger to make him a colonel in the Boer Army. He distinguished himself at least once when he and his 2nd Irish Brigade fought a rearguard action for the rapidly retreating Boers in Natal.*

In the autumn of 1900, when the organized phase of the war was ended, Lynch was persuaded to visit America to plead the Boer cause. While there he made many friends, including Theodore Roosevelt who later was to be-

* *'The Times' History of the War in South Africa, 1899–1902*, by L. S. Amery, 1900–1909.

come President of the United States. He then went to Paris and the rest of his story has little to do with ballooning, but is worth completing for its intrinsic interest. While in Paris he successfully contested a seat for the British Parliament, representing Galway, his ancestral Irish home on his father's side. He never lacked courage and, fully aware of the risk he was taking, he came to England to visit Westminster. He was at once arrested, and after eight months in prison was tried for high treason, and condemned to death on 23 January 1903.

There was at once an uproar, especially in America. Theodore Roosevelt, who had now become President, appealed to King Edward VII. It is probable that the King would have intervened in any case, but intervene he did and granted Lynch a free pardon. The story was finally rounded off for its bizarre character in 1918, when the one-time Boer Colonel was made a colonel in the British Army.

It was when he was in Paris, just before leaving for England, that Colonel Lynch gave his astonishing lecture on ballooning, on 27 March 1902. Its title was: 'The role of English military balloons in the South African War, by Colonel Arthur Lynch of the Boer Army'.* The lecture was most remarkable for its insight into military ballooning. It is indeed a mystery how he came to know so much about British ballooning in the war, and far more than any single person on the British side. His opinions, moreover, though highly complimentary to both the Balloon Factory and the Balloon Sections, could hardly have been prejudiced by pro-British feelings. Furthermore, he knew from first-hand experience how the Boers felt about balloons, a matter on which there was always some doubt on the British side.

In considering the more important extracts† it is appropriate to refer first to one that pays tribute to Colonel Templer and the Balloon Factory:

I take this occasion to say that the English take pride in themselves, and perhaps not without reason, that they possess the best balloon service of all the armies in the World. Certainly they never demur at the inevitable expense, and they are always the first to make use of all the new inventions in the world of aerial navigation. They have adopted goldbeater's skin for the envelopes of their balloons, a material which is rather costly but impermeable and very light. In consequence the balloons are very small, their capacity being about 300 cubic metres; and this gives a great advantage for transport and economy of gas.

* The text was published in *l'Aéronaute*, April 1902, under the title: 'Du rôle des ballons militaires anglais dans la guerre de l'Afrique du Sud, par le Colonel Arthur Lynch de l'Armée Boër'.
† In preparing the extracts in English, I have made some use of a rough translation produced by Major F. C. Trollope in 1902 when he was Assistant-Superintendent of the Balloon Factory.

Tribute to the men who operated the balloons is no less encouraging. All four balloon sections are mentioned specifically, including the Improvised Balloon Section of Captain Phillips: 'The balloons have been of great value to the English on several occasions, above all at Ladysmith, Colenso, Modder River and Fourteen Streams.'

He is clearly aware that the 2nd Balloon Section had its tail cut off by the beseigers of Ladysmith, but pays tribute to the part that got through: 'The part of the section which was able to enter Ladysmith rendered great service there.'

On the way in which balloons fulfilled their special task, Colonel Lynch was obviously able to speak with first-hand knowledge:

As everyone knows, in modern warfare with smokeless powder it is difficult to determine the position of a battery or infantry unit that suddenly opens fire. You are hit without the satisfaction of knowing who is your adversary or where the firing comes from. But observations made by balloon often enabled the English to note exactly the position of a battery, a laager, an encampment, or some fortifications; or even troop movements made in preparing for a major attack.

Colonel Lynch extends his theme to cover manoeuvres on a larger scale:

The wider and more general service which balloons rendered the English was also very important. They were so well informed about the Boer positions that they could divine the purpose of a combined movement, and it was thanks to their troop dispositions made in the light of such knowledge that they repulsed the attack at Platrand, or Caesar's Camp, a flat-topped mountain which overlooked the town of Ladysmith.

Particular examples are given in generous measure. Lord Methuen at Modder River (1st Balloon Section) depended mainly on balloons to discover the always elusive enemy. Fourteen Streams (3rd Balloon Section) held the record, it was thought, for long balloon action with one inflation, despite the continuous fire of the Boers, who were left with feelings of frustration. As for Paardeberg (1st Balloon Section), he refers to the defeat of General Cronje as the greatest disaster of the war. In this battle accurate information was the most valuable commodity on both sides, and thanks to the balloon the British Army had more than its share.

Perhaps the most forceful words of all may be used to sum up the arguments for balloons:

The Boers took a dislike to the balloons. All other instruments of war were at their command. They had artillery-pieces superior for the most part and handled more skilfully; they had everything possible in the way of telegraphic and heliographic apparatus; but the balloons were a symbol of scientific superiority on the side of the English which seriously disquieted them.

36

2 The Road to Farnborough 1901-6

1 A new start

1901-2

Whatever reluctance the Army may have had in using balloons in South Africa there was never any doubt, after the experience gained there, about the need for balloons in any future army. Even before the war had ended the War Office had staked a claim for a balloon force of considerable size. Thus the Army estimates for the financial year 1901-2 contained a requirement for six balloon sections, five of them fully operational. Not all that the Army wanted was granted at once, but it was only a matter of a year or so before the purely military needs were satisfied.

Such increase in military strength naturally called for an expansion of the organization for producing balloons and ballooning equipment. For the Balloon Factory this meant, among other things, a move away from the cramped quarters at Aldershot to some less congested area. The need for expansion was universally recognized so far as manufacturing went; but in the early days the need for scientific research and systematic experiment was less widely appreciated.

Templer had barely had time to settle down after his work in South Africa when a serious attempt was made to curb his many activities and to put the Balloon Factory under the control of Aldershot Command as a military organization. The first approach was made by the Financial Secretary to the War Office, Lord Stanley,* in September 1901. The main complaint was that Templer had done other work besides making balloons, notably his work on steam traction engines. Furthermore, he did not appear to be under the control of the General Officer Commanding, Aldershot.

Now Templer had indeed been made directly responsible to the War Office at the time when he had been formally appointed to the newly-created post of Superintendent of the Balloon Factory, i.e. in 1897. Although relations remained close and friendly, the Balloon Factory (a manufacturing and

* Later the 17th Earl of Derby.

37

research unit) thereby became detached from the Balloon Section (a military operational unit), which remained a normal part of the Corps of Royal Engineers within Aldershot Command. For some years, moreover, the Balloon Factory had undertaken other work besides ballooning, such as the development of steam traction, usually with the concurrence of the War Office and often at their instigation; and had also performed many tasks of a mechanical engineering nature for Aldershot Command, since Templer had created some of the best mechanical engineering workshops in the country.

On the face of things, the Financial Secretary objected to Templer's enterprise when he addressed the following minute to a member of the staff of the Inspector General of Fortifications, on 25 September 1901:

Can you tell me under whose authority the Balloon Factory is. I am given to understand that certain work has been done by the Factory for R.C.D. Woolwich – is this so? I think the Balloon Factory, being situated in Aldershot, should be under the control of the G.O.C. [General Officer Commanding] Aldershot, – that their work should be entirely confined to making and repairing balloons – and that no expenditure should be authorized unless it has the sanction of the G.O.C. Aldershot. I would like to have an account of all monies spent in the last two years.

Thus it was implied that the Balloon Factory should become a mere supplier of balloons for the Army in much the same way as a bicycle-maker would supply bicycles. All work outside this field, however important, should stop at once; and original research, even in ballooning, should not proceed without the consent of the G.O.C. Aldershot. Finally, the Financial Secretary seems to have been unaware that Britain had been at war; and that expenditure at a factory working day and night in order to win that war could not be used as a criterion for peace-time.

The post of Financial Secretary was a political appointment in those days, and the War Office had to take his remarks seriously, however stupid they might appear to be. He should not, however, be judged harshly and have the light of modern knowledge beamed upon him. He could genuinely have been seeking to clarify issues that had become confused; and, in any case, he was only revealing the general lack of knowledge and understanding of aviation and applied science that was the greatest obstacle in the way of the early pioneers. The minute was answered with meticulous care by Colonel Charles M. Watson, a distinguished soldier and diplomat who had had considerable practical experience of ballooning.* Though shortly to retire from the Army,

* C. M. Watson (1844–1916) became Sir Charles in 1905. His contribution to military ballooning in the last century was second only to that of Colonel Templer himself; and his *Professional Paper*, produced in 1902 with the title 'Military Ballooning in the British Army', has become

he was at this time Deputy Inspector-General of Fortifications, and the following is the essential substance of his reply dated 23 October 1901:

The Balloon Factory at Aldershot is under I.G.F. [Inspector-General of Fortifications] in the same way that the factories at Woolwich Arsenal are under the D.G.O. [Director-General of Ordnance] and the Brennan Torpedo Factory at Chatham is under I.G.F. The arrangement was made some years ago and has worked satisfactorily.

From time to time we have been asked to do work in the Balloon Factory for other departments, and as this was for the good of the public service the requisitions have always been met where possible. The cost of the work so done is always shown in the annual accounts of the Factory.

The expenditure for the last two years has been abnormal on account of the Wars in South Africa and China: the one balloon section which existed before the war in South Africa having been expanded to six. The strain on the Factory was great but all demands were met.

This reasoned case seems to have annoyed the Financial Secretary, who wrote to the Permanent Under-Secretary on 24 October 1901 making proposals for something approaching a financial dictatorship:

This is not satisfactory, to me at all events, and I cannot see what a balloon factory has to do with water mains* (unless this is a balloon engineer's job) and steam transport. I think that the Balloon Factory should be put directly under G.O.C. Aldershot, and that the Factory should be confined to balloon work. Yearly estimates must be put forward and the amount required must be seen and approved by me on the advice of the G.O.C. Aldershot. I shall pass no other accounts for the future except those so approved if the views I have expressed meet with the concurrence of the military authorities.

The matter was then referred to the Secretary of State for War, St John Brodrick.† He agreed that the Balloon Factory should be kept clear of Steam Road Transport and other mechanical engineering activities and that the

---

a classic history (see Note 3 of Appendix A). He was even more famous, however, for his work with the Egyptian Army, which led to his being made a Pasha – see *Watson Pasha* by Hanley Lane-Poole, 1909. In 1915 Watson produced Volume III of the *History of the Corps of Royal Engineers*.

* Presumably this refers to the almost legendary story illustrating the incredible mechanical ingenuity of Templer. The Army, when engaged in some large-scale manoeuvres, found itself without a water supply. Templer was asked for help; and he not only provided pumps and mechanical power (from his traction engines) but also, using his special knowledge acquired in developing hydrogen cylinders, laid steel pipes fitted with a quick-action joint of his own invention.

† St John Brodrick (1856–1942) later became 9th Viscount Midleton (1907) and, still later, 1st Earl of Midleton (1920). He was Secretary of State for War from 1900 to 1903.

G.O.C. Aldershot should supervise the Balloon Factory. The Inspector-General of Fortifications, General Sir Richard Harrison,* was then presented with a *fait accompli*, he not having been told of the approach to the Secretary of State. He thereupon wrote to the Permanent Under-Secretary on 4 January 1902, expressing his disagreement:

> I do not know how far past history has been considered. I venture to draw attention to the fact that the Factory was originally under G.O.C. Aldershot; but the arrangement was so unsatisfactory that it was given up in 1897 under the authority of Lord Lansdowne.
>
> The Balloon Factory, like all other factories, works for the whole Army at home and abroad – not only for Aldershot Command.

Whether it was through this minute alone or through some other cause is uncertain, the policy agreed by the Secretary of State was reversed as if by magic. Someone in a high place must have seen the danger signal, with the prospect of War Office policy for research, development, and manufacture, coming under control of the local military commander. The reference to the authority of Lord Lansdowne must have carried considerable weight, moreover, since not only had he been Secretary of State for War at the time when he gave his ruling, but he was still an active and powerful figure as Secretary for Foreign Affairs.† In any event, action proceeded as though the existing Secretary of State had given no ruling whatever.

After all this controversy it is most remarkable how all concerned got together to settle the future of the Balloon Factory in a rational way. Argument seems to have cleared the air, and even the Financial Secretary tried to be helpful. There was, however, one change made by way of compromise: the Balloon Factory was to become the overall responsibility of the Chief Superintendent of Ordnance Factories. This seems not at all unreasonable, but the change was never actually implemented, since by the time all was ready the entire War Office was being re-organized.‡

The unfulfilled plan, however, had a far-reaching and, indeed, a beneficial influence upon the future of the Balloon Factory. Not only did the Chief

---

* General Harrison also appears later in Section 3 of Chapter 3.

† Lord Lansdowne (1845–1927), the 5th Marquess, was Secretary of State for War from 1895 to 1900, having earlier in his career (1872–4) been Under-Secretary. He became Foreign Secretary in 1900 and held the appointment until 1905.

‡ The major re-organization of the War Office took place in the year 1904, and caused temporary dislocation at the time and some inconvenience to historians later. Many official posts disappeared whilst others were newly created. The Balloon Factory was put under the new directorate of Fortifications and Works, in the department of the Master-General of the Ordnance.

Superintendent of Ordnance Factories (who was expecting to take over in due time) collaborate in the planning of the Balloon Factory, but he brought into the picture H. F. Donaldson, who was shortly to become his successor. Donaldson was at that time Chief Mechanical Engineer to the Ordnance Factories, and an engineer of outstanding merit.* To him and Colonel Watson was delegated the responsibility of deciding the immediate future of the Balloon Factory.

As a result of these deliberations it was decided to move the Balloon Factory away from Aldershot as soon as practicable. It was not proposed to move every item of equipment. Essentials for ballooning were to go, such as the balloon shed, gasholders and hydrogen-making plant; but general mechanical equipment was to stay behind as the nucleus of a new repair depot for traction engines. With these were included, somewhat tentatively, internal-combustion engines, which were just becoming practicable for Army use. The whole concept of the move as developed by Watson and Donaldson in collaboration with Templer was realistic and practical; and it is remarkable how a series of arguments that began so inauspiciously ended so sensibly.

There still remained one task to perform, namely, to choose a site for the new Balloon Factory. This Watson and Donaldson set out to do with the help of Templer. About twenty acres (8 ha) of clear ground were estimated by Templer to be required, with thirteen acres as the reserve minimum. These figures seem ludicrous now when compared with the main R.A.E.'s eleven hundred acres (450 ha) of the present day.† In addition to the specified area it was considered necessary to have a good supply of water for cooling purposes, and nearness to a canal or river was thought to be essential. It is not certain whether the investigators were told to go outside the Aldershot Command area, but it is suspected that they were advised to do so if possible.

The first choice of the investigators was Weedon,‡ which is a village about

---

* H. F. Donaldson (1856–1916) became Chief Superintendent of Ordnance Factories in 1903. In 1916, as Sir Hay Donaldson and Technical Adviser to the Minister of Munitions, he accompanied Lord Kitchener on his tragic voyage to Russia in the critical stages of the First World War. Their ship, the Cruiser *H.M.S. Hampshire*, was sunk in somewhat mysterious circumstances on the night of 15–16 June 1916, and all on board were drowned.

† In metric units, one hectare (ha) is approximately $2\frac{1}{2}$ acres.

‡ The village of Weedon, sometimes known as Weedon Bec or Beck, has historic associations with the Napoleonic Wars. In 1803, by special act of Parliament, work began on the erection of the Royal Military Depot there. Money was spent on the Establishment to the extent of £100,000 per annum for some years, and provided the most spacious barracks in England, preceding Aldershot Command by half a century. An important part of the establishment was a pavilion built to be the residence of King George III if Napoleon should be successful in invading England, and it has been suggested that there was provision for housing the British

eight miles (13 km) west of Northampton. It has an Ordnance depot and barracks there, and was tentatively regarded as very suitable. Detailed investigation which followed, however, led to the conclusion that, while in most other respects excellent, Weedon had the disadvantage that there would be great difficulty in housing the work-people in the neighbourhood.*

Some place unspecified in or near Rugby was next selected. The investigators were reasonably satisfied that they would be able to find accommodation for the work-people, although at one stage Templer was accused of being unduly optimistic about this. As it turned out, however, while there may have been room for the people to live, there was insufficient room for them to work, since the required twenty acres could not be found.

As everyone knows, of course, Farnborough was the final choice, though *choice* is hardly appropriate to describe the way in which the Balloon Factory eventually appeared there. For the time being, however, we must pass on to other things and leave Colonel Templer still looking for his twenty acres. A note in his handwriting has come to light, dated 4 June 1902, in which he says he is still looking and thinks he has found a place near Woking . . .

2   The inquiry of 1903

Direct records of activity at the Balloon Factory during the period 1901 to 1906 are too scanty and too fragmentary for them alone to give us a clear picture of what was accomplished in the way of original work. After the South African War there was inevitably a period of re-organization combined with deep thought about the future. This applied in some considerable degree

---

government also. The location was near to being the furthermost point in Britain from the sea, which appears to have been one reason for its being chosen as a refuge originally. Curiously, this was also an argument in its favour for balloon work, since being blown out to sea was a danger that had always to be avoided with a balloon.

* Many of the key workers at Aldershot were local women, specialists in goldbeater's skin and fabric, and it is doubtful whether many of them would have left the Aldershot–Farnborough district anyway. This argument, however, seems to have been kept in the background, and as things turned out the issue never arose.

to the whole Army, but especially so to the Balloon Factory, which had before it the drastic proposals for a completely new start with much new equipment and in a new place. Research and development did go on, but in a somewhat erratic way; and the keeping of records was probably the last thing most people had time to think about.

By great good fortune, however, there is compensation to be found in an unexpected place – in a report by a prosaic and routine Army Inquiry held in 1903.* Committees of inquiry are often regarded with some suspicion as to their real purpose, but this one was absolutely above-board and genuine. Ostensibly the objective was to make recommendations on future policy for military aeronautics. In this the Committee fulfilled its task; but from the historical standpoint it did much more, for it pulled out, as it were, pieces of history that would have been overlooked and perhaps lost for ever. Even the fragmentary records already mentioned become more intelligible when re-examined in the light of the Committee's systematic investigations. It is proposed, therefore, to consider the Committee's report less as an instrument of policy than as a contemporary source of historical information.

Terms of reference. The Committee was formally constituted on 8 June 1903, and issued its final report on 4 January 1904. The terms of reference as laid down were as follows:

To report generally upon the extent to which it is desirable to attempt to improve and develop military ballooning, having regard to the experience of two wars† and to progress made in this service both by our own country and other nations.

It is clear from what happened afterwards as well as from the actual wording that these terms were meant to have the widest interpretation. Thus all aspects of military ballooning were to be considered: military operations, balloon manufacture, design, and research; with individual consideration to both the Military Establishment and the Balloon Factory. Furthermore, the term 'Military Ballooning' in those days was usually understood in Army circles to comprehend all forms of aerial activity, including balloons, kites, airships and aeroplanes.

* The report bears the title: *Final Report of the Committee on Military Ballooning – 1904.* I refer to it as the report of the *1903* Committee because all the investigations and even the writing of the report were carried out in 1903. The reference to 1904 in the original title, merely because the report was issued on 4 January 1904, could be seriously misleading for an age when the pattern of military aeronautics was changing rapidly.

† The Boxer rising in China (May 1900) is presumably being counted as the second of the two wars, the first being that in South Africa. Although balloons never entered into combat in China, they were the subject of elaborate preparations.

Constitution. The Committee was composed of the following members:

Colonel P. T. Buston D.S.O., R.E. (Chairman)
Brevet Lieut.-Colonel H. H. Wilson D.S.O.
Major G. M. Harper D.S.O.
Mr C. Harris
Brevet Lieut.-Colonel J. E. Capper C.B., R.E. (Secretary)

This was certainly not a team of light-weights. Colonel Buston, who later became Brigadier-General, had commanded the Royal Engineers of the 6th Infantry Division during the South African War. Lieutenant-Colonel Wilson was at that time Assistant Adjutant-General at the War Office. He was later to become Field-Marshal Sir Henry Wilson, Chief of the Imperial General Staff, who was assassinated outside his London home by Irish terrorists on 22 June 1922.

Major Harper was Deputy Assistant Quartermaster-General. He also was destined for high rank, becoming Lieutenant-General Sir George Harper, Commander-in-Chief of Southern Command. Not much is known about Mr Harris, except that he was given a watching brief for the Finance Branch of the War Office.

From the aeronautical standpoint, however, the most important figure was the Secretary, Brevet Lieutenant-Colonel J. E. Capper, who later in life became Major-General Sir John Capper. More significant was the fact that he was to become, and remain for some time, the leading figure in British military aviation, replacing Colonel Templer in that role and becoming Superintendent of the Balloon Factory in his place. At the time of his appointment as Secretary he was in his forty-second year and entering a phase of great mental activity. As a Royal Engineer he had passed through the School of Military Engineering at Chatham, and then spent a few months under Templer at the Chatham Balloon Establishment – if the primitive organization existing at that time can be so called.* This was followed by a diversity of experience in military engineering in India and Burma. In 1899 he was sent to South Africa as wartime Assistant-Director of Railways. As often happened to Royal Engineers, however, he really made his name by leading a victorious fighting force in the field of battle. At the time of the Inquiry he had only recently returned from South Africa to take over the Command of the Balloon Sections in April 1903.

A notable omission from the list was any direct representative of research,

---

* Capper, in a fragmentary note that has survived, says this was in 1883. 'I was permitted to help him [Templer], as even then I believed in the military future of balloons. We designed and made the first military balloon in England – *The Sapper.*'

design, and manufacturing interests, for which Templer was the obvious choice. It is almost certain that Templer was left out because he was not a Royal Engineer and, as a militia officer, not even a regular soldier. The absence of Templer, deplorable though it may now seem, had perhaps one advantage in the long run, since both the War Office and the Treasury accepted the Committee's findings about the Balloon Factory as being entirely free from any professional bias.

More surprising was the failure to include on the Committee at least one of the balloon commanders of the South African War. This was consistent, however, with the appointment of Brevet Lieutenant-Colonel Capper as Commander of the Balloon Sections, in equal disregard of operational experience, and which many people could not understand at the time. Nevertheless, as things turned out, Capper proved himself eminently successful both as Secretary to the Committee of Inquiry and as Commander of the Balloon Sections.

Military Appraisal. The Committee thought it worth-while obtaining the views of military commanders in South Africa on the value of balloons in war. The testimony, which was submitted in writing, naturally took some time to collect; and the Committee's action in seeking it was probably evoked more by a desire to have records properly completed than to fill any real need for it on their own part. The fact that the Committee existed at all was tantamount to official recognition that balloons had a place in the modern army, and the chief concern was with the future rather than the past. Since the appraisal of military value is already covered in the previous chapter it is proposed to mention only one or two further points of interest.

Two of the wartime balloon commanders were called upon. One was Captain R. B. D. Blakeney R.E., who had commanded the 3rd Balloon Section, and whose name will always be associated with the Battle of Fourteen Streams. The other was Captain A. H. W. Grubb R.E. who as second in command of the 1st Balloon Section greatly distinguished himself at the Investment of Paardeberg. Both men were restrained in their claims, as though they wished to give the impression of mature judgement rather than unrestrained enthusiasm. Grubb pointed out the tremendous disadvantage of the slow travel of the oxen in the march northwards from Bloemfontein to Pretoria, a point hardly likely to have significance in any future war except as a reminder that speed of travel for a filled balloon was essential for an advancing army. Blakeney made the point that, while the officers flying balloons needed to be young and active, the balloon units as a whole should be under a mature officer of field rank.

Various types of artillery were represented at Major or Captain level. There was a slight air of truculence in acknowledging help from balloons but, on the whole, comment was favourable. It would appear, however, that gunners were not always aware when the information they had received had come from balloons, so that the balloonists often failed to receive the credit due to them. In addition, methods of communication were often imperfect, though this was a fault throughout the British Army, and not particularly associated with balloons.

The most favourable testimony came from two generals with a wider view of the strategic picture. One was Lieutenant-General Lord Methuen, in command at Modder River and on the left wing of Lord Roberts's Army. He was enthusiastic about the value of balloons in South Africa, and especially at the Battle of Magersfontein. He thought that a balloon greatly increased the safety of an army camp when an enemy was nearby. The other distinguished contributor was Major-General A. Paget, who had commanded the 1st Army Division. He was equally enthusiastic, and laid emphasis on what had been achieved by balloons at Fourteen Streams. This high-level testimony was rounded off by Rear Admiral H. Lambton who had been responsible for the naval gunners inside Ladysmith. He forecast a profitable future for balloons as an aid to artillery.

A world-wide survey. The testimony of wartime operators took three or four months to collect and was then placed in one of the appendices to the report. Meanwhile the Committee had more important things to think about. One of their first tasks was to determine the state of military aeronautics throughout the world. The examination of foreign countries was comprehensive and it is doubtful whether there exists anywhere so complete a review for that particular period. For the present purpose it is considered sufficient to consider the three main foreign countries producing original work, namely, France, Germany and the United States of America.*

France had her impressive factory and research establishment at Chalais-Meudon, on a most favourable site with a vast area of open land for experiments, which, incidentally, were usually made under conditions of greatest secrecy. Their spherical observation balloons were inferior to our own, mainly owing to their fragility and perishability; and their entire equipment was less serviceable from the military standpoint. The French establishment had not produced a dirigible since *La France* in 1884; but it had done, and was still doing, much fundamental research into the principles of airship design and operation.

German balloons, while not suffering from fragility like those of France, tended to be unduly ponderous and to require about twice the transport

* The other countries investigated were Russia, Austria and Switzerland.

effort of the British. On the other hand, Germany had made great advances in the development of the kite balloon. This piece of aerial apparatus, though a commonplace to us all nowadays, was relatively novel at the time. The basic idea was to combine the buoyancy forces of the balloon with the wind forces of a kite. This gave a wider range of permissible wind speed at which the balloon could operate. The Committee found that the captive spherical balloon could not be used with safety at wind speeds exceeding 30 miles per hour (50 km/hr), whereas the German kite balloon, it was thought, could be used in winds of 50 miles per hour (80 km/hr). The German kite balloons, moreover, were much steadier than the spherical balloons, and hence more suitable for telescopic observation; but their great weight was a serious disadvantage.

Curiously, the German Government had done virtually no work on dirigibles for which they were later to become so famous, but it was believed that they were financing private investigators. Schwartz was mentioned as one of these, but not Count Zeppelin who had made his first trial flight as early as July 1900.

The United States of America was mentioned as doing virtually nothing in the field of ballooning proper. They were, however, making large financial contributions to the work of a Professor Langley who was developing a *flying-machine* (aeroplane).* It is now well-known, of course, that Langley was the great but unsuccessful rival to the Wright Brothers, seeking to be the first to fly an aeroplane.

Of special interest is the mention of another American, though one this time domiciled in England: a 'Mr Cody'. He had evolved a man-lifting kite 'capable of raising a man to a considerable height'. Man-lifting kites were thought by the Committee to deserve considerable attention, being usable in winds too strong for captive balloons. This was probably the first official mention of S. F. Cody, who must await proper introduction in a later chapter of this volume. He is too important to dismiss with casual mention, and appears with Colonel Capper as one of the outstanding figures of early British military aviation.

Balloon Sections. A relatively straightforward task for a committee constituted on such purely military lines was to assess requirements in the way of men and equipment for the Balloon Sections. It would be inappropriate to enter into all the Committee's detailed investigations in this field, but there

* Strictly, an airship could also be described as a 'flying machine', but this term came to be used specifically for an aeroplane or airplane (U.S.A.). Langley himself described his machine as an 'aerodrome', an inappropriate word which fortunately did not come into general use in the Langley sense.

47

are points of special interest that have a bearing on the future development of military ballooning generally.

In the past there has been much confusion between the Balloon Sections and the Balloon Factory. Although they were mutually dependent, they were distinctive organizations. At the time of the Inquiry in 1903 the Balloon Sections were a combatant military unit under Lieutenant-Colonel Capper, who was responsible to the Royal Engineer organization within Aldershot Command. The Balloon Factory, a manufacturing and research establishment, came under Colonel Templer, who was directly responsible to the War Office in Whitehall. As already recounted, attempts had been made to upset this arrangement and make Templer and the Balloon Factory responsible to G.O.C. Aldershot Command, but without success.

For the strength of a Balloon Section in peace and in war, the Committee's recommendations are embodied in the following simplified table:

		Peace		War	
	Officers	2		3	
Mounted Men	N.C.O.s	8		8	
	Sappers	22	31	22	31
	Buglers	1		1	
Dismounted Men	N.C.O.s	1		3	
	Drivers	10		22	
	Batmen	0	11	6	32
	Shoeing Smiths	0		1	
Horses	riding	3	13	10	54
	draught	10		44	
Vehicles	Forage carts	1		1	
	General equipment wagons	1		2	
	Balloon wagons	1	9	1	10
	Tube wagons (hydrogen)	6		6	

It is interesting to note the part played by horses in military ballooning. It has been said that in one hundred years' time someone will invent a horse and think it wonderful! Steam traction engines were very useful for taking balloons long distances over roads and firm ground, but for ordinary cross-country work there was no substitute for the horse. Many years were to go by before mechanical transport could replace it, by which time the spherical balloon as a combat weapon was an extinct species.

The allotment of man-power in the recommendations was only a little more generous than that in force at the time. In the year 1903 there were

1. Lieutenant-Colonel J. L. B. Templer in 1898

2 *top left*. The British military balloon of 1899

3 *bottom left*. An operational balloon being filled with hydrogen

4 *right*. Colonel Templer with some of his men and a 'Steam Sapper': the Balloon Factory became almost as famous for its work on steam traction as for balloons

5 *below*. The steam traction engines used in South African War, known as 'Templer's Babies', are here depicted taking refugee children for an outing

6 *left*. The balloon inside Ladysmith during the famous siege

7 *below*. The balloon at Swarts Kop, which operated regularly for many days despite frequent exposure to gun-fire

8 *bottom*. Balloons being towed by bullocks near Kroonstadt

already six sections; but one was a cadre unit with only a nominal existence in normal peacetime. Another had no horses, but four were fully operational to peacetime standards. The committee worked on the basis that there would be five fully operational sections plus one cadre.

For balloons the committee recommended twelve per section, not counting numerous small balloons. They comprised:

$$\left.\begin{array}{l} \text{13,000 cubic feet (368 cubic metres)} \quad 2 \\ \text{11,500 cubic feet (326 cubic metres)} \quad 4 \\ \text{10,000 cubic feet (283 cubic metres)} \quad 6 \end{array}\right\} 12$$

It was generally thought at this time that the balloon of 10,000 cubic feet capacity was best for England, but that something rather larger was preferable for hot or elevated regions overseas.

Balloon School. In making detail recommendations for the Balloon Sections, the Committee were working to the same broad pattern as the existing system. They then went further in putting forward a more revolutionary proposal as a preferred alternative. This was to create what was described as a 'balloon school', which was to be a compact military unit more closely integrated than the six balloon sections. The school would be responsible for training officers and men, many of whom would move out after a time to make room for others, and they themselves would form a reserve. The total strength would be roughly equivalent to three sections of the type already defined, but with a rather more generous allowance of commissioned and non-commissioned officers. In event of war, the School would be able to send three full sections immediately into action, and then produce reasonably quickly three more from the reserve. The committee recommended a complement of large balloons appropriate to the full six sections plus twelve more for regular use by the School, making 84 in all.

This proposal has historic importance because it was eventually adopted. In April 1905 the Balloon Sections became the Balloon Companies, still under Colonel Capper; and in April 1906 the whole collection became the Balloon School with Colonel Capper now styled 'Commandant'. It is probable, however, that the group had effectively been operating as the Balloon School for some time before the change was formally recognized.

Under Colonel Capper the Balloon School did considerable experimental work either on its own or in conjunction with the Balloon Factory. When airships came along, moreover, it had a vital role to fill, since these needed to be handled by a fairly large and disciplined body of trained men, such as only the School could normally provide.

The first airship. The Committee treated the design and construction of a dirigible balloon (as the airship was then called)* as a matter of greatest urgency, this being a task for the Balloon Factory. So impatient about this were the Committee, in fact, that they issued an interim report on 24 July 1903, when they had only been operating a little over one month. The limitations of free and captive balloons were first reviewed. As might have been expected, the free balloon was ruled out as a military ancillary except for most exceptional conditions.

In assessing the value of the captive balloon the committee were almost too realistic, having much experience to draw upon – more than anyone else in the world. It is hardly necessary to go into details, most of which have already been covered, but mention should be made of one point that received great emphasis: the difficulty of transporting a filled balloon. In developed country there were trees, bridges, and even houses, that got in the way. The obstacle presented by overhead wires, however, which would be a paramount consideration today, does not appear to have been a matter of much concern in those days.

As regards the airship, the Committee made the mistake that has always been made throughout the ages: they compared the facts of hard experience from the past with visions of a theoretical ideal in the future. The airship was to be a wonderful affair with all the best features of a spherical balloon combined with the propulsion and steering of a ship. In the event, of course, the airship had its own limitations, which in many ways were more serious than those of the balloon.

The Committee was a courageous one, however, and did not shirk the responsibility of making recommendations through fear of being proved wrong, or even ridiculed. Requirements for an airship of the non-rigid type were laid down. They wanted the power of rising and falling possessed by a free balloon but without loss of gas or change of shape. They wanted to be able to operate at a height of 5,000 feet (1,500 metres), and thought that goldbeater's skin would stretch the required amount to allow for expansion as the airship rose; silk, the Committee realized, obviously would not.† Perhaps the most optimistic of the requirements, however, was one which

* At this time the *airship* (in the modern sense) was sometimes called a *navigable balloon* but more often a *dirigible balloon*, which was shortened to *dirigible*, a term still acceptable today. A glossary of aeronautical terms of the first decade of this century is given in Appendix F.

† It is rather being assumed that the reader knows all about the principle of the non-rigid airship, which is discussed at length in Chapter 7. The envelope of the airship needs to be kept blown-up like the tyre of an automobile though not, of course, to such a high pressure, and with hydrogen instead of air. When the airship climbs to altitude, however, the envelope is liable to burst unless the hydrogen is allowed freedom to expand, or a portion allowed to escape.

called for the airship to be able to fly against the wind on three hundred days of the year.

Most important of all, of course, was the emphasis on urgency already mentioned. An envelope of an elongated balloon suitable for a dirigible, said the Committee, had already been made at the Balloon Factory, and the Superintendent should be instructed to proceed immediately with his experiments and plans for construction of a dirigible balloon. The Committee went even further, and said that construction should proceed without waiting for a proper shed in which to build and accommodate it. The recommendation was made in the belief that erection could proceed out-of-doors with some kind of temporary shelter; but, as will be seen, on this important aspect of airship construction the Committee had to reverse its earlier findings in the final report.

The Balloon Factory. The Committee considered the future constitution and work of the Balloon Factory at great length; and said that they had obtained a vast amount of evidence, and much more than they thought necessary to publish. An unbiased person might well consider that another Committee should have taken over at this stage, composed of men with a greater knowledge of science and engineering. The Committee as it was constituted was in some degree preoccupied with the status of the Royal Engineers and influenced by Army rules and customs, which made it difficult to do full justice to research. One of the first things they recommended was that the Balloon Factory should stop all work on steam traction engines and other forms of mechanical engineering. Obviously Templer had not yet been forgiven for having been Director of Steam Road Transport in South Africa.* As a concession, however, he was to be allowed one steam engine and a wagon or two in order to take the filled hydrogen tubes to a safe place by road. They were considered too dangerous to be stored in the Aldershot built-up area, and had to be taken by road to Bourly, a place three miles away. At intervals, moreover, hydrogen tubes had to be taken to Salisbury Plain and suchlike places for manoeuvres; and the railways would not accept them owing to the danger of explosion.

Military labour was to be employed as much as possible inside the Factory

---

* This may be a little unfair. The difficulty of accounting financially for Templer's many activities may have been at the root of the trouble. In those days tidy and methodical accounting meant more than scientific discovery or even victory in battle! It is said that, in the later guerrilla period of the South African War, the British soldiers were continually being harassed by Boer commandos, but dreaded much more the commandos of the Treasury with their multiplicity of forms. One officer is supposed to have suggested that the forms be sent direct to the Boer leader de Wet, since he alone knew what had happened to the British stores.

in the interests of the Service, though no mention was made as to what should happen to the men in the event of war. It was also recommended that the Commandant of the Balloon School should be ex-officio Assistant-Super-intendent of the Balloon Factory. No explanation was given of how this fantastic proposal could be made to work and who would be under whom.

Despite the limitations of the Committee's membership, however, much of the work accomplished was truly excellent. The recommendations for scientific work and experiment were realistic and practical, though many were probably a recapitulation of what Templer was already doing or seeking to do. Among recommendations for the routine of the Factory was one that hydrogen should continue to be made by Templer's electrolytic process to the extent of one million cubic feet (28,000 cubic metres) per year. An additional recommendation was that a zinc-acid plant should be maintained for instruction of men of the Balloon Sections, since the process might have to be used in the field. The sale of oxygen, a by-product of the electrolytic process, was also advocated in the interests of economy.

The Committee did justice to the need for experimental work, recognizing the dual function of the Balloon Factory as a research establishment as well as a manufacturing organization. It went so far as to state specifically the main objectives:

> (a) A dirigible balloon
> (b) An elongated balloon
> (c) Man-lifting kites
> (d) Signal balloons
> (e) Mechanical haulage to bring down balloons from a height
> (f) Photographic equipment

The dirigible balloon and man-lifting kites were straightforward require-ments and are the subject of later chapters in this volume. In calling for work on the elongated balloon the Committee had in mind not necessarily the German type of kite-balloon but at least its equivalent. The objective was greater stability than had ever been obtained with captive spherical balloons. The small signal balloons of Item (d) had tremendous possibilities in the battlefield. Among other things messages could be broadcast over a wide area in codes based on size, shape, colour, etc., of free or captive balloons. The next item, mechanical hauling-down, was an operational necessity. The existing cable winches were beyond the range of man-power and the snatch-block method had to be used. In this a gang of men had to walk towards the balloon while holding down the cable by a pulley attached to a pole. The internal combustion engine had obvious applications in this field. The Committee barely touched upon the last item – photography. This subject had been neglected operationally in the past, probably owing to the difficulty of keeping a captive balloon reasonably steady.

The new site. It was probably this Committee that first recognized officially that the Balloon Factory was a research establishment as well as a factory. The Committee was emphatic, moreover, in stating that accommodation was inadequate for satisfactory work in either capacity and recommended re-construction on an entirely new site. In this matter it would be difficult to improve upon the wording of the report itself:

The Balloon Factory is at present on a piece of ground about $2\frac{1}{2}$ acres in extent. The buildings are placed close together; there is no room either in the factory or on land adjoining where any new building can be erected.

The balloon house door is only 22 yds from a road, on the other side of which are houses, and on which there are trees, and the balloon house is built at one side of the factory ground. Filled balloons cannot be taken out without risk of damage, except on calm days, owing to the small size of the doors and the proximity of the fence and trees.

The report then went on to say that the only satisfactory solution was to move the factory to some more suitable site with open ground close at hand. No recommendation or even suggestion was made as to where the new site should be. It seems to have been contemplated, however, that wherever the Balloon Factory went, there also would go the Balloon School or Balloon Sections.

Most significant as things turned out was the change of view concerning airship accommodation, between the interim report of 24 July 1903 and the final report of 4 January 1904. In the final report the urgency in building an airship was still pressed home, but the Committee now considered that an improvised shelter or wind-break would not give adequate protection during construction, and a proper airship shed was essential. Furthermore, said the Committee, construction of the shed, long known to be wanted, had been postponed over and over again in optimistic expectation of there soon being a new Ballon Factory in an entirely new place. In the light of this situation, the Committee recommended erecting the shed forthwith on any suitable site near at hand, to be moved afterwards when a proper home was found for the complete Balloon Factory:

The construction of a suitable shed is a matter of extreme moment, and we recommend that such a shed be at once constructed (at an estimated cost of £3,500) on the nearest convenient site to the existing factory, and that it be so built as to admit its removal hereafter if necessary at the minimum of cost.

It is not possible to leave this subject without mention of one of the greatest pieces of dramatic irony that can possibly be imagined. The Committee could barely have finished their deliberations leading to the production of the most comprehensive review of military aviation of all time, when the event occurred that was to render obsolete every major piece of equipment that they had recommended. On 17 December 1903, three weeks before the final printed report came out, Wilbur and Orville Wright made the first successful flights in an aeroplane. Curiously, none of the Committee's efforts was wasted in the revolution which followed. The organizations to which they gave official substance and recognition flourished exceedingly, and became in time the Royal Air Force and the Royal Aircraft Establishment.

3   The Farnborough terrain

For many years there has been a mystery in how Farnborough came to be chosen as the home for the new Balloon Factory and Royal Aircraft Establishment. The mystery apparently deepens when it is known that efforts had been made to place it elsewhere, and if possible outside the extensive territory of Aldershot Command. In the light of the 1903 Inquiry, however, the sequence of reasoning becomes plain.

By the year 1903 it had become imperative that Britain should build an airship for her Army. An airship, however, could not be built until there was an airship shed in which to erect and house it. There was no room for such a shed in the existing Balloon Factory, which was due for removal in any case, and unfortunately a suitable site for the new Balloon Factory (it was thought) had not yet been found. Therefore it was proposed to erect an airship shed locally, but to construct it in such a way that it could readily be dismantled and moved to a new site later.

There must have been many who believed this specious argument about future dismantling and re-erection, as indeed there would be today. It looked well in financial statements and annual estimates; and also in answer to awkward parliamentary questions, if any were raised. The War Office was being committed to building an airship, about which everyone agreed anyway; but the final choice of location of the Balloon Factory was being left open.

There is little doubt that Colonel Templer smiled and kept his own counsel; and it is difficult to believe that Colonel Capper was deceived. An airship shed, enclosing as it does a vast three-dimensional space, without the obtrusion of even a minor bracing wire to strengthen the building, is not a simple structure. On a rough estimate, moreover, it would cost about as much to pull down, transport, and rebuild as to construct a new one. Furthermore, there are costly foundations and access roads which cannot, of course, be transported. Finally there is the airship itself; by the time it is built there is so much equipment scattered around that a factory already exists there anyway. Thus it follows that wherever the airship shed was erected there also would go the new Balloon Factory.

The local site chosen for the airship shed, or in effect for the Balloon Factory, is shown on the map, Fig. C, page 29.* The choice was a good one and, while there may have been alternatives as good, this is unlikely. The new airship shed was near, but not too near, a main road. It was a reasonable distance away from the Aldershot–Farnborough barracks, and it was un-obstructed by built-up areas. The old Balloon Factory at Balloon Square (also shown on the map) was only two miles away to the south, with a good connecting road between. Finally, there was, by the standards of the time, sufficient manoeuvring space for an airship in the northern half of Farn-borough Common, which had already been cleared of trees, scrub, and under-growth, for use as an Army camping ground.

At this stage there has to be recognized what might well be described as the 'Farnborough miracle'. In 1904 no one could possibly have foreseen the unique possibilities of the site for aeroplanes. The new Balloon Factory was situated at the northern apex of a rough triangle bounded by the main Farnborough Road on the east, the Basingstoke Canal on the south, and moderately high ground on the north-west where now lies the National Gas Turbine Establishment. This area, covering approximately 1,500 acres (600 ha), was free from houses and other buildings except on the edges. The obstacles were mostly natural and removable, comprising trees and rough scrub with marshes and ditches. Furthermore, the ground was reasonably level except at the edges, and it was possible to draw a straight line over two miles long on nearly level ground in a roughly south-westerly direction from the Swan Inn to Eelmoor Flash (Fig. C). Thus all was prepared for the ultimate transformation to the Royal Aircraft Establishment with its many runways

---

* Fig. C, page 29, is a sketch that I have been able to produce from old maps. The date is round about 1908-9, but the terrain was not very different from that in 1904. A few trees had been cut down in the meantime, and Laffan's Plain tidied up to give a reasonably clear, though very rough, surface. In addition, it is probable that access from Farnborough Common to the Plain had been improved, and the gap through the woodland made wider.

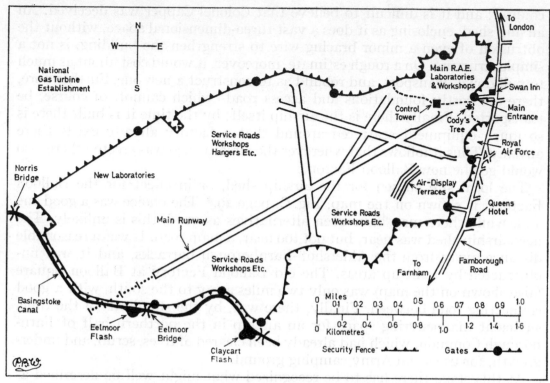

The following labels appear on the map:

To London

National Gas Turbine Establishment

Main R.A.E. Laboratories & Workshops

Swan Inn

Control Tower

Cody's Tree

Main Entrance

Royal Air Force

Norris Bridge

New Laboratories

Service Roads Workshops Hangers Etc.

Air-Display Terraces

Main Runway

Service Roads Workshops Etc.

Queens Hotel

Service Roads Workshops Etc.

Basingstoke Canal

To Farnham

Farnborough Road

Eelmoor Flash

Eelmoor Bridge

Claycart Flash

Miles
0.1 0.2 0.3 0.4 0.5 0.6 0.7 0.8 0.9 1.0

Kilometres
0.2 0.4 0.6 0.8 1.0 1.2 1.4 1.6

Security Fence ▲▲▲   Gates ●●●

(D) Plan of the modern Royal Aircraft Establishment at Farnborough which now occupies some 1,100 acres

and extensive laboratories and workshops, as illustrated in the simplified map of Fig. D (above).*

The transformation, of course, did not occur at once. Over the years that followed the construction of the new Balloon Factory, the ground immediately to the south was extended for aeroplane flying, and Laffan's Plain was also used. Until the outbreak of the Second World War, however, much of the wooded areas survived. The area was mostly common land to which the public had free access, and it speaks well for all concerned that no member

* The map of Fig. D gives the main essentials of the modern R.A.E., with sufficient external landmarks to show its relation to the outside world. In the north-east corner, on the site of the old Balloon Factory, lies the main concentration of buildings, which includes the administrative headquarters. On the airfield itself, of course, the main features are the concrete runways; but round the periphery there is much space occupied by secondary buildings, hardstandings for parked aircraft, and service roads, which cannot be shown in detail. In recent years there has been a trend towards developing a second area of main laboratories and workshops in the Ball Hill area to the north-west.

of the public was ever killed or injured by aircraft. In 1912 S. F. Cody established a legal precedent by colliding with a cow during a landing run with his aeroplane. The cow was killed and Cody nearly so. In the legal action which followed, the owner of the cow (Mr Maynard) was awarded £18 damages. In the present state of the science of aviation, said the judge, the man flying an aeroplane did so at his own risk and peril, and was liable for any resulting damage. Cody himself, however, was acquitted of evil intent, negligence, or even carelessness; and the right to fly on common land was not disputed.

The days of free access, however, were terminated drastically when the Second World War broke out in 1939. An area which eventually grew to approximately 1,100 acres (450 ha) was sealed off, and today there is a security fence about seven miles (11 km) in length (see Figs. C and D). Cove pond – or 'reservoir', to use its more dignified name – was filled in, and the whole area drained subterraneously. Concrete runways were constructed that were not greatly dissimilar to those of today, though naturally there have been improvements and extensions. The main runway, which goes roughly south-west against the prevailing wind, is approximately 7,500 feet (2,300 metres) long, or nearly 1½ miles, and there is still a good clearance at each end before the boundaries are reached. This runway follows roughly the course of a shallow valley, and rises, but only slightly, towards the south-west. The rising ground on either side has proved invaluable for building sheds, offices, and laboratories, while the slope of the edge of Farnborough Common provides natural terraces for the Farnborough Air Displays.

Thus it came about that the balloon men of 1904, in seeking a place for an airship shed, unconsciously laid down plans for an establishment that has proved invaluable in two world wars and is still today one of Britain's greatest assets. From the standpoint of modern aviation this suitability of the natural terrain is largely fortuitous, but not entirely so: the availability of so much unoccupied land, free of serious obstructions, goes to the credit of Army planners working over a century ago. Many people have shown interest in the still earlier history of the Farnborough terrain, and an outline of such history is certainly a great help in the understanding and appreciation of the work of the early aviation pioneers.*

It was in the year 1853 that the British Government decided that there was a need for a large concentrated 'camp' for the British Army, vastly more extensive than any which then existed. Plans were therefore made for building permanent barracks to hold at least twenty thousand troops;

* For a full account of the early history of Aldershot Command the work of Lieutenant-Colonel H. N. Cole should be consulted in his *History of Aldershot* (1951).

specifically: three regiments of infantry, two regiments of cavalry, two troops of horse artillery, and a company of sappers (Royal Engineers). More important than this, from the standpoint of later developments in aviation, were parallel plans to obtain control of a vast area of land for manoeuvres, including the outright purchase of at least ten thousand acres.

The scheme was set out by Lord Hardinge, then Commander-in-Chief of the British Army, in a memorandum dated 26 September 1853. After a rigorous survey of all possible locations for the new camp, the present Aldershot Command area was selected as the most suitable. One of the most important of the reasons given was the existence of vast areas of blasted heath, waste land, and open common land. Action was urgent, however, because attempts were being made to enclose much of it, and bills were already before the House of Commons to achieve this.

The project went ahead with a speed that has been rare in British history, and for this there were two main reasons. One was the personal interest of Prince Albert, the Prince Consort. Here was no dilettante dabbling in Army affairs, but a vigorous mind concerned at the perils to which Britain exposed herself by neglect of her Army. The other reason was the Crimean War, which Britain entered on 24 March 1854, only six months after Lord Hardinge's memorandum. The deplorable inadequacy of Britain's military resources which thus was revealed produced a bitter sense of realism that transcended all the usual arguments for further consideration and delay.

In the implementation of the plan, the barracks were built only on the east side of the Farnborough Road, and included part of Farnborough as well as Aldershot Town. This left a long wide stretch of undeveloped land on the western side extending southwards from Cove almost to Farnham. North of the Basingstoke Canal (Fig. C, p. 29) was the R.A.E. terrain, comprising Jersey Brow, Farnborough Common, Cove Common, Ball Hill, and Laffan's Plain. On the south of the canal lay Long Valley and Caesar's Camp. Long Valley was a barren sandy waste, often causing realistic misery to soldiers in the desert sandstorms of summer and the soggy Flanders mud of winter. Caesar's Camp had been a prehistoric mound with earthworks long before the Romans built a fortress there. Both these places acquired early aeronautical associations; Long Valley becoming useful for flying man-lifting kites, and as a relatively safe place for the primitive Farnborough aeroplanes to fly over, while Caesar's Camp provided a convenient taking-off place for Lieutenant Dunne's model gliders.*

Of special interest is Laffan's Plain, which lay just north of the Basingstoke Canal and within the modern R.A.E. Boundary. It has acquired a

* See Volume II of the present History.

romantic aura through its use by Cody as a flying ground from the beginning of 1909 until his death in 1913. Laffan's Plain, however, was famous long before aeroplanes existed, being Britain's national parade ground and often the scene of great military splendour. Perhaps its greatest occasion was the review by Queen Victoria of 27,000 troops on 1 July 1897, in celebration of her diamond jubilee.

Laffan's Plain was an artificial clearing, and as such much more clearly defined than the neighbouring heaths and commons. It was named after Major-General Sir Robert Laffan in the early nineties. As a Captain, Laffan had drawn up the original plans for the new Aldershot camp in 1854 and some years afterwards. He later earned the gratitude of both the Army and the populace when he served as Chief Engineer to the Command in 1866 to 1872. While in office he went to great trouble to make Aldershot a liveable town, and planted greens and trees wherever possible. In appreciation, his name was given to the famous parade ground as a memorial.

King Edward VII held a parade on Laffan's Plain in July 1903, and for many years there was a hut there known as the 'King's Pavilion', which proved somewhat of a hazard to the early aeroplanes. From about the beginning of the century, however, the Plain seems to have been neglected and in danger of reverting to its wild state. Deterioration was arrested by the action of General Sir Horace Smith-Dorrien when he became General Officer Commanding in 1907. Smith-Dorrien was the first British general to recognize the military future of the aeroplane, and in his term of office at Aldershot (1906–12) he did much to the benefit of military aviation; though he did this unostentatiously and few knew of it. It is perhaps ironical, therefore, that his first contribution to aviation was made unconsciously, in the clearance of Laffan's Plain for Army manoeuvres.

Smith-Dorrien has described what he did in an interesting paragraph in his memoirs written in 1925:*

I had not been to Aldershot for many years, and did not expect to find it so overgrown with trees as seriously to restrict the ground available for military training; but there they were, the country between Government House and Norris Bridge [i.e. Laffan's Plain] was a forest. The trees had to be got rid of. My Chief Engineer told me that it would take years for the Royal Engineers to cut them down. So I ordered two Divisions to carry out an operation designed to necessitate taking up a position on the edge of the wood and clearing such a field of fire as would cause the disappearance of the obnoxious trees. All went according to plan, and in six hours the trees were down. This is how Aldershot became possessed of a flying ground between Farnborough Common and Norris Bridge.

* *Memories of Forty-eight Years Service*, by General Sir Horace L. Smith-Dorrien (1925).

4   Building the Airship Shed
1904-5

On 5 May 1904, Sir John French, in Command at Aldershot, wrote to the War Office asking for authority to proceed with preparing the ground for the proposed airship shed at Farnborough.* There was perhaps a justifiable air of impatience at Aldershot. Four months had elapsed since the printed report of the 1903 Balloon Committee had been issued, which stated that construction of an airship shed was extremely urgent.

The letter refered to the airship shed as the 'Elongated Balloon Erecting House', and it was stated that the 'balloon' had been ready for some months. It is to be inferred from this that the envelope of the first British military airship (which later became *Nulli Secundus*) was ready for rigging and for the installation of the control surfaces, car, and engine.

It is of some significance that this initial approach to the War Office, and also most of the further communications about the airship shed, were made by Aldershot Command and not by the Balloon Factory. Both the Command and the Factory were concerned in the engineering work that had to be done, but Templer and the Balloon Factory were still supposed to be responsible directly to the War Office, now represented by the Directorate of Fortifications and Works. Templer was thus placed in an awkward position through divided allegiance and uncertain authority, and could never be sure of who carried design responsibility for the airship shed.

---

* Sir John French signed this letter as Commander of the 1st Army Corps. About a year later he was designated 'the General Officer, Commander-in-Chief, Aldershot Army Corps'. This change arose out of re-organization of the British Army in 1905. The Country as a whole was divided into Commands, e.g., Southern Command, Scottish Command; and only Aldershot remained an Army Corps. It was customary, however, to refer to Aldershot as a Command in the same way as the others.

Sir John D. P. French (1852–1925), who became 1st Earl of Ypres in 1921, was in command at Aldershot from 1902 to 1907. He had previously acquired great distinction as a cavalry commander in the South African War. Sir John was the original Commander-in-Chief of the British Expeditionary Force in France in 1914, but was replaced by Sir Douglas Haigh in 1915.

60

The letter to the War Office was dealt with by the Director of Fortifications and Works, Colonel R. M. Ruck, and he certainly acted expeditiously.* The Airship shed had been included in the Army estimates for 1904/5, but strictly these had to be passed by Parliament before action could be taken. Unfortunately, for some political reason or other, discussion in the House of Commons had been held up. Colonel Ruck therefore got the Treasury to agree to action proceeding in anticipation of Parliamentary approval. On 17 June 1904 he wrote the Commander-in-Chief, Aldershot, stating that preliminary work could proceed; and this authority appeared to cover design of the airship shed as well as preparation of the ground on which it was to be erected.

It took some time to work out the preliminary design, which in those days was no easy task, and drawings for the new airship shed were not sent to the War Office until 19 September 1904. With the drawings went also the estimate of cost, which came to a total of £8,900. From this point, however, everything went wrong. The 1903 Balloon Committee had estimated only £3,500,† which was raised to £3,600 in the later official estimate. The War Office could reasonably have started afresh and sought approval for greater expenditure; and there is no doubt that technically this would have been the right thing to do. Politically, however, this might have been unwise since there was danger of the project being stopped altogether. In any event, the Director of Fortifications and Works decided to go ahead and see what results came in from interested contractors.

The project was at once put out to tender to twelve engineering firms, ten of whom submitted. The tender of the firm ultimately selected, Joseph Westwood & Co. Ltd, came to £3,250. At first sight this appears well within the prescribed £3,600, but on the interpretation of the War Office it eventually fell far short of being so. What followed in the way of misunderstanding would have rivalled any comedy on the stage, had it not been so serious. First, the War Office realized that they had not allowed for the foundations,

* Colonel (temporary Brigadier-General) R. M. Ruck (1851–1935) became Major-General in 1908 and Sir Richard in 1920. At the War Office he carried responsibility for the Balloon Factory, first as Deputy Inspector-General of Fortifications (1902–4), and then as Director of Fortifications and Works (1904–8). He showed still wider interest in aeronautics, however, and served as Chairman of Council of the Aeronautical Society from 1912 to 1919; and it was during his term of office, i.e., in 1918, that the Society became, as it is today, the *Royal* Aeronautical Society.

† Templer seems to have been blamed for this original low estimate, somewhat unfairly. He got the figure from an engineering firm, and it was intended only as a rough guide. It is almost certain, moreover, that it related only to the essential structure, and did not include, for example, preparation of the foundations.

which were to be constructed by Aldershot Command engineers. For this work the Command had estimated £760, which reduced the available sum for the main structure to £2,840. Next the Command found that they had underestimated the cost of the foundations by £60, which reduced the available sum to £2,780.

Messrs Westwood appear to have been informed of what was going on, for on 21 October 1904 they wrote to say that if, as they now understood, the War Office only wanted a building that would last a few years then they could produce something cheaper. They offered to do the work for £2,760, i.e., £20 less than the amount available. Everything now seemed satisfactory, but then it was discovered that the War Office, in sending out the tender, had forgotten the doors, which were the most critical part of an airship shed. An estimate for these, which in the time allowed could only have been a guess, came to £300. This reduced the permissible cost of the main structure to £2,460.

At this stage the staff of the Director of Fortifications and Works took drastic action. Over-marking in red ink, they quickly reduced the width of the shed on the drawings and sent these to the contractors with a request for any possible further reduction in price. Pressure was brought to bear on Templer to agree to this ruthless action, and if he did so agree it must have been with great reluctance. His written endorsement to the proposal is so unenthusiastic as to be almost ambiguous: 'I acquiesce in these recommendations.' The Aldershot Command do not appear to have been consulted at all.

Messrs Westwood felt able to reduce the thickness of some 18 gauge sheet to 22 gauge, as well as reducing the width of the shed as instructed, but would not go further lest they imperil the safety of the whole structure. The new tender, however, came to £2,475, just £5 under the permissible maximum. Instructions to proceed with the airship shed at this price were issued to the firm on 8 November 1904. In the contract it was stipulated that the work must be finished in sixteen weeks, with a penalty of £2 2s per day for exceeding this time. This time limit had been imposed, not for any urgent technical reason, but merely to ensure that the money was spent in the current financial year, i.e., before 31 March 1905.

Aldershot Command were presented with a copy of the contract as a *fait accompli*. They expressed dissatisfaction in a letter which pointed out that a structure that had already been cut down to the minimum could scarcely be regarded as sound when reduced still further. They also implied that Templer had been forced by undue pressure to change his views against his better judgement. There was considerable justification for these strictures, and the shed was never really wide enough. But Messrs Westwood did their part and it successfully resisted the elements for many years.*

As things turned out the airship shed was not completed on time owing to delay in making the foundations. Under a very deceptive surface, the subsoil was found to be practically a bog. Sufficient firmness was eventually obtained in a most unusual way. The excavation was filled up by old wooden gun carriages from ships or fortresses. Being made of teak they did not rot and presumably are still there, although the airship shed has been pulled down. The delay does not appear to have been serious, and in a letter dated 14 March 1905 the Command asked only for an extension to 30 April, with transfer of £1,000 from the old to the new financial year.

The new building seems to have been an imposing structure and to have aroused considerable interest in aeronautical and structural engineering circles. A full description was published in the *Royal Engineers Journal* in 1906.† A photograph was included (Fig. 9) showing the doors being hauled into position. They were the most difficult part of the project and were said to be the largest in existence anywhere in the world at that time. A later photograph (Fig. 15) taken in 1910 shows the shed alongside the 'balloon house' with the airship *Beta* flying overhead.

The overall effect was not dissimilar to that of a Cathedral.‡ It may have been this association which produced the curious structure at the closed eastern end of the building. This took the form of a six-sided apse with a domed top, and is to be seen as it was in 1959 in Fig. 10. It was alleged to have been incorporated for economy and to give additional structural strength, though neither reason seems very convincing.

For the record the following were the more important dimensions:

Overall

Length	160 feet	49 metres
Width	82 feet	25 metres
Height	72 feet	22 metres

* The firm are still in existence, and I was able to get in touch with the present Managing Director. Despite the drastic pruning of costs here described the firm made a profit of between £200 and £300. The low cost of steel at that time was an important factor, and within a few years it was realized that never again would a structure of this size be built at anything approaching the price. Apparently steel bars from the mills cost £6 per ton. Later inflation masks the significance of this figure, but it was very low even for those days.

† 'Shed for Dirigible Balloon at Aldershot'. Communicated by the Director of Fortifications and Works (Colonel R. M. Ruck). *Journal of the Royal Engineers*, July–December 1906.

‡ Except, of course, that the inclined bracing members, sometimes called 'rakers' and corresponding to buttresses in a masonry structure, were designed to take tension in a strong side wind, like the ropes of a tent. Templer designed very substantial anchorages for these.

Airship Space

Length	160 feet	49 metres
Width	42 feet	13 metres
Height	64 feet	19½ metres

Doorway

Width	42 feet	13 metres
Height	64 feet	19½ metres

The cost of the building without doors and foundations was, as given in the contract, £2,475. The doors, originally estimated at £300, cost £562.

For many years the airship shed was the most imposing building in the Balloon Factory. It was extended westwards to about double the length in 1912 (see Fig. 11), and became generally known as the Beta Shed. In the next few years three more airship sheds were built and in time pulled down. The Beta Shed, however, survived until 1960, when it was demolished. It had by that time become an historic relic. Photographs were taken before the work of demolition began, and those reproduced in Fig 10 and Fig. 11 are two of the most interesting. Ostensibly built to last 'a few years' it had lasted fifty.

5   The new Balloon Factory
1905-6

We now move forward in time for a moment, to an event occurring fifty years after the period we are considering. The day is Thursday, 7 July 1955, and Her Royal Highness Princess Margaret is arriving at Farnborough by helicopter (see Fig. 12). The occasion is the Golden Jubilee of the Royal Aircraft Establishment in its Farnborough home, and the Princess has come to open a programme of demonstrations that is to last three days.

Never before had the R.A.E. been so unrestrained and liberal in showing what it could do and what it had done in the past. Inside the laboratories the Princess saw all kinds of apparatus – such as that illustrated in Fig. 13 – and experiments never dreamt of fifty years before; while out of doors, on the airfield once known as Farnborough Common, there was even more to see. With help from the Royal Air Force and the Corps of Royal Engineers, the latest adventures in aeronautical science were shown side by side with the best possible reproductions of aeronautical equipment of half a century before. It seems to have been universally recognized that the R.A.E. people showed themselves to be masters of pageantry in their own scientific field. Few could have known, however, of the difficulty they had in deciding in which year to hold the Jubilee Celebrations owing to doubts as to when the Balloon Factory could genuinely be regarded as having made a new start in its Farnborough home.

The main source of information when the matter had to be decided appears to have been the collection of historical records that I have named for convenience the *R.A.E. Chronicles.** These were some notes compiled just after the First World War from original R.A.E. documents, for the use of Sir Walter Raleigh when he was writing his official history *The War in the Air*.† The record committing R.A.E. to having settled in Farnborough in 1905 is forthright in acknowledging the paucity of information:

1905: The papers this year refer almost entirely to accounts. It was a period of transition from the old to the new sites.

A special historical investigation for the Jubilee was undertaken in 1954 by Mr D. E. Strike, who was at that time in charge of the R.A.E. Central Registry. He made full use of the Air Ministry archives and, after an exemplary piece of research, reached the conclusion that precise dates for the removal operation from Aldershot to Farnborough could not be determined:

Having made a most exhaustive search of old files and papers available to me, I am of the firm opinion that positive dates governing the removal of the Balloon Factory from Aldershot to South Farnborough are nowhere now recorded. I infer, however, that although the movement commenced in 1905, it was not until the middle of 1906 that the factory became really operative.

After considering these findings, and also the views of several other people, Sir Arnold Hall, who was Director of R.A.E. at the time, decided upon 1905 as the foundation year of the new *R.A.E. Farnborough*.

On the evidence available to Mr Strike it would be impossible to disagree with his conclusions. There has always been an element of mystery about

* These historical notes are reviewed as a contribution to R.A.E. history in Note 1 of Appendix A.

† *The War in the Air*, Volume I, published in 1922, was an introductory volume to a series of six dealing with aviation and the First World War (1914–18). Sir Walter died when he had completed this first volume, and the remainder were written by H. A. Jones.

what happened in 1905 and probably always will be to some extent. There is now, however, additional information available which goes a fair way towards clarifying the somewhat confused picture. In brief, the men of the Balloon Factory were undoubtedly in complete control of the Farnborough site by the end of 1905, although they did not renounce all claim to the old Aldershot site until the Summer of 1906.

Furthermore, considerable work was accomplished in 1905 using the Farnborough site as a base. Neither the writer of the *R.A.E. Chronicles* nor Mr Strike seem to have been aware of the work proceeding on the building of the airship shed. The reason for this is that the main responsibility for organizing the project – at least as regards paper work – rested with the Royal Engineers of Aldershot Command, and their records never reached the archives of either the R.A.E. or the Air Ministry. It is now clear, however, that Royal Engineers and Balloon Factory men were working on preparation of the site as early as the autumn of 1904, and that work on the new airship was proceeding at Farnborough in the summer of 1905.*

As is not unusual in such cases, the nearest approach to a coherent story of the move is to be traced in financial records, which have survived where others have been destroyed – if they ever existed. It was on 13 February 1904 that Templer sent in his estimate for dismantling the old Balloon Factory and re-building on the northern end of Farnborough Common.† The estimate, which did not include construction of the airship shed, came to £19,000, but Colonel Templer claimed a credit of £4,000 for the buildings and equipment that were to be left behind for use of the Royal Engineers of Aldershot Command.

On 21 March 1905, when the airship shed was almost finished, Templer exploded a financial bombshell by saying that he required £500 for an access road to it. The road had, in fact already been built, and the money spent, since the airship shed could not have been erected without it. It was 600 yards long and had been difficult and expensive to making owing to the atrociously boggy land. Templer maintained that the road was an essential and general service for the whole Balloon Factory, and should be charged against this, not set against the airship shed alone. Aldershot Command

---

* See Chapter 7, 'Templer's Airship – *Nulli Secundus I*'.

† In correspondence about this time the new site for the Balloon Factory at Farnborough is often referred to as Swan Inn Plateau. The name, however, is given on early ordnance survey maps to a minor plateau by the side of the Farnborough Road about a quarter of a mile south of the Swan Inn. This plateau has been occupied by the R.A.F. Officers' Mess since 1915. The Factory site was about the same distance from the inn but due west of it. The discrepancy is thought to have been caused by some geographical misunderstanding.

demurred, and eventually the Director of Fortifications and Works accepted the charge against a general headquarters vote. The whole affair, apparently so trivial, high-lighted the anomaly that Aldershot Command had been given a great measure of financial control over the two projects – the airship shed and the Balloon Factory – without any direct interest in the future of either.

It was not until 7 July 1905 that the War Office made a definite allotment of money for the new Balloon Factory; and then, to Templer's consternation, it was only for £10,000 instead of his required £19,000. On 30 August 1905 the War Office explained that this allotment was part of a more general one of £100,000 to Aldershot Command for expenditure on various things, which included steam traction, Royal Engineer workshops, and electric lighting, as well as the new Balloon Factory. This in turn was only a part of a still greater allotment of £240,000, going further afield in the Command to places such as Borden and Blackdown.

On 8 September 1905 the Aldershot Command asked Templer what he proposed to do with his £10,000, and what he intended to delete from his £19,000 plan. Reference, it is to be noted, was still to the future, and the word to go ahead had not yet been formally given. On 14 November there was a further financial query but this can be interpreted as a straight-forward matter of book-keeping, and the general tenor of the correspondence indicates that the work of removal and new construction was at last under way.

With the airship shed and the main access road already built, the construction of the new Balloon Factory was not a very difficult task. The *R.A.E. Chronicles* have some useful comment at this stage:

> The original Balloon Factory at Aldershot was situated between Alison's Road, South Camp, and the Basingstoke Canal. It covered a space of 150 yds by 100 yds, and the buildings included a lecture room, offices, machine shop, foundry, carpenter's shop, electrolysis plant, gasometers and balloon shed.
>
> The gasometers and balloon shed were removed to the new site at South Farnborough, but the other buildings and some of the plant were left standing, and are now in use by the Inspector of R.E. Machinery.

To this interesting account there should be added that the electrolytic plant and the foundry were also moved to Farnborough.

When the move was completed the new Balloon Factory must have looked something like the plan drawn in Fig. E,* though some of the smaller units

* I have drawn this plan (p. 68) from information derived from many sources, including some personal testimony as well as old maps, drawings and photographs. Original plans of the factory, or even parts of it, do not appear to have survived. The 1/2500 Ordnance Survey map published in 1911 has been particularly useful, and this is hereby acknowledged.

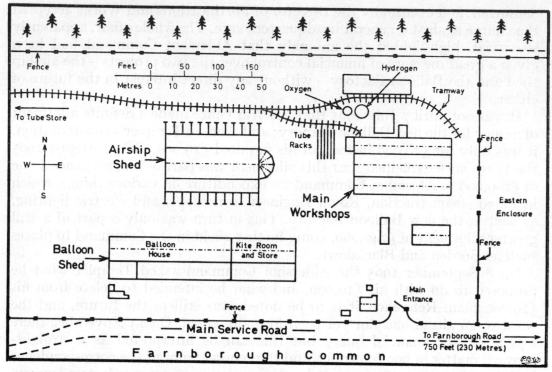

(E) Plan of the original Balloon Factory at Farnborough (1906). No proper plan of the original Factory has been discovered, and that shown here has been deduced from study of several miscellaneous documents

may have been added somewhat later than 1906. The principal building to be newly built was the main workshop. This covered an area of about 12,000 square feet (1,100 square metres) without the various off-shoots and annexes. Much of it has survived to this day but it has been so modified and absorbed in a great complex of workshops as to be virtually unrecognizable.

The only large building to be brought from Aldershot was the 'Balloon Shed'. This was carefully dismantled and re-erected alongside the airship shed as shown in Fig. 15. This photograph gives a good indication of the general shape of the building, and it will be noted how the main high-roofed portion is buttressed by a lower brick-walled annexe. A side view of the balloon shed is given in Fig. 14.

The western portion of the main high-roofed part of the balloon shed was known as the 'Balloon House', being somewhat like an airship shed in having a large space free from structural obstructions (see plan in Fig. E). It was used for fabricating balloon and airship envelopes. The eastern end of the main building was partitioned off and had two floors, the ground floor being used as a store-room and the upper floor being described as the 'kite room'. The annexe had accommodation for women handling goldbeater's skin, and included a place known as the 'skin room'. Some rooms in the annexe were also partitioned off for use by officers of the Balloon School.

For the record, the principal dimensions were approximately:

Overall length	275 feet (84 metres)
Overall height	45 feet (14 metres)
Overall width	62 feet (19 metres)
Length of Balloon House	180 feet (55 metres)
Width of Balloon House	36 feet (11 metres)
Height of doorway	28 feet (8½ metres)

When the airship shed was lengthened in 1912, the balloon shed was extended westward by about 75 feet, which brought the two doorways in line with each other. The balloon shed is still there (known as Q3 Building), though scheduled for demolition thirty-five years ago. It has no balloons in it now, of course, but is divided up into offices, laboratories and workshops.

In addition to these three large buildings there were a number of small ones as shown in the plan (Fig. E). There were two gas-holders, one for hydrogen and one for oxygen. These must not be confused with the vastly greater gas-holders which appear in some later maps (1910 onwards). There was a tramway which appears to have been used mainly for transporting loaded cylinders (tubes) of hydrogen or oxygen to a store situated at a safe distance from the main factory buildings. The area shown in the plan is about seven acres, but there was another eight acres to the west and seven acres to the east. This gave about twenty-two acres within the boundary fence, thus coming close to Templer's original requirement for twenty.

It is interesting to see that the specially-surfaced main service road came outside the boundary fence, and to this the public had free access. It was not perhaps a good thing for a military research establishment, and it gave rise in later years to many imaginative accounts in the newspapers about what was happening inside, as seen through the iron railings. The whole lay-out clearly demonstrates very careful planning, with a regular formation of buildings running approximately due east to west, and with the airship shed and the rest envisaged by the designers from the start as integrated parts of a single establishment.

There was an interesting sequel to the removal from the old site in Aldershot. After the balloon people had left, the Royal Engineers named their new mechanical engineering centre *Balloon Square*, and until a few years ago there was a plaque on the wall of one of the buildings which read:

> BALLOON SQUARE
> The School of Ballooning
> which was then a branch of the
> ROYAL ENGINEERS
> was founded here in
> 1892

In this way the Royal Engineers endeavoured to remind people of their contribution to British military aviation, which tends to be forgotten and which some people believe has never been properly recognized.

In 1963, however, not only the historic Balloon Square but also the whole of the Royal Engineers Establishment south of the Basingstoke Canal became due for demolition. The original Balloon Factory had left behind a small balloon house that had been used for the fabrication of balloon envelopes, and it was decided to destroy this with appropriate ceremony. On 27 March 1963, a balloon was made to take off for the last time from the Square while the Band of the Royal Engineers played, 'Will ye no come back again.'

The affair did not go off entirely as planned since the balloon showed how temperamental a balloon can really be. She was first balanced for lift* (see Fig. 16) while paratroops stood at attention, and then Brigadier D. W. Reid, Chief Engineer of Southern Command, made an appropriate ceremonial speech. While he was speaking, however, the sun came out and after a time went in again, so that hydrogen was lost, and meanwhile the slight breeze treacherously increased in force. As soon as she was released the balloon showed a determination to take a more active part than had been intended in the demolition ceremony. Instead of rising vertically, she swung sideways and the car struck the condemned balloon house violently. The situation was saved only by the Captain (Wing Commander G. Turnbull) throwing overboard a whole bag of sand, after which the balloon escaped out of the Square to freedom (Fig. 17).

* Exact airborne balance is first obtained, after which a precise lifting force is ensured by taking out a prescribed weight of sand-ballast.

70

3 The Last Years of Colonel Templer 1901-6

I   Disillusionment

The position of Colonel Templer following the war in South Africa was extraordinarily anomalous. The success of balloons in the war was largely attributable to his pioneer work, but he received little recognition. Honours were spread thickly over senior army officers, often for reasons difficult to understand; but Templer, with much genuine achievement to his credit, got nothing at all. He was indeed allowed to become a full colonel in the militia, but this was little more than routine; he even obtained an increase in salary, but as will be seen this was tardily given after much humiliating argument. Many of those who knew him well in the immediate post-war years thought that he was badly treated.

Brigadier-General Blakeney, who knew Templer intimately, left behind a few notes about the man he admired so greatly.* According to him, jealousy was the cause of most of the trouble, and especially on the part of the Royal Engineers. Up to the time of the South African War, however, there is virtually no evidence of jealousy on the part of the Royal Engineers. Records show how well they worked with him and respected him. After the war things were somewhat different. Possibly the selection of Templer as Director of Steam Road Transport rankled a little. Even so, there were not a few Royal Engineers of high rank who backed up Templer all the way.

Young men were coming along, however, 'who knew not Joseph'. The glories of Templer's past were to them only legendary stories told with all the imagination that clings to a romantic figure. According to some authori-

---

* R. B. D. Blakeney is earlier on record as the Commander of the *3rd Balloon Section* during the South African war. The notes he wrote about Templer were lent to me by Colonel Templer's daughter, Mrs Ursula Goold. Unfortunately these notes have a limited value because the writer was too involved emotionally to give an objective study. He provides, however, an interesting illustration of the loyalty and admiration Templer inspired in those who worked with him, and of the indignation that was engendered by the cavalier way in which he was treated.

71

ties, moreover, a new type of soldier was coming along. There was a reaction to the South African War, and a change of values. To the new school of officers, 'manoeuvring for position' meant something quite different from the tactics and strategy that was taught in army text-books. Into this new world Templer did not fit at all. He was devoted to his work for aviation, and within his own field could exercise remarkable shrewdness; but with his blunt straightforward manner he had no skill or liking for diplomacy.

His difficulties with Aldershot Command in general are not easy to assess, and all too easy to exaggerate. He could perhaps have been an annoyance to those in the Command who liked to have a regular and tidy organization. There are stories of how he tore out huge trees by the roots on Aldershot common when testing realistically the power of his steam traction engines. There are other stories of how he ploughed up large areas of common land when developing new methods of drainage and in testing his pipe-laying inventions. There are even stories about his reckless horsemanship; for interest in mechanical transport did not prevent him being a great and fearless rider.

Politically, of course, he was always, after 1897, in a potentially explosive situation. As already discussed, he and his Balloon Factory occupied an independent enclave within the territory of Aldershot Command, and were directly responsible to the War Office. Whether this worried most people, however, is doubtful; and it is unlikely that, even in the later stage of his career, the Royal Engineers were much concerned about it.

Amidst these minor uncertainties however, one thing stands out without the least shadow of doubt: he displeased the Commander-in-Chief, Sir John French. This was the most dangerous thing Templer could possibly have done, for in the early part of this century probably no one had so much power to make or destroy the career of a soldier as Sir John French.

The climax to Templer's troubles came with his compulsory retirement in 1906. On the face of things there was nothing wrong in this. He had reached the age of sixty, and he himself does not appear to have seen anything intrinsically objectionable. It was the shabby way this event was brought about that is indefensible. Perhaps also there was an element of sadistic cruelty in allowing Templer to devote years of his life struggling to create the new Balloon Factory, and then handing it over to some one else just as he was on the point of finishing his task; for, like Moses, Templer was allowed to see the Promised Land but he was not allowed to go there.

2   Templer's visit to Paris
December 1901

Templer is thought to have arrived home from South Africa early in 1901 and to have returned to duty in February. He probably did not become fully effective until June, however. According to Blakeney's notes he had suffered for some time from an internal complaint. For this an operation was necessary after he got back to England. Recovery, however, was complete, and he became once again the outstanding figure in British military aeronautics, though officially this seems to have done him no good at all.

Detailed accounts of Templer's work from 1901 to 1906 are not at all complete, since he did not have much use for diaries or other written records. This dislike of writing was his great weakness, and he was in this way himself partly responsible for the inadequate recognition given to his creative and original work. He was not in any sense unlettered, however, and when he had to send in reports they were usually clear and well-written.

Probably Templer's first public engagement was his talk to the Aeronautical Society on the part played by balloons in the South African War, which he gave to the Aeronautical Society on 15 July 1901.* In December of the same year he visited Paris, and from the reception he received it is clear that he had now become an international figure. He wrote an interesting report for the War Office (dated 2 January 1902) which fortunately has survived.†

Among others whom he met was the great Alberto Santos-Dumont, who had only recently flown round the Eiffel Tower in his No. VI airship (19 October 1901). Some writers have rather deprecated the significance that has been given to this particular event. It captured the imagination of ordinary people, however, and in those days an event of this kind was more likely to influence British official policy than any reasoned statement by a professional engineer or soldier. Templer, at any rate, seems to have been impressed, and he spent some time just looking at the Eiffel Tower and the course that Santos-Dumont had followed. Perhaps he decided that in the airship world Santos-Dumont was the greatest master of them all.

* 'Balloons in the South African War', *The Aeronautical Journal*, October 1901.
† Curiously, Templer does not give the date of his visit, but it was almost certainly in December 1901.

Templer also saw some work by Le Chambre, who was a balloon manufacturer and at that time was making a new balloon for Santos-Dumont. In this field, however, he decided that he himself held the laurels, and recorded in his report: 'But no foreigner can make a man-carrying skin balloon which can hold hydrogen and does not separate.' At the same time he recognized the advances made by the French in the manufacture of silk for balloons, and brought back samples.

Templer was able to meet his opposite number from the great French Government establishment at Chalais-Meudon, Colonel Charles Renard. Although most courteous, Colonel Renard would not allow Templer to visit the French establishment. He provided the information, however, that they were expecting to produce a dirigible balloon in about sixteen months time.*

Templer returned home after calling upon many other famous people in the aeronautical world, and then wrote his report. In this he made two pronouncements of historic significance. One was simply a reassurance that Britain was ahead of Europe in captive balloon work, both in manufacture and operation. The other pronouncement gave credit to Santos-Dumont for having established the value of the dirigible balloon, so that he (Templer) could now recommend that Britain should go ahead in this field.

3   Templer's appeal

1902-4

In the years which followed, Templer spent much of his time building an 'elongated balloon' as the first stage in the construction of an airship. Towards the end of 1902, however, he became concerned about his own future. Since 1 April 1897 he had been Superintendent of the Balloon Factory at a salary of £700 per annum. After a preliminary letter in October 1902 he wrote to the War Office on 29 December 1902 asking for clarification of his

* It is interesting to note that Colonel Templer was eventually allowed to visit the French Balloon Establishment – in October 1903, but unfortunately direct records have not survived. I was fortunate in being allowed to peruse the War Office records of Templer's activities in the War Office Library, but the file for the visit was unaccountably destroyed by the Public Record Office before I had finished with it. I can only quote, therefore, the number, date and title – 'File 7616/1147, 12 October 1903, Colonel Templer's visit to French Balloon Establishment'.

position, especially in respect of his tenure of appointment and retirement pension. He also asked for an increase in salary.

In view of what happened afterwards the precise wording is important:

As I shall have completed a term of six years in the appointment of Superintendent in the Balloon Factory on the 31st of March next, I should be much obliged if you would be so good as to let me know in what position I stand as regards tenure of the appointment, and also as to the rate of pension which will be due on retirement. If I am to continue for a further period it appears to me that I should receive an increase of salary, as the work has extended very much and responsibility increased since my appointment in 1897.

His case was strongly supported at the War Office by the Inspector-General of Fortifications, Sir Richard Harrison.* It was owing to Templer, he said, that we were in the lead of European nations in the air. If he was to resign, British military ballooning would receive a severe check, and it was essential that work should proceed on the elongated balloon, i.e. airship. These realistic arguments did not impress the Accountant-General and the Director of Contracts, who seemed to regard themselves as authorities on military effectiveness as well as on finance. To them and many others, unfortunately, Templer's duties were normal routine and, in their view, could be done by more or less any officer in the Royal Engineers. In consequence the increase in salary was not agreed. Sir Richard Harrison said, however, that he would raise the matter again later; but when the time came he was no longer Inspector-General of Fortifications. So far as is known, no one bothered to tell Templer or even to answer his letter.

In April 1903, Colonel Capper was appointed Commanding Officer of the Balloon Sections, and in June he became Secretary to the special Balloon Committee already discussed. Templer has not often been mentioned in this connection, but he must have worked hard to provide the Committee with much of its technical material about the Balloon Factory. By November (1903), however, he had still heard nothing from the War Office about his own future. On 12 November 1903, therefore, he wrote to the Inspector-General of Fortifications pointing out that he had not had a reply to his request of a year ago.

In response to this letter the matter was re-opened. By this time there

* General Sir Richard Harrison (1837–1931) was a Royal Engineer with a distinguished record. He had served as Commanding Royal Engineer at Aldershot 1886 to 1888 and had been Inspector-General of Fortifications from 1898 to 1903, thus covering the whole South African War. At the time under discussion he was approaching his retirement, which took place in 1903.

was a new Inspector-General of Fortifications, Major-General W. T. Shone.*
He put forward a case even stronger than his predecessor, if this were possible. His final sentence in a long and carefully written statement reads:

> We cannot afford at the present time to lose the services of Colonel Templer and I
> would invite attention to the large sums now expended by France and Germany in
> endeavouring to manufacture a satisfactory dirigible.

The understanding shown by this Royal Engineer, when approaching the
end of his active military career, is most remarkable. His realization of the
need to press ahead in aviation, and his appreciation of a man like Templer,
provides at least one answer to those who in later years have decried the
contribution of the Royal Engineers to military development of the air
weapon. The impact of men like General Shone upon the financial adminis-
trators at the War Office, however, was as disturbing as a snow-flake falling
gently to the ground; and men like Templer were regarded merely as an
untidy nuisance. The outcome was that Templer was curtly told by the
Finance Branch that his salary was to remain unchanged, and that his
pension would be equal to half his pay. If his airship should prove a success,
however, consideration would be given to the possibility of an award. The
financial people did not even take the trouble to tell General Shone what
they had done.

Templer then wrote a long letter, dated 22 January 1904, to the Inspector-
General of Fortifications, appealing against the financial decision. In this he
gave an account not only of his actual responsibilities but also of the original
work he had accomplished. It is one of the best accounts of Templer's career
that have survived, and it is regrettable that he had to be insulted in this
way to persuade him to produce such a valuable historic document. The
letter served two distinct purposes: it gave General Shone the ammunition
he wanted, and it told him how he had been by-passed by the Finance
Branch.

In a letter to the Financial Secretary (W. Bromley-Davenport), General
Shone set out in full detail the case for proper recognition of Templer, and
pointed out how parsimonious Britain was becoming compared to France
and Germany. He mentioned also, though somewhat incidentally, the generous treatment that the War Office had extended to Louis Brennan for his

---

* Another distinguished Royal Engineer of long experience. About this time Major-General
Shone (1850–1938) was promoted to Lieutenant-General and in 1906 he was awarded a knighthood. He ceased to be Inspector-General of Fortifications when the post was abolished in the
re-organization of 1904. The new post of Director of Fortifications and Works was filled by
General Shone's deputy, Colonel (acting Brigadier-General) R. M. Ruck.

torpedo invention.* Above all, however, he was determined to fight this battle to the bitter end, and he asked that the whole correspondence be referred to the Secretary of State for War:

I feel compelled in this case to ask that the Secretary of State should see the papers as the decision is an extremely important one as affecting very seriously the future development of military ballooning in this country, a service in which we have up to the present time been pre-eminent although accompanied by modest expenditure.

The matter was not referred to the Secretary of State, for the Financial Secretary at once capitulated. In a note dated 11 February 1904 he put his views on record:

It seems to be agreed that in one form or another an increase of emoluments is due to Colonel Templer. On the whole I think the Inspector-General of Fortifications is right. Please ask Treasury to sanction increase to £900 a year. It will be necessary to explain that this increase will be taken into consideration if the question should arise of any reward to Colonel Templer for inventions upon which he is engaged.

It is remarkable how the attitude to Templer improved as the subject ascended to the higher echelons of financial control. There was not only the Financial Secretary himself, from whom the matter seems previously to have been kept, but also the Lords of the Treasury who had to be consulted. They showed the utmost willingness to give Templer proper recognition.

There were, of course, a number of details to settle of no great interest, but the final outcome was impressive. Templer had his salary increased to £900 per annum from 1 April 1904. He was awarded a minimum pension of £400 per annum upon retirement. Finally, there was to be an increment of £10 on his pension for every year of further service from 22 March 1904 up to five years.

Thus it came about that in the Summer of 1904 the outlook for Colonel Templer was most promising. He had received recognition not only as one

* The Brennan dirigible torpedo is of interest to philosophers with a mechanical turn of mind as an outstanding example of the classical Greek paradox. In this example the torpedo could be propelled forwards by means of a cable pulling it backwards. It was developed first for the Navy, but was passed on to the Army for harbour defences. The brief case-history prepared for General Shone in 1904 could be of interest as having been compiled from original documents that may since have been destroyed. The award of £110,000 in 1887 is probably a record for a British invention.

1883	Award for expenses	£5,000
1883–7	While working out his invention	£1,000 per annum
1887	Award for invention	£110,000
1887–96	Salary as Superintendent of the Brennan Torpedo Factory	£1,500 per annum

carrying great responsibility, but also as a pioneer and inventor in his own right. He could look forward to two of the greatest projects of his life: the construction of the first British military airship, and the creation of a new aeronautical establishment such as had never existed before. Although fifty-eight years old, moreover, he had been given to understand that if all went well he would be allowed at least five years of service to achieve these objectives.

4   The court-martial
1905

The attack upon Templer was launched by Sir John French, Commander-in-Chief, Aldershot, in October 1905. One of Templer's men was court-martialled in Aldershot for a technical offence. The circumstances were briefly as follows. The Special Balloon Committee of 1903 had recommended that surplus oxygen, produced as a by-product in the manufacture of hydrogen by electrolysis, should be sold to private industry if possible. Templer does not appear to have been keen to get involved in such commercial activity, but his Superintending Clerk, a warrant officer, showed a certain amount of enthusiasm for reducing the net cost of hydrogen by this means. With his Chief's consent he carried out some preliminary negotiations with a particular firm, and in doing so he made a mistake which was picked up by the Command. In the course of negotiations he made a number of railway and other journeys at his own expense. Instead of presenting an official claim, however, he accepted monetary compensation from the firm with whom he was negotiating.

According to the best evidence now available, the prosecuting counsel at the court-martial firmly stated that he was making no charge of corruption and no suggestion of financial loss to the Public Purse. The procedure of receiving payment, however, was irregular and warranted a conviction for 'conduct prejudicial to good order and discipline'. The prisoner was found guilty and the final confirmed sentence was loss of seniority in his present rank.

During the trial, evidence was given that the Superintending Clerk had carried considerable financial responsibility at the Balloon Factory for many years. In all that time the official auditors had never found the slightest evidence of irregularity in procedure or discrepancy in the accounts. This simple testimony, however, intended merely to substantiate the honesty and integrity of the accused man, was later to be used to arraign Templer for incompetent administration.

On 19 October 1905, Sir John French, as Commander-in-Chief at Aldershot, sent the following letter to the War Office:

The District Court Martial held here on the 6th and 7th instants for the trial of Superintending Clerk H. J. Jolly, Royal Engineers, disclosed such a disregard of administration duties on the part of Colonel J. L. B. Templer, as Superintendent of the Balloon Factory, that I feel it is necessary in the interests of the public service, and of Warrant or Non-Commissioned Officers who may be placed in the same position as Mr Jolly was, to recommend that in future the Balloon Factory should be placed under the charge and control of an Officer on the Active List.

While feeling that I should fail in my duty as General Officer Commanding in Chief did I not make this recommendation, I should explain, that I in no way wish to underrate the great services rendered to the State by Colonel Templer, for I most fully appreciate all the good work he has done, and in making my recommendation, I do so only because I consider that this Officer is not sufficiently conversant with the system of Military administration to enable him to control as efficiently and according to the rules and regulations of the Army such an institution as the Balloon Factory as would an Officer who is on the Active List.

I recommend therefore his being relieved of the control of the Factory, his services being utilized in their most valuable form, i.e. Expert Adviser, retaining his title as Superintendent, but the administration duties being delegated to Colonel Capper, Royal Engineers.

The disclosures I refer to are contained in the attached, being a copy of the evidence as given by Colonel Templer before the Court Martial. It will be seen that Mr Jolly has been permitted to draw cheques amounting to about £60,000, and also to negotiate contracts and practically make all arrangements for carrying them out. By the evidence of Lieutenant Colonel Trollope it also transpires that during a period of five months, this Warrant Officer signed bills amounting to about £40,000.

As the accounts of the Balloon Factory have frequently been audited by Auditors from the War Office, and on each occasion have been found correct, it speaks well for the integrity and ability of Mr Jolly, and it was on account of the undue responsibility which had been placed on him and which he had not abused, coupled with his previous excellent character, that influenced the confirming officer in varying the sentence from reduction to Sergeant to reduction on the list of Warrant Officers from the date of signing the sentence of the court.

[Signed]   J. D. P. French
Lieutenant-General
Commanding-in-Chief
Aldershot Army Corps.

This attempt by the Commander-in-Chief to gain administrative control of the Balloon Factory by substituting his own nominee involved grave injustice to Templer. No one at the court-martial appears to have had in mind anything derogatory to Templer when testimony was given about the responsibility carried by the accused man. Yet the Commander-in-Chief was prepared to use such indirect testimony as evidence against Templer, as though he were being accused. Templer would indeed have fared better if he himself had been court-martialled; for then *all* the evidence would have been forthcoming, and he would have been allowed to explain his actions and to defend himself against the unfounded accusations.

Even the limited evidence apropos Templer that was produced at the court-martial was in his favour if it is interpreted without distortion or evasion. An official transcript of the evidence has proved unobtainable, but a representative of the local military newspaper was present and he followed the proceedings closely. *Sheldrake's Aldershot Military Gazette** for 13 October 1905 gave a full account of the court-martial, extending to nearly ten thousand words.

The first impression on reading the account is the comparative mildness of the charge against the prisoner, which is scarcely consistent with the Commander-in-Chief's picture of a man driven to desperation by Templer's overloading him with responsibility. Since a matter such as this can be largely a matter of opinion it is useful to have on records the actual words of the *Gazette*:

He [the prosecuting counsel] hoped he had made it clear that there had been no effort on his part which would suggest that the prisoner had done anything improper which would have the effect of making the funds of the Public Service suffer. . . . He did not suggest that there was anything corrupt or fraudulent conduct in what the prisoner had done, but he held that if it was found that the charges brought against him were proved, it was conduct prejudicial to good order and military discipline.

An even more important piece of evidence was brought out through intervention of the Court, almost as though the President of the Court wished to anticipate the possibility of Templer's loyal support of his man being used against him. Templer was asked by the Court as to the chain of authority in the control of the Balloon Factory's finances. Templer is recorded as having replied:

The reason why prisoner was able to sign cheques for such large amounts was because he was my chief officer at the Factory. It was his duty, even though he was not an officer. I have represented this to the auditor, but no objection was taken. His signature to the drawing and signing of the cheques was always taken.

* Now incorporated in the *Aldershot News*.

9 *top*. The first airship shed nearing completion

10 *centre*. The east end of the first airship shed

11 *bottom*. The enlarged Beta Shed before demolition in 1960: the original airship shed was lengthened in 1912, and although intended to last only a few years, survived for nearly fifty

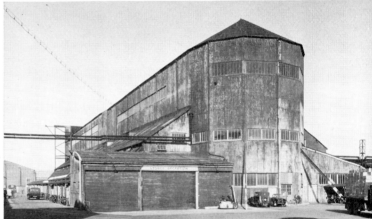

12 *top*. Princess Margaret arrives by helicopter for the Golden Jubilee of the Royal Aircraft Establishment at Farnborough on 7 July 1955

13 *bottom*. Princess Margaret on a tour of the laboratories at the R.A.E.'s Jubilee celebrations in 1955

14 *top*. The old balloon shed in 1908 (with the airship shed in the background):
it was moved from Balloon Square, Aldershot, in 1905/6, and has survived to
this day

15 *bottom*. The old balloon and airship sheds in 1910. This picture shows the two
earliest aeronautical buildings side by side, while overhead flies airship *Beta I*,
which gave the airship shed its name

16. The last ascent from Balloon Square, in 1963, when the old buildings were demolished

Thus Templer had taken all reasonable steps to ensure that financial control of the Factory was satisfactory, not merely in his own opinion but also in the opinion of the recognized financial authority.

Of great significance also was the testimony of Lieutenant-Colonel Trollope. He had been Acting-Superintendent of the Balloon Factory during the latter part of the time that Templer had been in South Africa as Director of Steam Road Transport, and continued as Assistant Superintendent for some months after Templer's return. He testified not only to the good character of the prisoner but also to the smooth and efficient administration of the Balloon Factory's finances.

The letter of the Commander-in-Chief passes from the unreasonable to the ridiculous, however, when the evidence of Colonel Capper, Commanding Officer of the Balloon Sections, is examined. He had not only trusted the prisoner in the past but would do so, if occasion arose, in the future also:

His opinion was that the prisoner was altogether an exceptional man; and he considered him, and always should consider him, worthy of every trust. When he had first come in contact with the Balloon Section he was rather surprised to find a warrant officer in charge of such great responsibilities, but after he had been there some time and had a closer acquaintance with Jolly he had felt that in the case of this man the confidence reposed in him was fully justified.

In this last piece of evidence alone is a complete answer to the Commander-in-Chief's accusations. The man to whom he would now delegate administrative responsibility was Templer's strongest supporter in the action that had been taken. Furthermore, if he himself was ever in a situation of the same kind he would act in the same way – 'he considered him [the prisoner], *and always should consider him*, worthy of every trust.' It seems incredible, therefore, that the Commander-in-Chief could have read all the evidence at the court-martial. No one concerned with Templer's future, moreover, appears to have done so either. As for Templer himself, there is nowhere the slightest indication that he was told anything about the attack being made upon him. On the original letter signed by the Commander-in-Chief there remains to this day a query raised by someone at the War Office. It is written in pencil opposite the statement that the prisoner had been allowed to draw cheques to a total of £60,000. Preceded by a question mark it reads: '? During Colonel Templer's absence in South Africa.' It would indeed be most ironical if all the larger cheques to which the Commander-in-Chief objected had been drawn while Templer was away in South Africa as Director of Steam Transport, and so not responsible at the time for the affairs of the Balloon Factory. Such is indeed not only possible but even likely, though it would be difficult to establish at this late date. The prisoner did actually testify, however, that the larger cheques had only been drawn by him in Templer's absence. If Templer himself had been on trial, examination or cross-examination would soon have produced the facts; but attacked as he was in this indirect and underhand way, he was never given the opportunity for correcting indisputable errors of fact, to say nothing of defending himself against false accusations.

5   The retirement of Colonel Templer
      1906

The Aldershot letter placed the Director of Fortifications and Works, Colonel R. M. Ruck, in a difficult position. Templer and the Balloon Factory were his responsibility, and even an *attempt* at replying to the charges made by the Commander-in-Chief would be tantamount to acknowledging his right to interfere. Furthermore, any inquiry into Templer's alleged incompetence in administration would at once reveal that any blame rested upon the head of the War Office director himself. Templer had several times explained to the War Office exactly what responsibility was being carried by his Superintending Clerk. He had even protested against the man continuing as a warrant officer, and had asked for his promotion to commissioned rank as a lieutenant. Thus, for example, on 22 January 1904, Templer said in a letter to the Director of Fortifications and Works:

With regard to S. C. Jolly, who is now thoroughly *au fait* with all the work here and has the whole charge, and also financial responsibility and maintenance, of these works, I beg to ask that he be made Lieutenant and Quartermaster, Royal Engineers.

There is no doubt that Ruck's predecessors under the old regime, Sir Richard Harrison and General Shone, as Inspectors-General of Fortifications, would have fought the issue. Colonel Ruck, however, was personally very vulnerable. The Commander-in-Chief, Aldershot, had tremendous influence in Army circles. At almost any moment Colonel Ruck might find himself under him in the normal course of Army transfers. A protracted argument between the War Office and Aldershot Command, moreover, could do no one any good. Ruck therefore decided on subtle diplomacy. Templer would reach the age of sixty in about six months time, and Ruck simply passed upwards a recommendation that he should be retired on his sixtieth birthday, almost as though this were a normal routine unconnected with the Commander-in-Chief's allegations. At the same time he avoided answering the Aldershot letter for as long as possible. When ultimately the Command got restive, he simply replied that Templer was on the point of retirement, without any mention being made of the allegations against Templer contained in the Commander-in-Chief's original letter.

It does not necessarily follow that Ruck was actuated entirely by motives of self-preservation. After what had happened, Templer's position as Superintendent of the Balloon Factory would have been difficult to maintain, especially when he had passed the age of sixty. He was, in effect, king of a small island surrounded by the vast area of Aldershot Command. He could scarcely undertake any major project without calling upon the Royal Engineers of the Command. Furthermore, success in his own dedicated work depended upon the closest co-operation with the Balloon Companies. In these circumstances the manifest antagonism of the Commander-in-Chief might well have made Templer's future position impossible. Ruck may therefore have been choosing what he considered the best way out and, in any event, he probably eased his conscience by arguments of this kind. Acting realistically if apparently harshly, he then did his best for Templer: in particular, he did not spread around the War Office the Commander-in-Chief's charges of administrative incompetence, but for all practical purposes suppressed the letter.

The proposal to retire Templer, however, introduced many procedural complications. His was a special appointment for which retirement at sixty was not in any way automatic, as many Army people might genuinely have believed. In response to his earlier request for enlightenment as to his tenure of office and retirement pension (as already described) he had been told: pension of £400 per annum with an additional £10 for every year's service after 22 March 1904, up to five years.

Before receipt of the Commander-in-Chief's letter, moreover, there had obviously been no intention at the War Office of retiring Templer. His retirement in the middle of the move from Aldershot to Farnborough was particularly inopportune. Furthermore, longer notice would have been given if retirement had been foreseen; for, despite the almost desperate haste to clear things up, he was given only a little more than four months' warning. The letter notifying him of pending retirement was dispatched on 10 January 1906.

Before this letter could be written, however, there were a number of legal points that had to be cleared. Templer obviously must have believed that he had five years to run from the specified date of 22 March 1904. As it turned out, however, there was an element of ambiguity in the wording of the letter of appointment, and the War Office found they could get by on a legal quibble. The main points were put on record by the Military Secretary to the Master-General of the Ordnance, Colonel Ruck's immediate superior, in a note dated 21 November 1905:

I do not think any of the articles in the Royal Warrant are applicable to Colonel Templer . . . as his employment has been quite exceptional.

I do not think that any injustice will be done to him if he is given notice [of retirement on 27 May 1906] at once.

He may perhaps regard the tenor of the letter of 7/4/04 . . . as implying a promise of an extra five years from 22/3/04.

Whether Templer did feel that he had been badly treated will perhaps never be known. He was a dedicated man, and at the time was deeply involved in creating the new Balloon Factory and in building his new airship, *Nulli Secundus*. He had been led to expect sufficient length of service to see both projects completed, and apart from any personal considerations retirement must on this account have been a disappointment. He may have obtained some consolation, however, from the prospect of being re-engaged as part-time adviser, which was first mentioned as a possibility in the retirement letter of 10 January 1906.

It took some time to work out the terms of Templer's new appointment as Adviser, and to choose his successor as Superintendent. A letter was at last written to Templer, on 26 May 1906, the day before his sixtieth birthday This asked him to hand over to Colonel Capper and offered him a post as Adviser at £300 per annum in addition to retired pay:

I am directed to request that you will be so good as to hand over your duties as Superintendent to Colonel J. E. Capper, Royal Engineers. I am further to inform you that approval has been given for your retention for a further period, if you agree, as Adviser in connection with Balloon Experiments etc., with pay of £300 in addition to your retired pay.

The letter was prepared too late to reach Aldershot in time, and a summary was sent by telegram. There were signs of hasty preparation, since no mention was made of the fact that Templer was expected to work only one third of his time. When this point had been clarified, Templer accepted the new offer in principle. Work on the airship, however, was so urgent, and the need to make full use of the summer so important, that he spent the first four months of his first year working practically full-time.

After one year had gone by the advisory appointment was renewed for a further year at the express request of Capper; and that was the end. Templer had served as the great pioneer of military aviation for thirty years, since his first appointment as Balloon Instructor in 1878 with a grant of £150 to build Britain's first military balloon. As he passed out of aviation in 1908 he received neither reward nor recognition. All that has survived as tribute is a note in an official file:

Colonel Templer's services were dispensed with from the 1st inst. – 27.4.08.

6   The new Superintendent – Colonel J. E. Capper

1906

When the War Office decided that Templer should be retired they found themselves in a difficulty. There had been no build-up of a successor. Templer had become almost a permanent institution. There was no one left in the War Office or indeed in the whole British Army who could remember a time there had been no Templer at the head of military ballooning in its research and manufacturing aspects. To the War Office, the obvious choice for a successor was Colonel Capper. He had already distinguished himself by his post-war re-organization of the Balloon Sections, and had acquired much credit for his work as Secretary of the 1903 Special Balloon Committee. He had, moreover, been in great measure responsible for the development of man-lifting kites and for preliminary negotiations with the Wright Brothers concerning their newly invented aeroplane.*

At the time, however, there were other plans for Capper; he was wanted for new developments in the purely military side of ballooning. At last it had been decided to re-organize the Balloon Companies (previously Sections) as the Balloon School, on lines recommended by the 1903 Balloon Committee. The change actually took place before Templer's retirement, on 1 April 1906. On this day Capper became Commandant of the newly formed Balloon School. This was followed by his appointment as Superintendent of the Balloon Factory when Colonel Templer retired on 27 May 1906, the two posts then being held simultaneously.

* See Volume II of the present History.

Behind this dual appointment lay also another purpose. Having lost Templer, military ballooning was in danger of losing Capper also. The post of Commander of the Balloon Companies carried the rank of Major only; and, although these were to become the new Balloon School, no great change of responsibility was to be incurred. Capper himself had been known as Lieutenant-Colonel owing to brevet rank acquired in 1900 as a personal distinction for exceptional service in the South African War. At the time these matters were under consideration, however, he had just been appointed *substantive* Lieutenant-Colonel (5 October 1905) and in the normal way should move on to another appointment.* There are still in existence many pages of arithmetical calculations purporting to show that without incurring additional expense it would be possible to appoint a Lieutenant-Colonel to the dual post, with enough in hand to appoint also a Captain as Assistant-Superintendent. With the financial aspect cleared, the combined posts were deemed to warrant a Lieutenant-Colonel in sole command.

Thus it came about that Capper found himself Lieutenant-Colonel with the dual responsibility of Superintendent of the Balloon Factory and Commandant of the Balloon School. He had under him two captains, one filling the normal Balloon School post as second-in-command, and the other filling the newly created post of Assistant-Superintendent of the Balloon Factory. This new post, however, was not filled on a permanent basis until 8 May 1907, when Captain Alan Douglas Carden R.E. was appointed.†

There were naturally some grounds for concern at having one man in charge of both the Balloon Factory and the Balloon School. Templer had devoted much of his life to maintaining for balloon manufacture and research a reasonable measure of independence from the purely military and operational interests. Capper, however, seems to have realized the dangers that could arise from this fusion of control, even though he personally believed in it in principle. Thus, while people at the War Office and elsewhere spoke of amalgamation of the Balloon Factory and the Balloon School, he never went anything like so far. Although the two basic organizations came to share many facilities on grounds of economy and efficiency, they were kept significantly distinct and separate.

---

* Capper was promoted in his brevet rank to full Colonel about three months later (28 January 1906).

† The Superintendent-cum-Commandant received a total emolument of £944 per annum, which comprised £594 basic pay of a Lieutenant-Colonel plus a special allowance of £450. This special allowance replaced special Command pay of £50 plus Engineer's special pay of £255.

The Assistant-Superintendent received a total emolument of £477 per annum, which comprised £277 basic pay of a Captain plus £200 extra in lieu of £109 Engineer's pay.

It might have been expected that as a soldier Capper would have been disposed to neglect the manufacturing and research aspect of his combined responsibilities. There is no evidence, however, that this was so. He was regrettably lacking in scientific knowledge and training, and his understanding of mechanical engineering was rudimentary, but he was never guilty of conscious neglect of the research or manufacturing aspects of his work.

In his purely military role as Commandant he was generally regarded as an unusually rigid disciplinarian, but he undoubtedly held the respect and loyalty of his men.* It is unlikely, however, that his stern military bearing was much help in dealing with civilians in the Factory; and he never seems to have understood the human side of the mechanic at the work-bench as Templer obviously did.

The manner in which Colonel Capper had come to be Superintendent was in many ways unfortunate for him. The sudden deposing of Templer was hard on both men. While it is natural to regard Templer as the chief victim, Capper had to take over the Factory without warning when it was in a state of disorganization brought about by the move from Aldershot to Farnborough. Furthermore, the new airship, which was generally regarded as the Balloon Factory's main aeronautical objective, was quite outside Capper's experience and understanding at the time, since it was entirely Templer's own creation. Fortunately Templer was willing and helpful, and instead of taking umbrage he worked practically full-time on the airship for the first few months after his official retirement.

There were, moreover, sinister undertones to the new appointment that would have shaken a weaker man than Capper. Gossip recounted how Capper had got rid of Templer by wire-pulling and trickery. Suspicion in the circumstances was not unnatural, but there is not the slightest evidence to suggest that it was justified. Templer appears to have behaved admirably, moreover, and did nothing to undermine the authority of his successor. In his turn, Capper also behaved in an exemplary manner, for he never flaunted his new position, and for a long time people were not aware that Templer was no longer Superintendent.

It is good to be able to record also that, despite many stories to the contrary, these two pioneers of aviation remained friends. As evidence of this there are two personal letters which by some happy accident have survived.

---

* Capper's fierceness on parade seems to have been a byword, rivalled only by his kindness in ordinary life. I interviewed one man, now of mature years, who served under him at Farnborough as a sapper. He told me how he had a serious accident which necessitated a long stay in Aldershot Military Hospital. Every week, and never failing, his Commandant made the journey to see him.

The first, dated 5 November 1906, is from Templer to Capper while he was staying at the Cromwell Hotel, South Kensington. Templer had had to give up his official residence in Aldershot and was looking for a house in London; and his letter reads:

My dear Capper,

I can come down any day you want me. I am thinking of going to Paris next week, and to Swansea on Wednesday when I fancy they will be starting to make the tubes [hydrogen cylinders].

I have worked on the dirigible and will come and explain to you when you are ready. I shall be in London again on 4th of December.

I have taken, or nearly taken, a house near here. We are only waiting for the agreement.

With best regards to you both from the wife and myself.

Yours sincerely
James Templer.

To this Capper replied:

My dear Templer,

Thanks for your letter. I will be delighted if you can come down to Farnborough station on Thursday, and come and lunch.

The car is not running,* but if you will let me know what train you are coming by, I will probably be able to send the trap to meet you.

Yours sincerely
J. E. Capper.

There are unfortunately few good photographs of Colonel Capper taken about this time, but there is a good one taken about five years after he had left Farnborough, and this is reproduced here as Fig. 18.† He had then just been promoted to the rank of Major-General, in 1915.

* A more or less normal state for an automobile in those days; the horse-and-trap was much more reliable.
† Kindly provided by Mrs Edith Previté, Colonel Capper's daughter.

4 Cody and His Kites 1861-1908

1   Introduction to Cody

The early life of Samuel Franklin Cody is mostly legend. So also, some people would say, is the rest of his adventurous life; but from about the turn of the century we now have documentary evidence for all the most important events in which he took part. This applies, fortunately, to most of his work for aviation: from his work on kites, which led to his becoming probably the greatest authority of all time on man-lifting kites, to his work on aeroplanes, by which he became the first man to fly in Britain.

The history of his early life, however, is very much a collection of tales told by the fireside: stories told to his family and friends when Cody was in a relaxed mood, and then remembered after a fashion by his listeners long afterwards. In these circumstances accuracy is the last thing to be expected; but in Cody's case there are indications that the legendary history is basically true. What tends to strain the credulity of most of us is the romantic background of Cody's early life in America. For generations young people (and their elders) have been entertained by stories of Cowboys and Indians; and even today the Wild West takes a generous share of patronage in novels, on radio and on television. It is fascinating to know, therefore, that in Cody we have the genuine article: he really was a cowboy; he really was attacked by Indians; and he really did lead a fantastically adventurous life in the Wild West before he came to England.

Much of the story of Cody's early life that now follows is an edited version of the account given in 1953 by G. A. Broomfield in his book *Pioneer of the Air*.* At the time of writing of his book, Broomfield was a close friend of the Cody family, and especially of Vivian Cody, who was Cody's second son. Broomfield appears to have had access to the few documents that existed and of course, to the memories of Vivian and his wife Eva. He had, moreover, memories of his own about conversations with Cody. As a young man he had

* A later and fuller account of Cody's early life was produced in 1965 by Air Vice-Marshal A. Gould Lee in his book *The Flying Cathedral*.

E.A.F.—4*   89

been very close to Cody, from late in the year 1909 to the time of Cody's fatal accident in 1913; and during much of this period he acted as an assistant mechanic when Cody was working as an independent aeroplane designer and pilot on Laffan's Plain. Some confirmation of the Broomfield story is to be found in the Cody obituary written by C. G. Grey, the famous aeronautical journalist.* Grey's references to Cody's early life were based on actual talks with Cody, whom he knew intimately.

Cody was born in Birdville, Texas, probably on 6 March 1861.† Birdville has long since been absorbed into the thriving town of Fort Worth, but in Cody's time it was merely a dot on the edge of a vast prairie. From very early childhood he was, with one brief exception, occupied with horses; so that he almost lived in the saddle. He had barely reached adolescence when he became a cowboy, and an expert with a lasso. He also spent some time as a buffalo‡ hunter and became a crack shot with a rifle. Another occupation was the catching and taming of wild horses, and he was a genuine 'bronco-buster'.

He deserted, for a time, the equestrian life when in 1883 he went gold prospecting in Alaska and Yukon. He had to return after two unsuccessful but – as things turned out – not entirely wasted years. He ended his time in America with about two years' service in Adam Forepaugh's Wild West Show, in which he gave exhibitions of trick riding and shooting. He then came to England in 1890.

Cody now became a professional entertainer on his own account. He first toured the music halls with demonstrations of trick riding and shooting, and other skills acquired during his roving American life. In his shows both Mrs Cody (Lela) and their two sons, Leon and Vivian, played active parts, although the boys were less than ten years old. Cody himself usually appeared as an over-dressed and over-glamorous version of a cowboy, though he was obviously able to play the part with greater realism than most of his rivals. Behind the obvious showmanship, however, lay exceptional skill with a rope, a gun, or a horse. After about two years of this he went to Europe with a wild west show of his own (1892). It was at this stage that he became mistaken for the famous 'Buffalo Bill', an error which persists in the minds of

---

* See *The Aeroplane*, 14 August 1913.

† Broomfield was specific about this date for Cody's birth, and it is thought to be the one recognized by Cody himself. There is, however, an element of uncertainty and I have found evidence suggestive of both 1860 and 1862. C. G. Grey, incidentally, compromised with 'about 1861', so he must have had some doubt. At the time of Cody's birth, it is of interest to note, Texas had only recently become part of the United States, having been annexed about fifteen years before.

‡ 'American buffalo', strictly the bison.

many even today. The true Buffalo Bill **wa**s William Frederic Cody, a man **a** good deal older than our Cody. In addition to the coincidence of surname**s** there was, it was said, a similarity in build and facial appearance of the two men. Now the genuine Buffalo Bill had organized Wild West shows some years before our Cody entered the field; and he was, in fact, one of the greatest showmen there have ever been. Our Cody, apparently, deliberately fostered the mistake in identity, and went to great trouble to produce the same facial appearance, especially the long hair, beard and moustache of his prototype.*

Cody spent considerable time on the European Continent, and when interest in wild west shows began to wane he rang the changes with a great variety of equestrian and shooting events. Thus, for example, he was highly successful in organizing chariot races in Italy; and in France and Germany he was equally successful with a novel kind of marathon racing in which he on horseback challenged a man on a bicycle. Altogether he entertained people in many countries, including France, Germany, Switzerland, Italy, Sicily, Malta and North Africa.

He settled down finally in England, the country he seems to have regarded as his home,† in 1896, and continued his music hall shows with all his cowboy tricks. He was again assisted by his family, all of whom appear to have become box-office attractions in their own right. A new recruit, still too young to take an active part in the shows, was Frank Cody who had been born in Switzerland.‡

After the family had been back in England for about two years, an event occurred which was to initiate a complete change in Cody's life and lead eventually to his becoming a professional kite designer and instructor. This was the production by the Cody team of a melodrama called *The Klondyke Nugget*. Before this remarkable story is told, however, it is worth-while considering briefly the significance of Cody's early life, as here outlined, in relation to his later pioneer contributions to British aviation.

It is clear that the concept of Cody merely as an ignorant showman and

* The relation between the two Codys has been the subject of some controversy. I have received testimony that they were blood relations and other testimony that they were not. Some have testified, moreover, that they were great friends while others have said they were bitter enemies.
† It is on record in official correspondence that Cody regarded himself as English almost from the moment of his first arrival in England in 1890, although he did not become legally naturalized until 1909.
‡ According to the memorial over his father's grave in Aldershot Military Cemetery, Samuel Franklin Leslie Cody, better known simply as Frank Cody, was born on 7 September 1895. He was killed in aerial combat as a pilot in the Royal Flying Corps in France on 23 January 1917.

cowboy must be dismissed once and for all. He obviously had ability and intelligence combined with a practical outlook that seem to have produced success in whatever course he set his mind upon. He had also unlimited courage and perseverence, and an extraordinary degree of resistance to physical hardship. The last qualities have never been contested, but his ability and intelligence have often been questioned. What is perhaps more important is that some of his greatest achievements in aviation were often stated to be mere showmanship, as though irrefutable facts were really examples of some ingenious conjuring trick that deceived everyone.

Against him at the start was his eccentricity in dress and behaviour. He was often suspected of being a charlatan owing to his long hair, his outsize cowboy hat, and other stage-like peculiarities. One of the best portraits of him is a composite picture which he had made for a poster advertising his kites (see Fig. 20). This shows most clearly his long hair, beard and moustache; and there is one of his kites underneath, with the letters F.R.M.S. to indicate that he was a Fellow of the Royal Meteorological Society. He was a heavily-built man and is said to have weighed fifteen stones (210 lb = 95 kg). Altogether he was an impressive figure, and perhaps even more so in later years when dressed as the more conventional Edwardian citizen whose portrait is reproduced in Fig. 19.

In some ways the unconventional Cody of his early kiting days represented the antithesis of both the Royal Engineers and the Royal Navy, yet both came to accept him, and even to respect and like him. The dilettanti of aviation may have been suspicious at first, but members of the Aeronautical Society treated him well. In the light of records in the *Aeronautical Journal*, they must often have listened patiently to his sometimes rambling comments, and they not only made him a member in 1903, but awarded him the Society's silver medal in 1909.

His showmanship has often been held against him, and has distorted the vision of his critics. Until he became a government servant he had to do a certain amount of advertising in order to gain interest in his kites. After leaving Government Service in 1909, moreover, he was compelled to act the part of an aeronautical showman in order to obtain money for his aeronautical work, since he had sacrificed his earlier sources of income when he made aviation his profession. Never would he allow his undoubted skill as a showman, however, to debase his work for aviation; for it was to this that he dedicated the later years of his life.

Perhaps most important of all was the influence of his early life upon his flying skill. The man who won the Military Aeroplane Competition against all comers in 1912 was one of the finest pilots who have ever lived. He had the balance and sense of timing of an acrobat, and the quick eye of a sharp-shooter. He was, moreover, a superb horse rider; and many of those who were responsible later for providing pilots for the Royal Flying Corps have stated with conviction that a good horseman was already half way to being a good aeroplane pilot. The extent to which these qualities were *developed* during his life as a cowboy and entertainer, and the extent to which they were *inherent* is immaterial to the argument. What is certain is that Cody possessed almost superhuman reflexes and quick responses, even at the age of fifty. Cody was forty-seven years old when he first flew an aeroplane, and it is doubtful whether he could ever have become such a good pilot, or even a pilot at all on such primitive aeroplanes, if he had not had long experience as a cowboy and showman.

Since this introductory dissertation on Cody has tended to become a character study of the man himself, it is not inappropriate to mention, paradoxical though it may seem, that Cody was at heart a very modest man. As evidence of this there is nothing more convincing than the letter he wrote to Colonel J. D. Fullerton, Secretary to the Aeronautical Society on 2 December 1908. About six weeks before writing (i.e. on 16 October 1908) he had flown an aeroplane for the first time by anyone in Britain, and he was writing about his talk to the Society, arranged for a few days later (8 December 1908). There is indeed a charming modesty about a man who, after such success, could say: 'I should very much like to have done something worth talking about.' At the time of writing he had had an accident with his motor-car, not long after the narrow escape in the termination of his first flight. Cody himself had had his usual good luck in both cases but, as will be seen, Mrs Cody was not so fortunate:

Pinehurst
December 2nd [1908]

Dear Colonel Fullerton,

Many thanks for kind enquiry. As usual the newspapers have tried to make a sensational article [about the motor accident]. There was no great damage to the car, nor to the horse and cart that drove into me sideways on; but unfortunately one of the shafts of the cart ran into Mrs Cody's side, fracturing her ribs internally. Our doctor is quite satisfied with her progress and assures me she is quite out of danger. Naturally, she will be confined to her room for some weeks, but this will not deter me from attending on the eighth.

Do not attach too much importance to my story [of the flight]. I trust that you understand that I should like to show the four or five slides which I presented to the Society some two and a half years ago. I am afraid I shall not be able to have another flight until after the eighth, though I would very much have liked to have done something worth talking about.

Believe me
Dear Colonel Fullerton
Yours truly
S. F. Cody.

2 Kites and the Klondyke Nugget

1898–1903

The Klondyke Gold Rush began in the year 1896, and in three or four years some thirty thousand people were existing in what had previously been a frozen, barren and empty land. After years of unprofitable prospecting, gold was at last found in large quantities in the neighbourhood of the Klondyke River. This lies not far from the Arctic Circle in the Canadian Province of Yukon, and close to the boundary with Alaska.

Stories about the Gold Rush and the dreadful 'Yukon Trail' reverberated throughout the world. It was not a simple story; and it did, in fact, assume at one stage almost epic proportions. There was not only a tale of vast wealth acquired in almost no time at all, but also a tale of human endurance under conditions of great hardship; and to all this was added the evil actions of men impelled by greed.

The universal interest in stories about the Klondyke seems to have been regarded by Cody as an opportunity to launch out into an entirely new dramatic venture. When he composed and produced his melodrama *The Klondyke Nugget* he must have been one of a very few authors who had had first-hand experience of the Klondyke region, which had been acquired in his two apparently wasted years out there in 1883 and 1884. It is doubtful whether the British public was sufficiently well-informed to appreciate points of detail about the Yukon, but they have a way of subconsciously recognizing realism in the background, without which melodrama becomes merely airy-fairy fantasy. In any event, despite the melodramatic exaggerations that came natural to Cody, there was something in the play which was to strike a genuine resonant note of sympathy in the hearts of tens of thousands of playgoers. In addition to his basic plot of the Klondyke, Cody threw in all he had in the way of Wild West experience; and he lost no opportunity for introducing his own three skills with horse, lasso, and rifle. The team of actors, of course, already existed in his own family, his near relations and his close friends, all of whom had worked together for several years in music-hall turns and Wild West shows.

For the story of the play that was to have such a profound effect upon aviation at Farnborough and, indeed, throughout Britain, we cannot do better than refer to G. A. Broomfield's account in *Pioneer of the Air* (1953):

In this blood-curdling melodrama, Cody himself played the villain, and his wife the heroine. His two sons, together with a nephew and niece, also took part. Cody, as Sheriff, gave a wonderful exhibition of his skill as a horseman, lasso artist, and rifle shot. During the play he precipitated the hero into a yawning chasm, accused him of murder, very nearly had him lynched, tied him to a keg of gunpowder, and did various other deeds of wickedness. The villain was finally eliminated in the last act during a ferocious knife duel between himself and a Redskin chief, the hero saving himself by jumping on horseback over a blazing bridge (the supports of which Cody had previously cut), carrying the unconscious heroine (Mrs Cody) across the saddle in front of him.

The Klondyke Nugget had its first public performance at the St George's Theatre Walsall in 1898.* It proved an immediate and sensational success. It is indeed unfortunate that so many writers have, by exaggeration of Cody's achievements, endeavoured to turn him into a legendary Robin Hood; for in consequence any attempt at giving the plain and literal truth in this case must appear as another dose of the same medicine. Nevertheless, this risk must be taken: *The Klondyke Nugget* in terms of popularity was one of the most successful plays that have ever been produced. People in the North of England and the North Midlands raved over it for years. Its success, moreover, was to carry with it a whole series of subsequent plays of the Indian-and-cowboy type, with titles such as: *An Indian Bride*, *Calamity Jane*, *Nevada*, and *Vera*.

The result of all this was that Cody acquired what must have been to him great wealth. The aeronautical significance of this wealth was that Cody came to be able to afford indulgence in what was to him a passionate hobby. Without it there would probably have been no Cody War Kite, and no Cody Aeroplane. The kites and all their ancillary equipment were indeed expensive, and Cody had to employ a team of eight men to operate the more advanced types of man-lifting combination. Although later he was able to draw upon the resources of the British Government, neither the Navy nor the Army were disposed to invest in mere ideas – some of which must have ap-

* An authentic contemporary account of the first performance is given in Appendix C.

peared fantastic at the time – and they insisted upon demonstrations of real kites that would really work. In this matter Cody was in much the same position as many other pioneers in aviation who needed money to get started. Sir Geoffrey de Havilland, for example, described in his autobiography *Sky Fever* (1961) how his grandfather set him up as an aeroplane designer-pilot by anticipating a legacy of £1,000. As with Cody the British Government engaged de Havilland (in 1910), but only when he could bring along with him material proof of his ability in the form of a primitive but flyable aeroplane.

The extent of Cody's fortune, much of which went up into the sky, may be judged from a manuscript note left behind by Captain R. G. O. Tupper R.N., and dated 8 April 1903. The matter at issue was part of some complicated negotiations with the Navy that are discussed later in this History. The particular objective was to determine fair compensation if Cody sacrificed his dramatic income in order to serve the Navy. Tupper decided that Cody was making a clear profit for himself of at least £1200 per annum. For a man with Cody's background, this was a considerable sum and equivalent to at least £7,000 per annum of present-day money; and it is to be noted, moreover, that income tax did not exceed one shilling in the pound (i.e. five per cent) so there was no question of the Government taking the lion's share in taxation.*

At this stage it is appropriate to record a fact which many people seem to have had difficulty in accepting – that Cody was unable to read or write. It does, indeed, seem incredible that the author of a successful play such as *The Klondyke Nugget* should be subjected to a handicap of this kind. The fact, however, is not only borne out by unimpeachable testimony, but it becomes increasingly evident as the story of Cody's aeronautical work unfolds. There are surviving letters in various handwritings, written at his dictation in the early days. Later, after his entering the Official Service, his letters were usually typewritten. Eventually, he managed to produce a rather clumsy signature of his own, but this was the most he ever accomplished in the way of handwriting. The circumstances are discussed in greater detail in Appendix B, with extracts from witnesses' testimony.

* Documents exist showing that in January 1909 Colonel Capper appealed on Cody's behalf against his being taxed at *one shilling* in the pound instead of *ninepence*, a privilege granted to Army Officers. The reply expressed agreement in principle but declared that it was then too late to claim because Cody had not filled in Form AF 01656.

3   From amateur to professional
       1901–4

Exactly when Cody became seriously interested in kites is a little uncertain, but it could hardly have been later than the year 1900. He began flying kites as and when his play-acting allowed. In consequence his kite-flying became known all over the North of England as he moved from place to place with his plays; and even, it is said, to Scotland and Ireland. According to some remarks he made later at a meeting of the Aeronautical Society on 2 December 1904, he spent one month on meteorological kite flying, attaining a height of 14,000 feet (4,300 metres); but his real interest was in man-carrying with multiple-kite systems, a subject in which he was soon to lead the world. It is also on record, as discussed later, that in October 1901 Cody wrote to the War Office drawing attention to his kite work and its military possibilities, although nothing much came of this initial approach.

In November 1901 Cody filed a provisional application for a patent – *Improvements in kites and apparatus for same* – and this was followed by the complete specification in August 1902.* To anyone already familiar with Cody's magnificent work with kites at a later date, the first encounter with this patent specification is a great disappointment. The provisional specification is unintelligible; and the final specification gives no more than the slightest indication of the great pioneering work which it was supposed to initiate. The patent specification is valuable historically, however, as illustrating both the limitations and the greatness of Cody as an engineer. Probably partly from inclination and partly from lack of any formal engineering training, he insisted on working everything out from first principles. In consequence some of his claims seem trite and unoriginal, and he was very much in the same position as a gardener trying to patent a wheelbarrow. On the other hand, Cody's original thought processes, often inspired by more than a trace of genius, produced some remarkable results. From time to time he discovered something everyone else had missed; and there is no doubt that, when perfected, his man-lifting kites were one of the best examples of such success.

As time went by Cody became increasingly famous for his kite-flying;

* British Patent No. 23,566, 1901.

and he began to find that his dramatic *work* was interfering with the kiting *hobby* that it was paying for. A letter to the Aeronautical Society from the Metropole Theatre Gateshead, dated 14 July 1902, illustrates very clearly what was happening. The Society had obviously been asking for a demonstration of kite-flying within reasonable distance of London for its London members, and Cody was pointing out that this was impracticable at the time:

To E. S. Bruce Esq.*   Metropole Theatre
Hon. Secretary to   Gateshead
The Aeronautical Society   July 14th [1902]
of Great Britain
Dear Sir,

I find it impossible to make any demonstration this Summer near London, as my theatrical enterprise keeps me pretty much in the North and Midlands. I have six weeks vacation which I shall devote to kite experiments near here.

I have sixteen kites ranging from seven to thirty-eight feet across. The seven foot kite carries a spread of one thousand and ten [square] feet [95 sq metres]. Three of these kites are of silk and the others of canvas. I have a great amount of wire cable, and from eight to ten miles of piano wire of various gauges. I have also two winding apparatuses. I have a staff of three men assisting me in my experiments which will take place within a few miles of Newcastle. Should any of the members of your Society be pleased to witness any of my experiments – both weight lifting and high flying – I will send you my exact address and shall be pleased to entertain them at any time.

I may mention that I have supplied Mr Bruce who is at the head of the Scottish Antarctic Expedition – which starts in August – with one of my No. 1 size aeroplanes.

Faithfully yours
S. F. Cody.

This letter is one of the most informative ever sent by Cody. The last paragraph is of special interest, and has rather amusing associations. He often used to call his kites 'aeroplanes', a not at all inappropriate term at the time, although it has since come to mean the modern powered aircraft. Now Cody did not include the year in the date at the head of his letter, and on the strength of the reference to his No. 1 size aeroplanes the Royal Aeronautical Society originally placed it as 1908, the year of his first flight with a powered aeroplane. The year of writing, however, is precisely identifiable

* Eric Stuart Bruce (not to be confused with the Mr Bruce mentioned in Cody's letter) became *Acting* Honorary Secretary of the Aeronautical Society on 21 October 1899 when the Secretary, Major B. F. S. Baden-Powell, left for South Africa. Bruce became Secretary on 17 July 1900, and it is largely owing to him that the Journal during his term of office was unique in the diversity of aeronautical material it produced. In my view, Bruce did much to smooth the way of the somewhat *outré* Cody into the scientific, if somewhat dilettante, world of the Aeronautical Society.

as 1902 by the reference to the Scottish Antarctic Expedition. The request that Cody should supply a kite for this expedition is clearly indicative of the recognition that Cody was steadily acquiring as an authority on kites.*

Further recognition for Cody as a pioneer in kite flying came from Patrick Alexander when he invited him to the Balloon Centenary celebrations at Bath on 8 and 9 September 1902. Patrick Alexander was at that time the great *entrepreneur* and patron of flight in all its forms; and he organized and paid for the celebrations.† On the first day (8 September) a balloon ascended exactly one hundred years after the celebrated balloonist and parachutist, André Jacques Garnerin, had made the first balloon ascent from Bath. Probably the whole affair was primarily a convenient way of getting together some leaders of aviation, and perhaps also an excuse for the sumptuous repast provided at the end of the first day. It is significant, however, that Cody was now regarded as one of the pioneers; and on the second day he was reserved for still greater distinction in being asked to give a demonstration of his kite flying. Aided by a steady easterly wind, he provided what Eric Stuart Bruce, Secretary of the Aeronautical Society, described as the *pièce de résistance* of the day.

While Cody was becoming increasingly famous for his kites, he was still well-known for his dramatic activities which were his main source of income. On 8 December 1902 he wrote a letter to the Aeronautical Society which, though trivial in content, has a certain interest:

S. F. CODY'S
KLONDYKE NUGGET CO.

To: The Secretary,   Grand Theatre
Aeronautical Society   Rawtenstall, Lancashire
                                        8.12.02

Dear Sir,

    I replied to your letter asking for my address but have not heard from you, so conclude my letter must have gone astray. My address next week is *Royal Court Theatre, Warrington*. Have you seen last week's *London News*.

Faithfully yours
S. F. Cody.

* The Scottish Antarctic Expedition under the leadership of W. S. Bruce left Scotland in the *Scotia* towards the end of 1902. Its objective was oceanographical research in Antarctic waters, and on return in 1904 the *Scotia Sea* was named after it.

† Patrick Y. Alexander (1867–1943) was originally a very wealthy man, but he expended most of his fortune in a lifetime of devotion to aviation and astronomy. He made direct contributions to both lighter-than-air and heavier-than-air flight, but he will be remembered most for the way in which he gained the friendship and the trust of the pioneers of aviation in the early years of this century, and spread around both information and encouragement to all who

'Klondyke Nugget Co.' is now engraved on Cody's notepaper and has clearly become almost a national institution. It is becoming equally clear that the tug-o'-war between kites and Klondyke must soon be resolved. Cody is too elusive with his ever-changing address, and no one can be certain where he is. This particular letter also illustrates a point that many historians have overlooked: Cody was not operating as a lone eccentric, but was in close contact with civilized thinking in the Aeronautical Society. In point of fact, he was soon to become a member of the Society, being made a member at the same time as Colonel Capper on 24 June 1903.

In February 1903 Cody made a decision that was to affect his whole future and, in fact, the future of British aviation: he offered his invention and his services to the British Navy. What then transpired is a story in itself, and is covered in appropriate detail later in this History (Chapter 6). The significant outcome was that in May 1903, after thorough trials on land and sea, the Admiralty declined his invention and his services, but ordered four sets of kites with the appropriate ancillary equipment.

The effect on Cody was remarkable, for he came out of the affair more confident in his kites than ever before. Once again we have as a record a letter to the Aeronautical Society that, while trivial in itself, gives valuable information about what was happening. Under an embossed reproduction of the flamboyant Cody bust illustrated in Fig. 20, the letter reads:

INVENTOR OF THE CODY WAR KITE
AS SUPPLIED TO THE BRITISH NAVY

July 12th 1903

Banqueting Hall
Alexandra Palace
Wood Green
London N.

To: Eric Stuart Bruce Esq.

Dear Sir,

The cheque for my entrance fee and membership was sent to you some time ago, but to date I have received no acknowledgement. Kindly let me know if you have received same and oblige.

Yours sincerely,
S. F. Cody.

Thus Cody has thrown away his Klondyke Nugget, at least from his notepaper, and is now the inventor of the War Kite and supplier to the British

---

seemed to need them. He was a friend of the Wright Brothers, and acted as their main channel of communication with the Aeronautical Society until they were able to visit Britain in person. He is also remembered in the Aldershot–Farnborough area for the observatory he built there.

Navy. There is still a difficulty over his address, but this is not likely to recur, for he has now a more-or-less permanent address at the Banqueting Hall of Alexandra Palace. Here he had his workshop, rendered necessary by the Naval order for sixteen kites. As a matter of fact, he did not stay long at Alexandra Palace, but soon moved to the Crystal Palace, Sydenham, where he found more suitable accommodation; and there is a letter in the Aeronautical Society collection from this address also, but it is undated.

The Naval Trials, as things turned out, proved to be only a preliminary to much more serious work for the Army, the story of which takes up a considerable share of the present volume. Cody arrived at Aldershot station with all his kiting paraphernalia on Saturday 4 June 1904. Farnborough Common, Laffan's Plain and Long Valley then became his operational domain, and so continued until his fatal crash on 7 August 1913. The arrival, moreover, was a preliminary to nearly five years official employment in which he began as Kite Instructor and ended as the first man in Britain to fly an aeroplane.

4   The evolution of Cody Kites

     1898-1904

When Cody began his experiments with kites, in the year 1900, he followed a period of intense activity in the kiting world. The last fifteen years of the nineteenth century saw a virtual Renaissance in which the kite was transformed from a philosophical toy to an engineering proposition. At the beginning of the present century only one aspect still remained in a primitive unfulfilled state – the lifting of heavy weights and notably of men for military observation. It was in this that Cody, in conjunction with the Royal Navy and the Royal Engineers, was to make his great and revolutionary contribution.

The first man to gain universal recognition for man-lifting was Captain (later Major) B. F. S. Baden-Powell.* He lifted a man ten feet (3 metres) in

* B. F. S. (Baden Fletcher Smyth) Baden-Powell (1860–1937) became a leading figure in early British Military aviation. In 1897, as Captain Baden-Powell, he revived the almost extinct Aeronautical Society of Great Britain, and became its Secretary. On 1 October 1899, as Major Baden-Powell, he embarked for the war in South Africa. He was able to join his brother,

1894, after which he achieved greater heights, probably reaching nearly 200 feet (60 metres) in 1895. Baden-Powell was also the inventor of the six-sided kite, intended to replace the more conventional shape resembling a distorted diamond with which we are all familiar. This particular kite was only one of several that Baden-Powell investigated, but it was the one he preferred and patented in 1895.* He found that there was a practical limit to the size of a single kite; and for man-lifting he used several, arranged in tandem.

It is perhaps not generally realized that the design of a kite, and especially one that has to take men up into the air, presents problems in stability and control that are at least as complicated as those associated with a modern aeroplane. The kite pioneers, moreover, were not only presented with a formidable task, but had to face it without the modern knowledge of aero-dynamics and testing facilities such as wind tunnels. The ordinary kite is liable to go berserk in a strong wind. It may swing from side to side in great arcs across the sky; and it may even climb vigorously until the cord is nearly vertical and then collapse like a punctured balloon. Most, if not all, the troubles can be overcome by fitting the well-known tail which, incidentally, works through its air-resistance or drag, and not its weight. Baden-Powell was convinced that his hexagonal kite was superior to the ordinary diamond-shaped one in respect of inherent stability, a conclusion which may well have been correct; but his suggestion that it did not need a tail at all is open to question.

For his more successful man-lifting experiments, however, Baden-Powell rather circumvented the problem of inherent instability by using two separate lines connected to stations some appreciable distance apart on the ground.† In this way the kites were held more-or-less forcibly in the correct position, but the whole arrangement was excessively elaborate and cumbersome. In point of fact, Baden-Powell's man-lifting work was a disappointment and never any practical use. His manifest failure, combined with a dubious but world-wide reputation as a skilled experimenter, was a great embarrassment to Cody later. He had to penetrate a barrier of disbelief when he produced a genuine and workable system. The attitude of many

---

Colonel Robert S. S. Baden-Powell, hero of the famous siege of Mafeking, when the relieving forces entered that city on 17 May 1900. From Mafeking he wrote to the Aeronautical Society, sending his resignation as Secretary. This was accepted but he was at once, on 17 July 1900, created President *in absentia*. His brother, Colonel Robert, eventually became Lieutenant-General Lord Baden-Powell and founder of the Boy Scout movement.

* British Patent 17,683, 23 September 1895, *Kites*. B. F. S. Baden-Powell, Guards Club, London.

† See 'War Kites' by B. F. S. Baden-Powell, *Aeronautical Journal*, January 1899.

people was: 'how can this cowboy-showman succeed where the great Baden-Powell has failed?'

The kite that was to prove superior to all others in the pre-Cody era, however, was the 'box-kite' invented by the Australian, Lawrence Hargrave, a brilliant but modest man who refused to take out any patent.* Fig. 21 shows a photograph of the one at present in the Science Museum, South Kensington. As is readily seen, the kite is simply an oblong box without ends and with about one third of each of the four sides removed from the middle. Alternatively, the kite may be regarded as two shallow boxes fixed one behind the other, but well separated, which is a useful concept since there were a number of variants in the way the front and rear elements could be connected: the two fore-and-aft booms, for example, were often replaced by four longerons running along the four edges.

Hargarave had a great respect for Baden-Powell, whose work he seems to have studied assiduously, but he was convinced that a flat kite could never be successful. He attributed the success of his box-kite largely to the sides of the box, which contributed to stability by resisting sideways motion. It is inconceivable, however, that even he could have foreseen how successful his kite would prove to be. It was, of course, much more than a kite in the previously accepted sense, having some of the attributes of an aeroplane as we now know it.

The reputation of Hargrave's kite was greatly enhanced by the American school of kiting, and especially by the meteorologists at the Blue Hill Observatory, Massachusetts.† In the last decade or so of the nineteenth century the Americans were well ahead of most other countries in kite work, and as soon as Hargrave's invention of 1893 became known they at once recognized its superiority, and afterwards would rarely use anything else. American interest, however, was mainly confined to meteorology and research into the nature of the upper atmosphere, heights of two miles (3 kilometres) and more being frequently attained. Some man-lifting was done, nevertheless, notably by Lieutenant R. G. Wise of the United States Army. In 1897 he

* Lawrence Hargrave was born in Greenwich, England, on 29 January 1850, but emigrated to New South Wales in 1866. He there had experience, first as an engineer-draughtsman, and then as a member of the staff of Sydney Observatory, both of which had an important influence on his aeronautical career. From 1883 he gave his whole time to aviation, subsisting on his private income. He accomplished much first-class work in engine and aircraft research and development. In results, however, he was mostly unlucky, except for his famous kite, which was one of the most perfect and successful inventions of all time. He re-settled in England (or thought he did) in 1899, but went back to Australia after six months. He died on 16 July 1915.
† See, among other notes and papers, 'The Chief Scientific Uses of Kites' by A. Lawrence Rotch, Director of Blue Hill Observatory, *Aeronautical Journal*, October 1901.

lifted himself about fifty feet (15 metres) using four Hargrave kites.* Hargrave in Australia also lifted himself, but only a few feet, using four of his kites. It was left to Cody to take man-lifting seriously, and in this there is no comparison between his work and that of his predecessors: he thought in terms of thousands of feet against their hundreds or less.

Cody's first significant efforts in kiting experiments, which began in the year 1900 – as already mentioned – were directed towards high-flying and meteorology: a kind of amateurish extension of the work at the American Blue Hill Observatory, without any man-lifting associations. The kites he used were mostly of the Hargrave type, at least aerodynamically, though probably with structural alterations in accord with his own original ideas.

Cody would have had little difficulty in obtaining the necessary data for design: Hargrave's kite was not only simple in its basic form, but it had been fairly well publicized among those likely to be interested. Especially important was the account of Hargrave's work given in the periodical *Engineering* on 5 February 1895, which included vital dimensions and illustrations.† In addition, the Aeronautical Society had published the essence of three classic lectures of greatest possible interest. There was, first, Hargrave's lecture delivered on 5 August 1896, to the Royal Society of New South Wales. This was remarkable among other things for the categoric statement that 'flat kites' were essentially unstable, which must have shaken Baden-Powell. The second of the trio was by Baden-Powell, delivered to the British Royal Society of Arts on 2 March 1898. As might be expected, this lecture dealt mainly with 'flat kites'; but it was distinguished by Baden-Powell's remarkable statement that he was 'unable to comprehend any very special theoretical advantage in the Hargrave kites'. Nevertheless he gave a lucid description of his rival's invention and demonstrated with an actual specimen. Finally, there was the third lecture, rendered possible by Hargrave's return to England in 1899. Hargrave addressed the Aeronautical Society on 26 May 1899, and he brought with him a selection of his kites. After the lecture he presented these to Baden-Powell; but he, while graciously accepting, passed them on to the Aeronautical Society.‡

---

* See *Aeronautical Journal*, January 1905, p. 13.
† 'Experiments on kites', a letter to the Editor of *Engineering*, dated 15 December 1894, from Lawrence Hargrave of Clifton, New South Wales. Published in *Engineering*, 15 February 1895.
‡ The three famous lectures were published in the *Aeronautical Journal* on dates as specified below:
　(1) 'On the cellular kite', by Lawrence Hargrave, April 1897.
　(2) 'Kites: their theory and practice', by Captain B. F. S. Baden-Powell, April 1898.
　(3) 'Kites and soaring machines', by Lawrence Hargrave, July 1899.

Cody was not long content to follow Hargrave, however, and by his own account soon tired of meteorological high-flying. With man-lifting in mind, he began modifying the Hargrave design, and achieved results so original as to justify their being re-named 'Cody Kites' and treated as a new species. A very good specimen photograph has survived and is reproduced in Fig. 22. It shows Cody with an assistant holding up one of his smaller kites. Clearly there could hardly be stronger evidence of how radical have been the developments from Hargrave's basic form as shown in Fig. 21. Naturally the wings are the most striking feature and their wide sweep in some of the large man-lifters (see Fig. 23) must have been a most impressive sight.

5   Design and operation of man-lifting kites

In the recorded histories of Cody's kiting work there is engendered disappointment at the small amount of information about the kites themselves. A general history must not be encumbered by masses of technical detail, but to proceed with the story of the kites without something being said about what they were and how they worked could be as dull as it would be unrealistic. In what now follows attention is directed to some of the more neglected aspects of Cody's work on kites, in the hope thereby that they may be given their proper place in aviation history.

Past vagueness about the design of Cody's man-lifting kites, it should be noted, is not without reason. Obtaining information about the 'War Kites' – as Cody called them – is not an easy process nor an exact one. There were no formal reports or technical papers such as would accompany comparable scientific experiments today. Cody himself, moreover, over and above the demands made upon him for military security, was inclined to be reticent, even secretive, about details of his designs. For this there appears to have been some justification owing to the reluctance of the War Office to acknowledge the *originality* of his inventions as distinct from his work as a kite manufacturer and kite-flying instructor.* More surprising, however, is the

* It has been suggested that, as in the case of Colonel Templer's retirement, the tactics of the financial controllers at the War Office verged on dishonesty. In any event, it appears significant that in 1912 an independent court of arbitration overrode the War Office and awarded Cody £5,000 for his kite inventions. This was additional to what Cody had already received as direct payment for his services and for equipment that he had provided.

lack of interest in the mechanical and aeronautical technicalities of man-lifting on the part of those actually engaged in man-lifting operations. 'Leave it to Cody', seems always to have been the order of the day; and those concerned were usually content to pull this cord or push that lever with implicit faith in Cody's instructions.

Nevertheless, it has been possible after several months of research to produce a reasonably complete story. The answer reveals some remarkable, if sometimes unconventional, engineering. There is naturally a strong Hargrave element in the basic design of the Cody kite, and the front and rear boxes reminiscent of the box-kite are always recognizable; but to these are added not only wings, but also hornlike projections at the edges of the boxes. These are clearly to be seen in Fig. 22 and in practically all the other photographs of Cody kites.

The 'horns' were a practical invention typical of Cody, and were integrally associated with the diagonal bracing struts about which Hargrave had very strong views. The Americans in their box-kites dispensed with diagonals altogether, but Hargrave regarded them as the best means of producing tautness in the fabric surfaces, such tautness being an essential requirement for both Hargrave and Cody types of kite.* In provision for tautening, however, Cody seems to have gone further than any of his predecessors. For this he used one pair of diagonal struts for each box element instead of the more usual Hargrave two, and they were made to project outside the boxes to produce the 'horns'. Attached to each projection was a roughly triangular piece of fabric terminating in a piece of stout cord that could be tightened by being pulled round the projecting end of the strut. The sides of the 'triangle', moreover, were reinforced and made to sag like a suspension bridge. In this way the system provided a practical method for producing the necessary uniform tautness of fabric surfaces. There was a further advantage in that the system could also be used for truing-up the kite – an important consideration when any lack of symmetry could lead to instability, with danger to life.

The wings were, from a structural standpoint, merely enlarged horns. The continuation of the diagonals, projecting from the top edges of the

* Hargrave's views on diagonal bracing were expressed in his 1899 lecture to the Aeronautical Society (see *Journal*, July 1899) and repeated in a letter to the *Journal* in July 1905. 'The American copies of my cellular kites have no diagonal struts, the corners being pushed out by horizontal and vertical pieces of wood. . . . This style appears to me barbaric. Horizontal pieces of wood adjacent to the horizontal surfaces must impair their efficiency . . .' As the inventor, Hargrave was in a privileged position; but I would have hesitated at criticizing the Americans, who seem to have known what they were about. A modicum of extra drag could be harmless for a kite and even beneficial by contributing to stability.

front box, provided the main spars for the wings. The fabric was tautened by the same basic process as that already described, but the slack was usually taken up on the horns opposite the wings. In some cases there were rudimentary wings sprouting from the rear box also. Aerodynamically, the natural inclination of the diagonals gave the wings the stabilizing dihedral of a true aeroplane. From many points of view, in fact, the Cody kite was more like an aeroplane in the modern sense than a conventional kite. Weight for weight, moreover, it had considerably more lifting power than its Hargrave prototype.

In some ways even more remarkable than his kites was Cody's ingenious method of using them for getting a man up to a height of 2,000 feet (600 metres) or more. Lieutenant R. G. Wise in America had been hauled up vertically by a rope passing over a pulley fastened to the main kite line. Hargrave, on the other hand, had attached himself direct to the lowest kite of a train of kites. Cody's method was more revolutionary and more imaginative, as well as being more effective: he created, in effect, an overhead railway leading up into the sky. An aerial ropeway was installed similar to those that are so common in Switzerland and other mountainous countries, except that instead of being fixed to the top of a mountain it was fixed to the sky by a battery of powerful Cody kites. Along this ropeway ran a small wheeled trolley or 'traveller' from which was suspended the 'car', usually a kind of armchair or basket designed to avoid too much risk of the man falling out. The trolley with its human load was then towed skywards by still another kite.

The whole array is illustrated in Fig. F (overleaf). Right at the top is the *pilot kite*. This is not a working kite in the sense of providing heavy lifting forces, but is intended to give guidance and stability to the train of kites below. Next down the line are the *lifter kites* which take the pull and weight of the main cable up which the trolley is to run. The number of lifter kites would vary from two to six according to wind strength and weight to be carried, though three may be taken as a practical average. Last of all comes the *carrier kite* with its trolley and car. At the bottom is the winch for paying-out and winding in the cable, and providing a firm anchorage for the whole system.

All the kites had basically the same type of *bridle*, the single line spreading into four branches connecting with four attachment points at the four lower front corners of the front and rear boxes. The bridle was symmetrical as regards left and right, but lengths were adjustable fore-and-aft while the kite was still on the ground. Adjustment was usually made with regard to the strength of the wind, since it was possible to control to some extent the angle of incidence or the inclination of the kite to the horizontal. All the kites flew well at thirty degrees, measured as the inclination of the main longitudinal members to the horizontal, but there appears to have been tremendous toler-

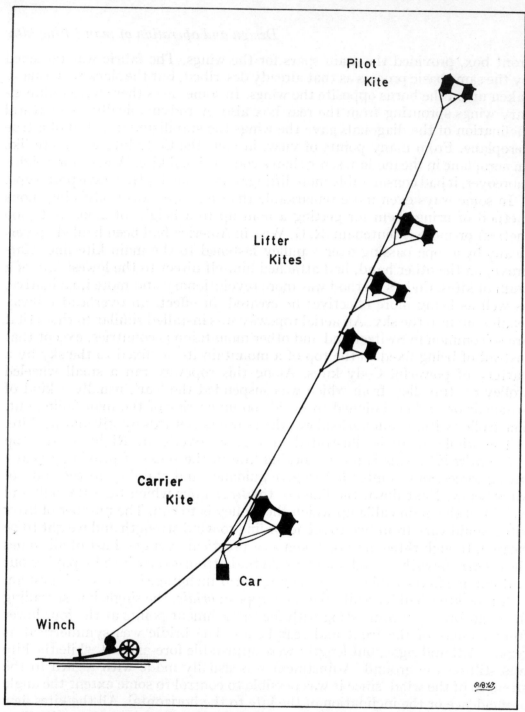

(F) The man-lifting array: Cody's method was to create an aerial ropeway anchored to the sky. At the top was the steadying pilot kite on a light line. Then came a team of lifters holding taut the heavy cable. Finally there was the carrier kite, pulling along the trolley with its suspended car

ance for satisfactory working. The pilot kite, it is believed, was often set at a smaller angle than the lifters, while the carrier kite had to have its inclination varied to the desired movement of the trolley.

There was a definite procedure for getting the main cable into the air ready for the trolley to go up it. First of all, the pilot kite was sent up on a light line of moderate length, say 300 feet (100 metres). The lower end of this pilot line was then tied to the upper end of the main cable. A fair length of this was then taken up into the air by the pull of the pilot kite alone, before any of the lifter kites had been sent aloft.

Each lifter kite had a smooth *nose-ring*, usually called the 'fairlead',* attach-ed at the centre of the front edge of the top front lifting surface, similar to that shown for the carrier kite in Fig. G (overleaf). The four-piece bridle was tied by a short length of cable to a *towing-ring*, usually known as the 'cleat',† which was designed to slide smoothly along the main cable. When a lifter kite had to be sent up its two rings were placed in position on the main cable. The kite was then released into the wind and blown upwards until it reached its prescribed position.

The method by which each lifter kite found its proper place on the main cable was as simple as it was ingenious. At suitable intervals near the upper end of the main cable were a series of stops known as *bulbs*, and these were more-or-less permanently fixed to the cable. They were roughly conical in shape and so designed that a smooth towing-ring would pass over them easily provided it was large enough. The bulbs, however, were of different sizes and disposed in continous steps upwards along the cable, so that the smallest was at the bottom and the largest at the top. The towing rings were graded in size to correspond, so that a ring would pass over any lower and smaller bulbs until it reached the one pre-selected for holding. The nose-rings, of course, were further up the line than their associated towing-rings, and would pass freely over all the bulbs. In operation the first lifter kite would be sent up with the largest towing-ring, to travel smoothly up the line until the topmost bulb was reached, whereupon the ring and bulb would jam, and immediately take the pull of the kite. The next lifter kite would follow with the next largest ring and take up its position one station lower than its predecessor.

* The term *nose-ring* is mine, and is chosen as being more descriptive, and less ambiguous, than *fairlead*. In engineering a fairlead is a smooth guide for a cable, and may or may not be associated with a change in direction of cable run.

† The term *cleat* used for the towing-ring is misleading, since a cleat is normally a device to prevent sliding, or otherwise for fixing the end of a line. An example is the bracket at the bottom of a flagpole. The towing-ring was, in fact, just as much a fairlead as the nose-ring. Probably the originators had in mind the combination of a ring and its stop when finally jammed together as described later.

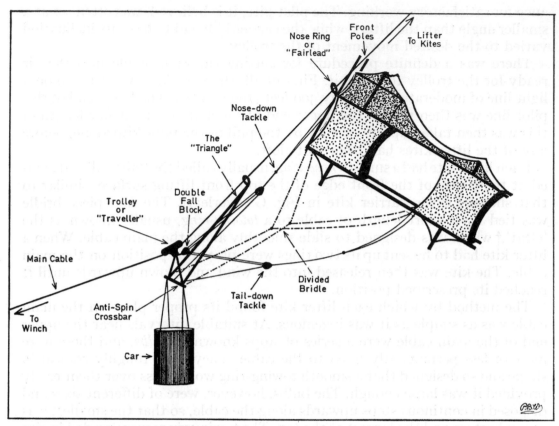

(G) A carrier kite with car and trolley. The carrier unit was a complicated affair. The trolley and car had a 'triangle' to prevent rotation; and a complex of control lines were brought from the kite to the 'crossbar'. The trolley had also a brake acting on the main suspension cable

The process would continue until all the lifters were up aloft. If necessary, further cable would then be let out to provide a clear way upwards for the man-carrier.

The complete carrier system is illustrated in the sketch of Fig. G. In its commonest form the trolley had two wheels running on and above the cable, and a single wheel placed centrally underneath. The necessary braking action was obtained, when required, by a lever pushing this underneath pulley upwards against the cable to produce a pinching action. From the trolley was suspended a simple but most important piece of equipment in the form of a *crossbar*. This served as an anchorage point for the miscellaneous collection of control lines, but its main function was to prevent rotation of the car suspended beneath it. Two poles attached to the ends of the crossbar passed upwards to a ring that would slide easily along the main cable, the unit being appropriately named the *triangle*. The kite was connected to the crossbar by the standard four-piece bridle, with one minor modification: in order to provide some constraint on rolling and yawing of the kite, the bridle was split into two, and the parts appropriately connected to opposite ends of the crossbar.

Under certain circumstances the bridle would have been sufficient to haul the trolley and its load upwards when the brake was released. This alone, however, was not sufficient to ensure that the kite could be made to go up and down at the will of the aeronaut sitting in the chair or basket. For this purpose two sets of block and tackle were provided: one set to enable the tail of the kite to be pulled down and the other to enable the nose to be pulled down (see Fig. G). The tail-down gear was straight-forward. Its tackle gave a mechanical advantage of three-to-one, and used the same rear attachment points as the bridle. When tightened it simply increased the flying incidence of the kite and hence the lifting force required for ascending.

The corresponding tackle for pulling the nose downwards was more complicated and its operation less easy to comprehend in retrospect; and most accounts on record are somewhat inadequate and conflicting. Cody appears to have experimented with countless schemes for pulling the nose downwards, the fundamental difficulty arising from the fact that facility for descent in a strong wind was marginal, and there was a genuine risk of the aeronaut being compelled to stay aloft until the wind dropped, or until the whole system could be hauled down. One of the more elaborate arrangements was that to be seen in Fig. 24, in which there are two men in the basket. In this case the maximum tilting power was obtained by running lines from the tops of the vertical poles – specially fitted to the nose of the kite – to the fall block situated just below the trolley.* Further reduction in lifting force was obtained by branch lines attached to the leading edges of the wings near the tips. Tension in these lines twisted or 'warped' the wings to reduce their angle of incidence over and above the reduction attained by the tilting of the kite as a whole.

Despite the complexity of the system, the procedure for launching and operating the carrier kite was fairly straightforward. After being connected to the main cable close to the winch, the kite, the trolley and the car were 'walked out' by a group of men. When the upward pull of the main cable was deemed adequate, the car was gently released. In order to climb the aeronaut

---

* In conventional engineering the fall block is the pulley-block attached to the weight being lifted, and usually carries a hook. In the present case the fall block was tied to the trolley, and was a double one since it was part of both nose and tail tackles.

had to slacken completely the nose-tackle, and tighten the tail-tackle, while gently easing the brake on the trolley. For descent the reverse procedure applied: the tail-tackle had to be slackened and the nose-tackle tightened. Ordinarily the kite would absorb most of the energy of descent, but the brake could be applied as necessary to prevent excess speed.

This concludes the broad outline of Cody's design and operational methods, while leaving out many of the variants introduced in the course of his ceaseless experimenting. There is just one matter of wider historical interest. Between 1906 and 1908, the Wright Brothers patented a scheme for wing warping involving the opposed twisting of opposite wings as a means of providing roll control of an aeroplane.* Cody claimed to have anticipated this for his kites in 1903. Cody's claim has not been universally accepted by historians, at least in its entirety. The absence of any written records by Cody – he being unable to read and write – is itself an obstacle to be encountered in the search for the truth. Cody could conceivably have been mistaken, and there seems little doubt that the Wright Brothers' invention went well beyond anything that Cody contemplated in 1903. It now seems *certain*, however, that Cody did use wing warping in 1903 for control of pitching, and he *may* also have tried it experimentally for control of roll. Whether this amounted to anticipation of the Wright Brothers' patents is arguable and the issue was never settled on a legal basis. It may be significant that, although the brothers successfully contested infringements in France and America, they never attempted any legal action when Cody introduced wing warping for control of roll into his powered aeroplanes.

These notes on the more technical aspects of man-lifting kites serve to show that something more than 'Cody Luck' is necessary to explain his undoubted successes. His skill at mechanical invention rose to the level of genius, and his understanding of fundamental mechanical principles transcended that of many professional engineers. In design of control systems he seems to have equalled or even surpassed many of the great pioneers of aviation throughout the world. Curiously, Cody's mechanical skill and ingenuity was given greater recognition in France than in England. One of the greatest contemporary authorities on kites, the Frenchman G. Houard, paid the highest tribute to Cody as the world's most successful pioneer in the man-lifting field. In his book, *Les Ascensions en Cerfs-volants*, published in 1911, moreover, he gave

* The Wright Brothers' patent was granted in the United States in 1906, and patent applications were filed in France in 1907 and in Britain in 1908. The subject of wing warping as developed by the Wrights, including reference to Cody's claims, is dealt with comprehensively by C. H. Gibbs-Smith in *The Aeroplane: an Historical Survey of its Origins and Development*, 1960.

17. The ceremonial balloon showed a reluctance to leave Balloon Square during the historic demolition ceremony, but eventually got away nicely for the last flight

18 *top left*. Major-General John E. Capper in 1915, after his departure from Farnborough

19 *below left*. Samuel Franklin Cody in conventional mood

20 *below right*. The poster-portrait of Samuel Franklin Cody (1904)

21 *above*. The Hargrave box-kite in the Science Museum, London. For ten years the box-kite invented by the Australian, Lawrence Hargrave, was superior to all others for lifting power and stability. Cody improved upon it to produce the most successful of all man-lifters

22 *left*. An early Cody kite displayed by Cody and an assistant. Cody put wings on to what was basically a Hargrave box-kite, and invented detail modifications such as the device for tautening the fabric

23 *left*. A Cody 'carrier' kite lifting a man

24 *below left*. Two men aloft in a balloon basket. This carrier kite was an advanced design capable of taking two men on this occasion. The photograph gives some idea of the multiplicity of control lines and the need for a cool head on the pilot

25 *below right*. Carrier kite taking off from Balloon Square (1904/5). So well-controlled and safe were the kites that in reasonable weather they could operate from the limited space within the square

more genuine technical information about Cody kites than the whole of British literature on the subject.*

It has to be remembered that Cody's kites were virtually aeroplanes in the modern sense of the word, with the one qualification that they were, in effect, propelled by a rope instead of an engine. It would be wrong to compare Cody as an aeroplane pioneer with the Wright Brothers, but it is simple justice to give recognition to the fact that Cody's winged kites were flying at least one year before the Wright Brothers made their first powered flights on 17 December 1903. It is in some ways surprising that, when Cody himself began work on powered aeroplanes, he followed the style of the Wright Brothers – for whom he had a passionate admiration – rather than a direct development of his own winged kites.

In judging the technical merit of Cody's kiting work, it is necessary to bear in mind how different the results might have been if there had been available modern research equipment in the way of wind-tunnels and strength-test frames that are taken for granted nowadays whenever a new aeroplane is designed. It was with this thought in mind that I decided to seek some genuine scientific information in the Farnborough relics of past researches. By great good fortune there came to light some wind-tunnel tests on what was alleged to be a genuine copy of a Cody kite.† The tests were made in 1938 when consideration was being given to kites as a possible alternative to the balloon barrage as a deterrent to low-flying enemy aircraft. In consequence, the tests had nothing to do with man-lifting or past history, otherwise they would have been conducted more usefully for the present purpose; but there is much of value, nevertheless.‡

These tests indicate that stalling, in the sense experienced with true aeroplanes, virtually did not exist, and that the kites could fly steadily over an incredibly wide range of inclination to the horizontal. More important, however, is the fact that the test results, given in precise mathematical terms, are consistent with the design details and methods of operation just described. Respect for Cody's skill and judgement is in consequence still further increased. Like his predecessor Hargrave, Cody seems to have achieved by intuition, systematic experiment and skilled observation – and perhaps a modicum of pure luck at times – results that can still withstand criticism in the fierce light of modern knowledge.

* Houard said that the limitation in the amount of technical information available on Cody kites was attributable to the stringent security measures of the British Government.

† I understand that the design of this kite was produced entirely from memory by the late Vivian Cody, the pioneer's second son.

‡ The tests were made and reported upon by K. G. Wilkinson and D. White of the R.A.E.

5 Kites in the British Army 1901-8

I   Early plans and policy
        1901-4

The great work on military kiting accomplished by the Royal Engineers under Colonel Capper followed naturally upon the work of the Navy during the year 1903, which is described in the next Chapter of this History. There was, however, some thought given to the subject by the Army before the Navy entered the field. In a somewhat back-handed way the war in South Africa stimulated interest in kites. The captive balloons used during the intensive early phase of the war had been sufficiently successful to warrant their being given a place in the modern army, and in the eyes of many people kites came into the same category, both being machines for aerial observation.

Cody is on record as having said that he had been impressed by the difficulties encountered in the operation of balloons in high winds during the war, and his declared objective was to produce observation kites that would fly in winds too strong for a balloon. It was left for Colonel Capper, however, to develop a co-ordinated strategy for the operation of both balloons and kites by the same Army units, so that balloons could be used in light winds and kites in the strong ones, at the discretion of the commander.

It was on 14 October 1901 that Cody is first known to have approached the Army, drawing attention to his new invention and its military potentialities. To this approach he received a somewhat non-committal reply and an offer to send an officer to attend the next experiment. There was, however, an understandable inertia in Army circles in respect of new inventions. The war in South Africa, which should have ended in the year 1900, dragged on until the *Peace of Vereeniging* of 1 May 1902. The whole British Army, moreover, was due to be completely re-organized, so that the development of kites was a very minor issue in the minds of most men at the War Office. Nothing further is on record as indicating Army interest until a note in the *R. A. E. Chronicles*,* where reference is made to a proposed demonstration by Cody that was to be witnessed by official observers from the Balloon Factory:

* The author of the *Chronicles* did not follow up this clue or make any further reference to the demonstration.

April 6th 1902: Superintendent of Balloon Factory [Colonel Templer] to Inspector-General of Fortifications. First reference to S. F. Cody. Proposed exhibition of box-kites at Seaham Harbour to which a representative of the Balloon Factory will be sent.

The scarcity of official information about kiting during the years 1901 and 1902 reflects to some extent the general lack of interest at this time. There is, however, sufficient evidence that Cody was making rapid advances technically with his kites, and Colonel Templer was taking some interest in an informal way. Towards the end of 1902, moreover, the Press was showing interest in military kiting: the *Illustrated London News*, for example, produced on 6 December 1902 a remarkably up-to-date picture of the man-lifting array. By the end of 1902, in fact, Cody was ready to offer his invention as a serious proposition to both the Army and the Navy.

Thus it came about that Cody gave kiting demonstrations on Woolwich Common on 12 and 13 March of the following year (1903) for the benefit of both the Services. There are indications that these Woolwich demonstrations were arranged originally in conjunction with the Balloon Factory, but as things turned out the Navy dominated the occasion and took the initiative away from the Army (see Chapter 6). Tests were quickly arranged to take place at the naval station on Whale Island and at sea; and it was after these tests that, as already mentioned, the Admiralty decided not to purchase Cody's patent for the kites, although they gave Cody a contract for four complete sets for use on ships at sea.

In this way it came about that the Army played virtually no part in kite development during the year 1903. This period of inaction, however, is no reflection on the Army of that time: the War Office and the Admiralty had agreed to co-operate, and not to duplicate, but to hand over to each other information as it was acquired. At that particular time, moreover, the Army were not well placed for taking on a new commitment such as man-lifting kites, owing to the general re-organization required as an aftermath of the South African War.

Action by the Army, when it came, however, was most timely; but it was initiated from an entirely unexpected quarter – by the Commander of the Western District of the British Army, Lieutenant-General Sir William Butler.*

* Sir William Butler (1833–1910) was Commander of the Western District from 1899–1905. He also commanded Aldershot District temporarily from 7 September 1900 to 9 January 1901, concurrently with his Western Command. He had had previous experience of Aldershot through having commanded the Second Infantry Brigade there, from 1893 to 1896.

The Districts were replaced by the Commands in the Army re-organization of 1904–5, and were roughly comparable, although they did not exactly correspond geographically.

Sir William first encountered Cody at Devonport, presumably when Cody was delivering kites to the Navy. Devonport lay within Sir William's military domain, and he had his Headquarters located there. He appears to have spent some time watching Cody flying kites, and was impressed by their military potential. As a result, he gave Cody a letter of introduction to Sir John French, Commander of the Aldershot District. Cody in due course presented himself, and Sir John at once became interested. On 2 May 1904 he wrote to the War Office requesting permission to examine Cody's proposals officially and to report upon them. This request was agreed without hesitation.

Sir John French then passed on the entire responsibility for investigation of Cody kites to Colonel Capper and his Balloon Sections. This left Colonel Templer and the Balloon Factory – responsible directly to the War Office – out of the formal picture. Colonel Capper, however, handled the situation with remarkable tact. A good deal of face-saving was achieved by bringing in the Royal Engineer Committee. Colonel Capper was an associate member of this committee, and was therefore able to put forward his own views, as well as those of his chief, informally in discussions. The Director of Fortifications and Works at the War Office, Colonel R. M. Ruck, was then prepared (as a general rule) to act on the Committee's recommendations.

2   The Army's preliminary experiments
1904

Once clear of political obstructions, Colonel Capper and Cody performed miracles in the way of planning what to do. It is most remarkable how two such diverse characters from the very beginning seemed to understand each other, and in a curious way also to respect each other. Eventually, after the inevitable official delays, Colonel Capper was able to invite Cody to come to Aldershot and Farnborough for proper trials of the kiting system. In a letter dated 27 May 1904, Capper wrote to Cody:

With reference to former correspondence I have pleasure in informing you that I am permitted to arrange with you to carry out experiments with your apparatus at your expense. I will be pleased to assist with labour and as far as possible with apparatus which may happen to be in store. I will be glad to know when you would like to bring the things here so that I may arrange accordingly.

The letter ended in a way that revealed how cautious Capper needed to be in order to avoid committing the War Office on future policy, and also indicated his determination to keep Sir John French and Aldershot Command in the picture:

You must understand that any expression of views that I may personally give as to the value of your apparatus after testing, or that the Commanding Officer may see fit to give, will be absolutely confidential and for the information of the War Office.

It was obviously a simple matter for the former showman to get all his complicated apparatus to the scene of operations. This was all unloaded by Capper's men on Monday 6 June 1904 at Aldershot Railway Station, having been dispatched from Cody's workshops at the Crystal Palace, Sydenham, London, on the preceding Saturday. It must have given Cody great satisfaction to join Colonel Capper, for his reception reached the highest standards of both courtesy and efficiency. Lieutenant R. V. D. Holwell R.E., Officer Commanding the 3rd Balloon Section, was put in charge of operations, with an N.C.O. and eleven men to work on the trials exclusively. The instructions given to Lieutenant Holwell on 1 June 1904 were clear and definite:

Please arrange to unload and bring up Mr Cody's apparatus from Aldershot Station on Monday morning next. Also give your personal attention to Mr Cody during these experiments, and place at his disposal one N.C.O. and eleven rank and file, with a riding horse.

The flight trials, all of which took place in June (1904), were remarkably successful. The thoroughness by which they were carried out is testified by the reports, of which a summary is given in the table on p. 118. Over twenty flights were made by eleven different people, not counting Cody's own flights. Lieutenant R. V. D. Holwell made most flights and reached the height of 1,300 feet (400 metres) on one occasion, which was the record for the series. After some initiation flights in which he shared the basket with Cody, Colonel Capper himself went up solo to a height of 1,000 feet (300 metres). On one occasion three men went up together. Among those who went up was Lieutenant P. W. L. Broke-Smith, who later as Brigadier Broke-Smith wrote his series of articles on early military aeronautics.*

The confidence inspired by these flights was astonishing and, as the reports show, no very special skill was ordinarily required from the aeronauts; and all ranks of the Royal Engineers were able to participate. Man-lifting flights

* 'The History of early British Military Aeronautics', *Journal of the Royal Engineers*, May–June–September 1952. See Note 5 of Appendix A.

Brigadier P. W. L. Broke-Smith (1882–1963) was just about the last survivor of the generation with direct operational experience of the man-lifting kites.

ASCENTS OF MAN-CARRYING KITES IN JUNE 1904

Date	Aeronaut	Height		Wind	Remarks
		feet	metres	speed	
7 June	Lieut. Holwell	100	30	17 miles	
	,, ,,	400	120	per hour	
	,, ,,	1,300	400	(27 km/hr)	
	Lieut. Broke-Smith	450	140		
8 June	Lieut. Holwell	350	110	20 m.p.h.	
	,, ,,	1,000	330	(32 km/hr)	
13 June	Lieut. Holwell	600	180	15 m.p.h.	Gusts of
				(24 km/hr)	25 m.p.h.
14 June	Sapper Shaw and	200	60	13–20 m.p.h.	Simultaneous
	168 lb. of ballast			(21–32 km/hr)	load
	Lieut. Holwell			13–20 m.p.h.	Three men
	C. S. M. Powell	80	25	(21–32 km/hr)	up
	Corp. Baxter				together
	Corp. Baxter	900	275	13–20 m.p.h.	
				(21–32 km/hr)	
15 June	Lieut. Holwell	600	180		
	C. S. M. Powell	900	275		
	Corp. Ramsay	900	275	18 m.p.h.	
	Corp. O'Rourke	700	210	(29 km/hr)	
	Corp. Hughes	200	60		
	Lieut. Spaight	300	90		
16 June	Mr Cody and	Several	—	25 m.p.h.	Together
	Col. Capper	short		(40 km/hr)	
		ascents			
	Lieut. Holwell	500	150	Nil at Ground	Flight
				20 m.p.h.	at night
				(32 km/hr)	
				at Height	
25 June	Lieut. Holwell	Short ascent –		40 m.p.h.	
	Corp. O'Rourke	300	90	(65 km/hr)	
	Lieut. Holwell	600	180	at	
	Col. Capper	1,000	300	1,000 ft.	
	L/C. Lamman	150	45	(300 metres)	

were said to be possible in any wind exceeding fifteen miles per hour (24 km
/hr). Conditions became rather difficult on 25 June, however, when the wind
reached forty miles per hour (65 km/hr) and the angle of the cable became
very steep, exceeding seventy degrees to the horizontal. Even so, conditions

were regarded as not too severe for an experienced operator. At the lower wind speed of thirty miles per hour (48 km/hr) the car was said to be as steady as a captive balloon in a wind of ten miles per hour (16 km/hr).

There were two interesting accidents, though results were so innocuous that it is arguable whether the word 'accidents' can rightly be used in any modern sense. Both were associated with something going wrong with the pilot kite. On 11 June 1904 a gust of wind carried away the pilot kite when Lieutenant Holwell was flying at 600 feet (180 metres). The whole array, however, had been set up in a most unusual manner. The wind being very light, there were four lifter kites and two carrier kites, that is to say two kites pulling the traveller with the basket. When the pilot kite got away the whole system began turning and swinging, but the overall effect was a gradual descent of the whole system until it reached the ground. Some of the kites were damaged but Lieutenant Holwell was not even slightly hurt.

The second accident was similar in character, though the initiatory damage was less severe. On 15 June, with Lieutenant Spaight up at 150 feet (50 metres), some stitching came loose on the pilot kite. Oscillatory motion supervened and spread downwards like a virus infection until it reached the basket. As before, the whole system, despite its dancing madness, descended fairly gradually. The basket with Lieutenant Spaight inside eventually hit the ground but only with what some of the witnesses described as a 'bit of a bump'. Both these accidents supported the conclusion reached in the earlier Naval trials: that the pilot kite was the most vulnerable part of the system, and quite a minor imperfection could lead to oscillatory motion and loss of control.

The mildness of the consequences of these accidents, however, gave great encouragement to all concerned.* Furthermore, the one danger they all feared, namely, breakage of the main cable, was soon to be proved by experiment to be a minor hazard also. A man-carrier was sent up, with ballast in the basket, to about 200 feet, and the cable was then released near the winch. The kite acted as a parachute and came gently to the ground with its suspended load.

Colonel Capper produced a note about the trials which brought out one or two points of technical interest. The pilot line was a thin steel wire one thousand feet (300 metres) long. The main cable was stranded and seven-eighths of an inch ($2\frac{1}{4}$ cm) in circumference, and was said elsewhere to have a failing

---

* Throughout the whole period of naval and military kiting with Cody kites I have not discovered a single fatal accident on record. There is a marked contrast here with the pioneering days of gliders and powered aircraft, where survival of a flyer for more than a few years was unusual.

strength of about two tons (2000 kg). The weight of the whole man-lifting system, excluding the winch, was only a little over 300 lbs (135 kg). Communication between the aeronaut and the ground crew was maintained by telephone, or simply by message bags being slid down the cable.

Perhaps the most unsatisfactory feature by modern standards was the winch, there being at that time no light and reliable internal combustion engine for use in the field. Nevertheless, the winch was a complicated affair, with subsidiary drums and pulleys for preventing the taut cable from pulling directly on the main storage drum. Without this precaution, the cable as it unwound would be liable to be nipped between adjacent coils, and complete seizure could result. The Cody winch had also sprung pulleys to smooth out jerks caused by gusts of wind. A winch with its crew and a kite is illustrated in Fig. 26. Very little trouble, however, seems to have been encountered by the ground crews and it was even possible to send up an array of kites from the confined space of Balloon Square, Aldershot as illustrated in Fig. 25.*

Colonel Capper sent in his report on 30 June 1904, which was only twenty-four days after Cody's equipment had been unloaded at Aldershot Station. He was wholly in favour of proceeding with the kites:

I cannot speak too strongly as to the excellence of these kites as regards their design and ability to perform what Mr Cody claims for them. The man-lifting kites will take a man into the air to practically any required height, and will keep him steady there so that he can observe. The danger, given sufficient skilled men to work the kites, is, I think, even in high winds, more apparent than real.

I unhesitatingly say that these kites permit of one ascending in the air with the utmost confidence. No other kites that I have read or heard of can approach them in steadiness and security combined with lifting power.

Capper finally makes two proposals. One is that a complete set of man-lifting kites and one set of signal kites should be purchased from Cody. The other is that Cody should be engaged as official instructor for three months, at a salary of £50 per month:

Mr Cody is perhaps the greatest living expert in the art of kite flying, and certainly understands his own kites to an extraordinary degree. . . . I recommend that an

---

* Cody appears to have understood the basis of winch design, but left no proper records; and the Royal Engineers do not appear to have been very interested in mechanical engineering. According to Brigadier P. W. L. Broke-Smith, the winch was not used for hauling down the kites, but only for cable storage and paying out; but I would query this being the universal practice. The alternatives to hauling down by winch were those developed earlier for the balloons: men walking outwards and pressing the cable down with a pulley or horizontal pole, or the winch wagon being pulled by horses and drawing the cable through a pulley fixed to the ground.

engagement be made with Mr Cody to act as Instructor to the Balloon Section in kite flying at a salary of £50 per month.

3   Cody as Kite Instructor
1905–8

Some weeks went by with no perceptible action by the War Office in response to Capper's letter. Cody, who was now committed to his new profession, was getting restive. He therefore wrote to Capper on 10 August 1904 asking for news. The request, however, covered only the initial paragraph of the letter; for Cody could not resist the opportunity for reporting progress to the man who, above all others, was able to appreciate his work.

In particular, there had been an accident of a kind that had never occurred before, but which inevitably was bound to happen sooner or later: at a critical moment a distracted aeronaut pulled the up-line instead of the down-line. The wind was blowing at fifty-five miles per hour (90 km/hr) at the time, and the carrier kite shot upwards and smashed into the lower lifter kite. Both kites were rendered inoperative as kites, though not, it would appear, as parachutes. With his typical enthusiasm Cody described how the man came down and landed gently on the roof of a house:

FROM: S. F. CODY, F.R.M.S.   Headquarters,
INVENTOR OF THE MAN-LIFTING WAR KITE   Crystal Palace,
AS SUPPLIED TO THE BRITISH NAVY.   London, S.E.
                                                                     August 10th 1904

Colonel Capper
Dear Sir,
   Some time has elapsed since my trials at Aldershot and I have not yet received any communication from the War Office re same. May I take the liberty of asking if you have had any reply to your official report which I presume was sent some time ago.
   I have had some very successful flights lately; last Saturday one of the men that was assisting me went up to a height of 1,500 feet and on arriving at the top he pulled the force line instead of the descending line, with the result that he forced the man-carrier against the bottom lifter, this being in a wind of about 55 miles an hour. Both kites collapsed, leaving one lifter and one pilot intact, though the combined weight of the man and two broken kites was too great for the pilot and one lifter. One would imagine

his descent would be somewhat rapid, but I am happy to say that this was not the case. The two kites swerved somewhat forward and landed the man quite gently on the roof of a house about 300 yards from the winch. Of course in the minds of the inexperienced this would be considered a failure in my apparatus, but in my opinion it is one of the most successful experiments that it has been my lot to witness.

The descent of the two kites was not quite so rapid as the descent of the sand bags when we tried them in your presence on Laffan's Plain,* the strain on the cable being reduced to nothing since the man during his descent came a little forward in the wind from his original position before the kites collapsed. I am telling you this because I think it may interest you, and it is one of the demonstrations I should like to give during my next visit to Aldershot. By the way, I have a new basket and my new cross-bar with the automatic brake on the steering gear works beautifully.†

I am, Dear Sir
Yours Obediently
S. F. Cody.

Action was proceeding, however, as fast as the machinery of government would allow. Colonel R. M. Ruck, Director of Fortifications and Works at the War Office, had already referred the whole matter to the Royal Engineer Committee, whose advice was now being sought on every issue. A special sub-committee visited Aldershot on 24 August 1904, with Capper present as an associate member. Cody attended to show his kites, and Capper is thought to have had a private talk with him after the meeting. At any rate, the outcome was that Cody sent off a letter the very same day to the War Office, stating his terms for patent rights and for his own personal services. He asked to be allowed to supply in four months time a complete set of man-lifting kites for £500, and to be allowed to serve as Kite Instructor for three months at £55 per month. For his patent rights he gave as alternatives either £8,000 outright or £5,000 plus an undertaking to employ him for ten years at £600 per annum.

There then followed for the next eighteen months or so, much tedious and time-wasting argument about terms of employment and reward, with Cody being engaged and then re-engaged at short intervals. The delays in technical progress, however, were not so serious as the bare statement of official

---

* This reference to Laffan's Plain as the scene of the preliminary trials is an interesting piece of information. In the other documents discovered by me, the precise location is never mentioned, though somewhere within the Aldershot Command is indicated. Laffan's Plain was, of course, the obvious choice, and this was probably taken for granted.

† It is not clear exactly how the *automatic brake* operated, especially in relation to the so-called *steering gear*, and I could only make guesses, which the reader could probably do just as well. I suspect that the words 'steering' and 'automatic' had, in Cody's mind, meanings slightly different from the usual.

dates and resolutions would imply, since both Capper and Cody were keen to get on with their work, and this work was usually proceeding by friendly agreement long before formal contract action was completed.

In the event, the Director of Fortifications and Works approved the purchase of the kites at £500 and Cody's engagement for three months at £55 per month without undue delay; but the contract for the kites was not placed until 25 January 1905, and Cody's three-month engagement began on 1 February 1905. The contract of employment, however, was later renewed for another three months which gave Cody a clear six months to the end of July 1905.

The work had not been proceeding more than a few weeks under the new arrangements when the Balloon Sections had their first accident since Cody had taken charge officially. The accident, which occurred on 17 February 1905, was attributable to a number of contributory causes, but probably the overriding one was an obvious weakness in the drill. The pilot kite was up aloft together with four lifters, when Lieutenant Holwell got ready to ascend. Just at the critical moment, however, either an air current or a drop in the wind lowered the pilot kite and rendered the whole system unstable. Lieutenant Holwell and those nearby failed to hear the warning cries of Cody, who was watching from a distance; and the carrier kite with its load was launched on its upward journey into chaos. In the turmoil that resulted, matters were rendered still worse by the winch coming adrift and being dragged thirty yards or so by the rebellious kites. Lieutenant Holwell suffered concussion through falling backwards when he hit the ground. According to Lieutenant Broke-Smith, who reported the incident at the time, his injuries were not serious. Nevertheless, it taught the whole unit a number of useful lessons: the winch should have been so firmly fixed that it could not have come adrift; Lieutenant Holwell would not have fallen backwards on his head if he had been in a balloon-type basket instead of a simple Cody chair; and, finally, the aeronaut would not have been sent up in the adverse conditions if there had been a proper system of signalling for the man observing the whole procedure some distance on one side, with the kites in the air and the men on the ground both in his range of vision.

Despite this rather ignominious episode, the Balloon Sections rapidly got into their stride as kiting specialists. There must have been great enthusiasm when, on 27 April 1905, Sapper Moreton reached the record height of 2,600 feet (800 metres). Capper was moved to write to the Royal Engineer Committee about this achievement.

We had a long cable on the kite for the first time today, and a Sapper reached the record height of 2,600 feet [800 metres] above the level of the ground, with a cable about 4,000 feet [1,200 metres] long. We have made a great number of ascents now and I do not think anyone connected with the kites is in anyway shy of going up.

Later, Brigadier P. W. L. Broke-Smith claimed to have surpassed this record, as a lieutenant in 1905. In his series of articles, written for the *Journal of the Royal Engineers in* 1952, he stated that he 'exceeded 3,000 feet'. Afterwards he altered this to a specific figure, 3,340 feet (1,020 metres), but he gave no date beyond stating that the event took place in 1905.*

Towards the end of the first six months of Cody's employment, i.e. on 22 July 1905, the General Officer Commanding, Aldershot, sent in a very favourable report to the War Office. As a result Cody's contract was renewed for still another three months on the recommendation of the Royal Engineer Committee. The salary was reduced, however, from £55 per month to £33.6.8, but was accompanied by the concession that Cody would be free to look after his other interests, within reason, outside the Service.

By October 1905, however, Capper became concerned with the various uncertainties about the future of kiting generally, and Cody's position in particular. He sought a definite policy, with plans to cover a reasonably long period to ensure stable progress. He even made what amounted to a confession of error in having previously asked for Cody's services for only short periods. The men of the Balloon Sections were not learning as quickly as he had expected, and Cody's continued presence was essential in order to avoid accidents. On 16 October 1905, Colonel Capper wrote:

I was wrong in thinking, as I originally did, that the use of these kites could very quickly be learnt, and that an examination of their construction [and behaviour] in the air would enable any intelligent person to fly them properly. I have had officers and men under instruction for varying periods from a fortnight to six weeks, and there is not one of them who at present is competent to put a flight of these kites in the air with certainty, nor to whom I would trust the responsibility of supervising when men are being lifted from the ground.

Capper, with the full backing of Aldershot Command, asked for Cody to be given a definite contract for three years' employment, with temporary employment on the old terms while the main contract was being negotiated. Eventually, Cody was given an extension of his current contract of engagement for a further five months. The choice of this period had special signi-

* Unfortunately I have not been able to find any official or other contemporary document confirming this record height. Cody in his lecture to the Aeronautical Society on 8 December 1908 (see the *Aeronautical Journal*, January 1909) refers to 3,340 feet having been attained on one occasion but does not mention Lieutenant Broke-Smith by name. I am personally unable to overlook the possibility that this figure quoted for height was an error.

ficance. The temporary arrangement was clearly made in anticipation of the creation of the Balloon School on 1 April 1906, with Capper as Commandant, and the plan was for Cody to enter regular employment on the same day. When Capper took this post he had already been promoted to Brevet Colonel (28 January 1906), and with his new appointment as Commandant he was shortly to become also Superintendent of the Balloon Factory. Colonel Templer was not, in fact, due to retire as Superintendent until his sixtieth birthday on 27 May 1906, but retirement and replacement by Colonel Capper was obviously a foregone conclusion.

The outcome of all this intricate negotiating was remarkably simple. From 1 April 1906 (for all practical purposes), both Capper and Cody in their respective ways operated simultaneously for the two organizations: the Balloon Factory and the Balloon School. Thus, while Colonel Capper became both Superintendent and Commandant, Cody became responsible for design and manufacture of kites in the Factory as well as being responsible for instruction in their operation at the School.

It took some time, however, to negotiate the precise terms of Cody's appointment to the post of 'Chief Kite Instructor'. Cody's own proposed terms were not considered acceptable. The War Office were not against employing Cody for a few years, even at a high salary, but they were reluctant to make an assessment of the monetary value of Cody's invention until its military utility had been more positively established. Matters reached a deadlock, which was eventually broken only by the personal intervention of Colonel Ruck. He had a quiet talk with Cody and persuaded him to accept a compromise. Cody was to be employed on a contract for two years and to receive a salary of £1,000 per annum plus free fodder for his horse. At the end of two years the contract was to be renewed *automatically* unless either party gave six months notice to the contrary. As regards a reward for Cody's invention, this was to be treated as an entirely separate issue which the War Office would consider on its own merits later if requested; and Cody would be allowed to raise the matter after one year's service under the new conditions. A rider was added that Cody would not, while receiving an official salary, communicate with any foreign government.

With Cody's future settled as from 1 April 1906, Capper at once gave thought to Cody's two sons Leon and Vivian. Not only were these two young men part of the Cody team, but they were in a position to go to any foreign government with such knowledge as they possessed. Capper therefore wrote to the Director of Fortifications and Works stating the position and asking to be allowed to recruit them. Authority came through in a letter dated 5 June 1906 to engage them at £2.5.0 per week. The appointment of Vivian, if not of Leon, turned out to have an importance that was probably un-expected. Never very interested in his father's work, Vivian struck out on a line of his own. He became the leading authority on fabric work, not only for kites and balloons, but also for airships and aeroplanes; and he was Head of the Fabric Division at R.A.E. when he retired in 1950.

Cody's own position in the Balloon Sections, now the Balloon School, was already well established through nearly two years of working contact. With typical thoroughness, Capper took steps to ensure that Cody had the same status in the Balloon Factory. He even went so far as to circulate the the following notice, dated 3 September 1906:

Mr S. F. Cody has been engaged by the British Government to supervise kite con-struction in the Balloon Factory, and to instruct the Balloon Company in Kite Flying.

Mr Cody's status is that of an officer of his Majesty's Army, though he has no military command. He is to be treated as an officer, as becoming the status in which he has been engaged, by all employees of the Factory.

In later years Cody was often referred to as Colonel Cody and, while not strictly entitled to such rank, he clearly had the salary and the status.

Now that the place of kites in the British Army had been properly recog-nized, especially as affecting their chief protagonists, Capper and Cody, it seems ironical that kiting work was becoming largely an uneventful routine, with much of the excitement of the pioneering days only a memory. The Balloon School continued to take part in Army manoeuvres, and kites were used whenever appropriate. Cody attended as occasion demanded, and fulfilled all his duties as Chief Kite Instructor. He became, it is said, a familiar figure on his white horse (for which, it will be remembered, he got free fodder) inspecting the kiting teams (see Fig. 27). But the experimental content of kiting had largely disappeared; and Capper and Cody became fellow conspirators in seeking new outlets for their originality.

Thus it comes about that we find odd letters written about this time (1906) dealing not with kites but addressed to such people as the Vacuum Oil Company, manufacturers of engine oil; the Reliance Rubber and Hardwood Company, makers of flexible pipes; Ludw. Loewe and Co. Ltd, machine tool makers; Brampton Brothers, makers of driving chains; the Rex Hallé Agency, motor accessory dealers; E. G. Wrigley Ltd, gear makers; and so on. Capper and Cody were obviously already thinking about powered aeroplanes, which in Britain were still to come; and about the propulsion system for the first British military airship. And so it was that, although for some years Colonel Capper remained Superintendent of the *Balloon* Factory and Cody remained Chief *Kite* Instructor, interest in kites, as with balloons, gradually faded away.

The story of Army kiting, however, is not quite complete without some mention of two rather special projects which somehow fitted in with the rest of the kiting work – the *glider-kite* and the *motor-kite*; and these come up next for brief consideration.

4   The glider-kite
1905

In the evolution of the aeroplane, as we know it today, we can recognize ancestry in both the simple glider and the kite. Neither, of course, were self-propelled. The glider had always to descend in relation to the surrounding atmosphere; and so apart from any initial impetus which it might be given, as in the throwing of a paper dart, flight was possible only in an upward air-current or over ground sloping downwards more steeply than the glider's natural descending flight path. The kite, on the other hand, was dependent upon the cable connecting it to the ground, so much so that some people have queried its right to be called a flying-machine at all. This possibly over-simplified representation of the origin of the aeroplane is necessary for a proper understanding of some of the aims of the earlier pioneers. Cody brought the kite to something nearer to an aeroplane than any other person, whereas it was from the glider that the Wright Brothers derived the first successful powered aeroplane.

In the Farnborough story there were two intermediate evolutionary types that preceded the first successful aeroplane in Britain, one being conveniently referred to as the 'glider-kite' and the other as the 'motor-kite'. Both originated with Cody but with some help from the Royal Engineers and the Balloon Factory. Cody himself took neither machine very seriously, but regarded them both as steps towards his true objective – the powered aeroplane. Of the two machines, the glider-kite was by far the more successful, and it is this which now comes up for consideration.

The way in which Cody succeeded in marrying two rather opposed concepts such as the glider and the kite seems little short of miraculous. The first problem to be solved with the ordinary glider is how to get it into the air so that it can then descend in controlled flight. Cody conceived the idea of sending it up first as a kite on a string, and then setting it free to glide down to the ground. If anyone were to succeed in this, of course, it must be Cody with his vast experience of winged kites. Nevertheless, the success he achieved in designing a man-carrying glider that could be flown also as a kite was indeed remarkable. Even if it be granted – though, however plausible this is largely supposition – that in designing the glider merely as a glider he made use of published experience of other pioneers, it still remains a matter for wonder that as early as the year 1905 he was able to reconcile in one machine the conflicting requirements for stability and control of both a glider and a kite. Cody himself had no illusions on this matter. At a meeting of the Aeronautical Society on 15 December 1906, it is on record that he said: 'I have now built it [the glider-kite] and am surprised at its success.'

In some ways even more surprising was the casual way in which the design was accomplished and the resulting machine tested. In 1905, when the glider-kite was made, Cody was giving most of his time to improving his officially-recognized man-lifting kite system whenever he was not actually engaged in instructing the men of the Balloon Companies in the kite-flying art. According to Cody's own statements, he made the glider-kite while on leave, presumably at his old Crystal Palace Works. Precisely when he started work on the new machine is uncertain, but there is definite evidence that it was nearing completion in July 1905. It was then brought to Jubilee Hill, which is situated at the southern end of Long Valley and a little to the north of Caesar's Camp, near Aldershot. Thereafter the Balloon Companies rendered great assistance, and the machine was quietly absorbed into the Capper organization.

There is not much documentary evidence in existence from which to derive a precise description of the glider-kite, but two or three photographs have survived which tell us a great deal. One shows the glider-kite in the air with a Royal Engineer Officer as pilot (see Fig. 28). The machine is flying as a kite with the cable still connected before being cast away for the transformation to a freely-flying glider.* Two other photographs show more details of the construction of the glider-kite (see Figs. 29 and 30). In these it is being held specially to display its main features by several men, among whom are Sappers of the Royal Engineers.

* There is inevitably a suggestion of artificiality or of deliberate posing in this photograph owing to the difficulty of photographing a machine in the air, especially at altitude. The glider-kite is probably much nearer the ground than appears, and there is a nearly horizontal wire on the left of the original picture that is probably there merely to steady the machine while being photographed.

The machine looked much more like the conventional biplane of later years than any of Cody's original winged kites, and there is scarcely a trace of the Hargrave box-kite at all. The structure is typically 'Codian' in its unconventiality; and if it had any advantages as a structure they are not easy to perceive. The pilot lay prone in a kind of hammock, with some fin-like projecting feet intended to give protection against excessive ground-impact on landing. The whole machine, less pilot and cable, weighed only 116 lbs (53 kg) according to one of Cody's earlier statements, though later increases are at least to be suspected. The total wing area was 807 square feet (75 sq. metres), and its tip-to-tip span was 51 feet (16 metres), so that for those days it was quite a large machine.

Aerodynamically the machine had a number of interesting features. Prominent are the triangular fins, sprouting everywhere like weeds in a neglected garden; and these seem to be the only reminder of the ancestral box-kite with its large side-panels or 'curtains' that contributed so much to stability. More important historically are the two small auxiliary surfaces lying below the bottom wings and somewhat to the rear. They were used both as elevators and ailerons. Their use as ailerons may well have been the the first *practical* application of the aileron principle in the whole of aviation history. It is conceivable that Cody thought of them quite independently of any other person, but they had already been invented by the Frenchman, R. Esnault-Pelterie, a year or two earlier.* It is, in fact, not at all unlikely that Capper helped in this, as in other matters of basic design, as a collector of information. From the time he became Commanding Officer of the Balloon Sections, Capper made it his duty to be *au fait* with everything aeronautical that was happening abroad and especially in France and America.†

A most interesting account of the glider-kite was given by Cody himself at a meeting of the Aeronautical Society on 15 December 1905, and reported in the *Aeronautical Journal* for January 1906. At this meeting Cody had two sporadic outbursts of speaking, without which there would still be a great deal of mystery and uncertainty about the whole project. Apart from several detail matters already discussed, Cody mentioned that he himself had

* The origin of ailerons is discussed authoritatively by C. H. Gibbs-Smith in *The Aeroplane: an Historical Survey of its Origins and Development*, 1960. As with many other important inventions, absolute priority is difficult to establish, but for ordinary purposes Esnault-Pelterie may be taken as the inventor. His ailerons were not at first a success, however, which is why Cody may be regarded as the first practical user irrespective of whether he discovered them independently or not.

† Colonel Capper's daughter, Mrs Edith Previté, says that her father was a friend of Esnault-Pelterie.

taken-off in his glider-kite at an all-up weight of 320 lbs (145 kg), of which 204 lbs (92 kg) was Cody, in a wind of only seven miles per hour (11 km/hr). He maintained, moreover, that flights were not chancy affairs, but could be repeated in reasonable winds *ad libitum*.

According to Cody, the machine was reasonably satisfactory from the very beginning, and did not require the long period of development associated with many of his new projects, for which it was necessary to be continually altering this and that until satisfaction was obtained. On the second day out, in fact, he sent up in turn at least eight men, so it must have been *easy* to fly as well as *ready* to fly.

Of the best glide accomplished, Cody (still speaking on 15 December 1905) said:

Our longest glide was 740 feet [225 metres] with a drop of 350 feet [107 metres], carrying one pound to the three square feet [1·6 kg per sq metre].

As to the machine's stability and controllability as a glider, Cody gave it high praise when recounting his own personal best glide:

My longest glide was 240 feet [70 metres] with the wind. It went down the valley and up again over some telegraph wires and landed right side up. It is absolutely impossible for it to turn over, no matter what the currents of wind are.

Yet with all this machine's virtues as a glider, it still was also a kite; and, whether it carried a man or bags of sand, it was sent up and flown first as a kite on every occasion:

The machine would glide forward thrown up as a kite; in fact it may be called a kite.

The hall-mark of genuiness on this unique project was placed by Colonel Capper himself at the same meeting of the Aeronautical Society:

I should like to say a word about this machine, which I have seen. It is a very pretty machine and most ingenious. It flies as a kite in the lightest of winds and seemed extraordinarily safe, and if you can get a machine that is safe, that is the first thing.

Colonel Capper's remarks about safety do not appear entirely consistent with various stories of a nearly fatal crash when Vivian Cody was flying in the glider-kite in the summer of 1905.* It is significant, however, that not only did Colonel Capper emphasize the safety of the machine, but Cody himself implied the same in his enthusiastic descriptions. On the other hand,

---

* G. A. Broomfield, in *Pioneer of the Air* (1953), says that the glider-kite with Vivian Cody on board turned over and over in an uncontrolled descent from 800 feet. A much more reasonable story is given by Air Vice-Marshal Gould Lee in *The Flying Cathedral* (1965), in which the glider-kite slipped sideways from a height of fifty feet.

there is in existence a written statement by Vivian Cody that he had a weakened back caused by a glider accident in 1905. It would seem, therefore, either that Capper and Cody were not disposed to condemn the machine on the strength of one particular accident, or else Vivian was injured in an entirely different machine.

5   The motor-kite
1907

The *motor-kite* was not quite a mythological bird, but of all Cody's creations it was by far the most mysterious. There are many stories about this so-called pilotless aeroplane, but they are mostly without documentary support and very little in the way of evidence. Yet this flying-machine did exist, and in any history of Farnborough aviation it could not possibly be ignored. It is necessary in the circumstances, however, to proceed on somewhat unusual lines, presenting evidence where there is any, alongside the stories that have evolved in the course of time.

Our detailed knowledge of this machine comes mainly from three surviving photographs, which are reproduced here as Figs. 32, 33 and 34. The machine was a biplane with its upper span much greater than its lower, so that nowadays it might be called a 'sesquiplane'; and its engine was a three cylinder twelve h.p. *Buchet*. It did not carry a man on board, and so far as is known was never intended to do so.

The machine was tested when taxying on the ground, and 'in flight' when sliding along a more-or-less horizontal cable suspended overhead from two masts. The circumstances of its design and construction were very different from those of Cody's earlier kites, since the work was accomplished while Cody was in regular employment by the War office. He had behind him, therefore, all the resources, not only of the Balloon School, with its organized man-power, but also of the Balloon Factory, which by the standards of the time was well equipped for all kinds of mechanical engineering jobs.

The name *motor-kite* needs special mention since it is the result of a historical complication. The name was given in 1966 by Mr C. H. Gibbs-Smith in his *Directory and Nomenclature of the First Aeroplanes*. Cody himself

131

called the machine his *power kite*, not at all an inappropriate name, but unfortunately he gave this name also to his first man-carrying powered aeroplane of 1908, which historically has far greater importance. There are reasons for believing that this has led to misunderstandings in the past; and some writers are believed to have confused the two. Apart from removing the ambiguity, however, the term 'motor-kite' has no special merit and none has been claimed for it.

The main reasons for the machine originally being called a kite were almost certainly political. After many difficult battles, Capper had been permitted to experiment with kites as well as to use them, and Cody's official position was that of Chief Kite Instructor. Any departure from the original work authorized by the War Office, however, was likely to incur the displeasure of some of the financial controllers, with the possibility of any particular enterprise being stopped altogether. Every conceivable thing that took to the air in Farnborough without the aid of gaseous levitation, therefore, had in the interests of British military aviation to be called a kite.

Nevertheless, there was a family relationship between the motor-kite and the normal Cody kite. Some writers, in fact, have described the motor-kite simply as a Cody kite with an engine in it, but this is going too far, as is clearly seen from the photograph reproduced in Fig. 34. The front box of the Hargrave–Cody configuration is preserved, but not the rear one. Instead, there are two fairly modern-looking fins at the rear together with a horizontal tailplane. The upper wings of the motor-kite, moreover, as is shown even more clearly in Fig. 33, are much larger than any ordinary Cody kite, the span being estimated at about 35 feet ($10\frac{1}{2}$ metres). The lower wings, moreover, though much shorter than the upper ones, are clearly in no sense equivalent to the triangular horns of the original Cody kite.

The propeller was well-designed according to the standards of the time, and it had the merit that the blades could be adjusted (when stationary) to give the best pitch setting established by trial and error. Being situated behind the wings (Fig. 34), the propeller had to be driven by a long shaft connected to the *Buchet* engine, which was placed well forward to give a reasonable position for the centre of gravity of the whole machine.

At some stage in the development of the motor-kite, Cody experimented with a forward biplane system of balancing planes, most reminiscent of the Wright Brothers' designs of powered aeroplanes. These balancing planes are shown in the first photograph (Fig. 32). Unfortunately, the picture has been heavily retouched at some time unknown, but there are no grounds for suspecting that it is not genuine. This biplane system in front has special interest because Cody never again used the biplane configuration ahead of the wings, but adopted a monoplane 'head-rudder' of his own invention for all his powered aeroplanes.

The first known reference to the motor-kite is probably the very brief entry in the *R.A.E. Chronicles*:

> Experiments carried out this year [1906] included:
> Attachment of engine and fan to kites.

The reference to the year 1906 instead of the more usual 1907 is of interest. It is possible that work upon the motor-kite actually began in 1906, but alternatively Cody may have made one or two preliminary experiments in fitting an engine and propeller into genuine Cody kites.

The earliest known reference to the motor-kite having flown *freely* as well as along a wire is contained in the *R.A.E. Historical Summary* of 1947:

> *Year 1907*: S. F. Cody produced his first power-driven aeroplane. This was a modified kite fitted with a 12 H.P. Buchet three-cylinder engine. It was first tested on a long wire supported between two 100 feet [30 metres] poles. A free flight was later made on the common and this must be recognized as the first flight of a power-driven heavier-than-air aircraft to have been performed at Farnborough.*

G. S. Broomfield in 1953 in his *Pioneer of the Air* developed the same theme, claiming free flight as well as flight along a wire:

> Later Cody fitted one of his kites with front elevators and a rudder, and installed a French *Buchet* engine of fifteen horse-power driving a front airscrew. Early in 1907 this was tested, at first captive on two wires suspended from posts 100 feet [30 metres] apart, and then in free flight on Farnborough Common, where it flew successfully for four and a half minutes, this being the first rising-off-the-ground power flight by a petrol engined pilotless aeroplane in England.

Still more impressive is the more recent account given by Air Vice-Marshal Gould Lee in 1965 in *The Flying Cathedral*:

> For the first tests, he attached the kite to a cable stretched between two masts 200 feet [60 metres] apart. These captive flights went well, and he next tried a free flight with only a cupful of petrol in the tank. With the rudder set for a circular trip, the kite climbed steadily to 200 feet [60 metres], flew bravely round, then, when petrol ran out, instead of dropping suddenly and crashing, as Cody feared it might, glided smoothly to earth, and came to a halt among the bushes without any damage.

Thus, according to this version of the story, the new aircraft not only made

---

* As explained in Appendix A, Note 4, I am unable to accept many of the statements in the *R.A.E. Historical Summary* without independent confirmation. Incidentally, the reference here to 100-feet poles is difficult to understand: why go so high and how did they get the motor-kite up there?

a long flight but also a circular one. Furthermore, flights of this kind were repeated often, and on one occasion in the presence of King Edward VII:

> Delighted that his expectations should be so finely realized, that he had produced the first powered, pilotless aeroplane to fly in Britain, Cody made numerous other flights, the longest being four and a half minutes. His success brought congratulations from his Army colleagues, and from even further afield, for among those spectators who came to watch the powered kite was King Edward VII.

For a number of reasons, despite the views that have been expressed, I have always doubted that this machine engaged in free flight away from its leader cable. The manifest technical difficulties and the general appearance of the machine are against it having the necessary stability, let alone an adequate degree of automatic control.

Mr Percy E. Crosson, who joined the Balloon Factory at the age of fourteen in 1896 and retired as Superintendent of Workshops at the R.A.E. in 1950, has added his personal testimony on this issue – when interviewed he was adamant that the motor-kite had never flown freely. Mr Crosson was also able to give some details of the leader cable along which the motor-kite ran. One end of the cable was fixed to a mast just outside the apse at the eastern end of the airship shed. This mast is to be seen in several photographs, particularly that reproduced as Fig. 14. The cable passed through a hole in the closed end of the shed and out through the open doorway at the other end, to another mast about one hundred feet (30 metres) away. Apart from a slight sag, the cables was horizontal; and according to Mr Crosson the actual flying was done inside the shed.

The last word, however, must rest with Cody himself – in his lecture 'Experiences with the "Power Kite"', which was given to the Aeronautical Society on 8 December 1908.* Although "Power Kite" refers specifically to his powered aeroplane, Cody spoke on many other matters from his aeronautical repertoire. Among these is an indisputable reference to the motor-kite as he points to a picture on the screen:

> This is a kite. I am just starting the engine and am trying to get out of the way. It was supposed to be let loose, but the authorities were afraid I might do some damage by letting it go up in the sky.

* *The Aeronautical Journal*, January 1909.

6 Kites and the Royal Navy 1903 and 1908

1   Cody approaches the Admiralty

1903

It was on 6 February 1903 that Cody first ventured to approach the Admiralty, writing from one of the theatres at which he was then performing:

KLONDYKE NUGGET CO.
Grand Opera House
Liverpool

6.2.03

Dear Sir,

Having completed and patented an 'Aeroplane', or superior design of kite, suitable for signalling purposes, transmitting messages and light articles from one vessel to another, also capable of taking a man up for the purpose of reconnaisance, especially adapted as a look-out to guard against submarines etc., I should be pleased to bring the same before your notice.

I do not ask you to assist me in carrying out designs, but am prepared to show you a complete apparatus suitable for the purposes mentioned. I have twenty of these models ready for use.

I am sending you by same post a few photographs of my latest experiments. My highest ascent with the meteorograph attached is 14,000 feet [4,200 metres]. The highest the apparatus has carried me – under my special system for use on ships – was 1,200 feet [360 metres].

I am prepared to demonstrate in the presence of any officials you may approve during the coming spring and summer.

Faithfully yours,
S. F. Cody.

From the response to this letter, no one could have foreseen the intelligent interest that the Navy was ultimately going to take in Cody's kites. Its reception was indeed cool, and all the more remarkable because the man who first turned down Cody's offer was one of the few men who eventually acquired a real understanding of the kiting technique. This man was Captain R.

Tupper, who at that time was an Assistant to the Director of Naval Ordnance at the Admiralty. He sent a reply to Cody on 2 March 1903, thanking him for his offer but declining it – for the time being at any rate.*

It would appear that Captain Tupper had been in touch with Captain George Le C. Egerton, who was in command of *H.M.S. Vernon*. At that time *Vernon* was the Torpedo School Ship at Portsmouth,† and Captain Egerton had undertaken to ascertain the views of Major Baden-Powell, who was President of the Aeronautical Society. Neither Captain waited, however for Baden-Powell's final verdict, and Captain Egerton expressed his views on 23 February 1903 in a note containing not a little unconscious irony:

I do not think we need try this at present. Major Baden-Powell recognized the difficulties of flying kites from on board ship and is thinking over the matter. *Mr Cody has probably no notion of these difficulties and would only waste our time.*‡

Whether or no Cody had any notion about the difficulties of flying kites from ships, he certainly seems to have had sound notions about how to deal with the British Navy. He would not accept no for an answer, and presented the Admiralty with a *fait accompli* in the way of the demonstration arranged to take place on Woolwich Common. Writing from Birmingham on 6 March 1903, Cody told the Admiralty:

In answer to your esteemed letter, I have great pleasure in informing you that I am carrying out experiments on the Woolwich Common next week in the presence of Government officials. It appears to me that this would be an excellent opportunity for your representative to witness operations. Of course, these operations would be some- what advantageously transformed when conducted from the deck of a vessel. If you can see your way clear to send a representative, kindly drop me a line to Royal Artillery Theatre, Woolwich, and I will telegraph you the exact time and place of the experi- ments.

Now it so happened that before the trials took place Baden-Powell's com- ments arrived. The gist of these was tersely but effectively expressed in a note by Captain Tupper that happens to have survived:

* Captain R. G. O. Tupper (1859–1945) had a career of distinction, becoming Admiral Sir Reginald Tupper and Commander-in-Chief Western Approaches. In the First World War he was for a time Vice-Admiral for the Atlantic Blockade, and later became Admiral Northern Patrol.

He served as Assistant to the Director of Naval Ordnance at the Admiralty from 1901 to 1903, and as Captain of *H.M.S. Excellent* (see later in this History) from 1907 to 1910.

† *H.M.S. Vernon* herself was a ship of 5,481 tons, but the School had also a whole fleet of small vessels: *Bloodhood, Starfish, Nigger, Devastation*, and six torpedo boats.

‡ The italics are mine.

'Major Baden-Powell says the kites are good.*

Such a message from such a respected authority, of course, turned all previous decisions upside down. Captain Tupper immediately tried to arrange for *H.M.S. Vernon* to send a representative, but events were moving too fast A telegram arrived at the Admiralty from Cody saying that tests were to take place tomorrow – 12 March 1903; and Captain Tupper thereupon decided to go himself.

The wind over Woolwich Common on Thursday 12 March 1903 was unfortunately very light. Two types of kite were on show: one had eight feet (2½ metres) wing spread or span, and was made of black silk, the other had seventeen feet (5 metres) span, and was made of calico. Owing to slackness of the wind, however, only the smaller kite was flown, and no attempt was made at man-lifting. The Navy was interested in this simple form of kite flying, with a view to sending up a wireless aerial. In those days, of course, radio communication was still primitive, and a long high aerial attached to a kite could appreciably extend the operational range.

In his report to the Admiralty, Captain Tupper was most enthusiastic with his commendation:

This is quite the best kind of kite I have seen, and I have every reason to think that it will be found of use for supporting an aerial wire for w/t purposes, and that it can be handled and flown from the deck of a ship or even a small craft. I have no hesitation in recommending a trial.

He mentioned also that Major Baden-Powell had been present at the demonstration.

Next day (13 March 1903) the wind got up a little and it was possible to fly the 17-foot man-lifters. Captain Tupper was hastily summoned to Woolwich Common and arrived at about three o'clock in the afternoon. The wind was so light, however, that in order to get the man airborne twenty-five men had to run at about two miles per hour holding on to the end of the kite line. In this crude fashion a man was lifted 150 feet (50 metres). The absence of wind, however, was in one sense advantageous: it reminded people that the same difficulty need not occur on a ship at sea, which could produce a useful wind artificially by its own motion. Tupper, in his report, expressed the opinion that operating from a ship would be quite practicable for reconnoitring at sea.

Captain Tupper also gave an interesting technical description of the man-

* Baden-Powell was often wrong in his technical judgements, the worst example being his failure in 1906 to recognize the successes of the Wright Brothers in America. His integrity, however, was beyond question and the chances of his being influenced by Cody's superior personal achievements were negligible.

lifting system, one of the best on record. There are, however, some discrepancies between this and the description given earlier in the present history (Chapter 4). The discrepancies are thought to be attributable partly to the very short time Captain Tupper had available for examination, and partly to Cody's earlier methods having been still in their embryonic stage and subject to later development. While this matter can in general be so dismissed, there is one item that may be specifically mentioned. The case is best described in Captain Tupper's own words: 'In order to descend, the man has a line to pull down the rear end of the carrier kite, which spills it; he then glides down controlling his speed with the brake.' This is, of course, a direct contradiction of the technique previously described as normal, in which the *nose* is pulled down for *descent* and the *tail* pulled down for *ascent*. Again there could be a misunderstanding, but a not unlikely explanation is that it was a practical method for descent in the abnormal circumstances of a very slight wind.

Captain Tupper's remarks about Cody are interesting:

Mr Cody is most anxious to be allowed to try his system on a vessel and wishes to place his invention at the disposal of the Admiralty. He says he has been in England for twelve years and considers himself an Englishman, and would be pleased to be naturalized if he could be employed by the Government in connection with his kites.

Finally, with Captain Tupper's recommendation that proper naval trials be undertaken there is introduced an air of mystery:

I have the honour to submit that the system might be very useful, and is worth a trial. A military officer of high rank witnessed this performance with me, and expressed the opinion to me that he considered it valuable for military purposes, and that it had great advantages over a captive balloon.

The name of this high-ranking officer, who presumably attended incognito, is unknown, and probably will now always remain so.*

At this stage the prospects for kites were greatly enhanced by the personal interest of Prince Louis of Battenberg, who was then Director of Naval Intelligence at the Admiralty.† In a note dated 18 March 1903, Prince Louis

---

* The distinguished visitor could well have been Lieutenant-General Sir William Butler, Commander of the Western District. It will be remembered (see Chapter 5, Section 1) that he showed great interest in kites and gave Cody a letter of introduction to the Commander at Aldershot, Sir John French.

† Prince Louis of Battenberg (1854–1921), son of Prince Alexander of Hesse, was born in Austria, but he became naturalized British in 1868 and entered the Royal Navy. In 1884 he married Princess Victoria, a grand-daughter of Queen Victoria. He was Director of Naval Intelligence from 1902 to 1905. Promoted to Rear-Admiral in 1904, he then advanced rapidly, being Commander-in-Chief Atlantic Fleet from 1908 to 1910; and becoming First Sea Lord

gave a masterly review of the situation and of the action which he thought should follow:

Having had the advantage of hearing Captain Tupper's personal experience, I feel that we ought to experiment with this apparatus ourselves, as it opens up two possibilities, viz:

(a) Lifting an aerial wire for wireless telegraphy, both ashore and afloat.

(b) Lifting a man to a considerable height from a ship under weigh for reconnoitring purposes.

It is therefore submitted to carry out the following:

1. To request Mr Cody to send his apparatus to Portsmouth.

2. To direct the Captain of *Vernon* to carry out trials with the 8 ft kite from a gunboat or destroyer for lifting an aerial wire.

3. To direct the Captain of *Excellent* to carry out at Whale Island trials with a man-lifting kite. If successful these could then be repeated from a vessel under weigh.

(Signed) Louis Battenberg.

Events now moved with incredible speed. Cody was most cooperative, and he himself proposed taking his men and equipment to Portsmouth for trials on land and sea. On 25 March 1903 clear instructions were sent by the Admiralty to the Commander-in-Chief of Ships and Vessels at Portsmouth:

I am commanded by my Lords Commissioners of the Admiralty to inform you that they have accepted the offer of Mr S. F. Cody, Ramsgate, to take his kites to Portsmouth for trial by the Captains of H.M. Ships *Excellent* and *Vernon*.

I am to desire, therefore, that you will direct the Captain of *H.M.S. Vernon* to carry out trials for lifting an aerial wire, from a gunboat or destroyer; and the Captain of *H.M.S. Excellent* to carry out trials at Whale Island with the man-lifting kites and for other uses to which kites may be put for Naval purposes, these latter experiments, if successful, being subsequently carried out from a vessel under weigh.

H.M.S. Vernon, the torpedo training ship, has already been mentioned in respect of the interest shown by her Captain, George Le C. Egerton. *H.M.S. Excellent* was a gunnery training establishment occupying the whole of Whale Island, an island on the eastern shore of Portsmouth Harbour.* As was the

---

of the Admiralty in 1912. He was allowed to resign as First Sea Lord at the outbreak of war in 1914. In 1917 he renounced his foreign titles at the request of King George V and became Marquis of Milford Haven. Earl Mountbatten of Burma is his youngest son. The late Princess Alice of Battenberg (Princess Andrew of Greece) was his daughter and the mother of our Prince Philip, Duke of Edinburgh.

* Whale Island (once called Waley) was little more than a bank of mud when first acquired by the Admiralty in 1853. Its first major use was as a dump for soil excavated in the process of extending Portsmouth Naval Dockyards. Later it was thought worth-while to level and drain the land, to produce a valuable island base. The story of Whale Island has been told by

custom, *H.M.S. Excellent* was also a ship, a sea-going gunboat of 508 tons, which gave the establishment its name and was in fact part of it. *Excellent* had also a large fleet of vessels of varying sizes on its strength.*

2   The Naval Trials of 1903

The first stage of the 1903 Naval Trials was concerned primarily with the suspension of aerials for wireless telegraphy, though some consideration was also given to the use of kites for visual signalling. In accordance with the Admiralty instructions, the responsibility for these trials rested with Captain G. Le C. Egerton, as captain of *H.M.S. Vernon*, the torpedo training ship. He decided to make his first tests of the kites on Whale Island before venturing out to sea. The island was by all accounts very suitable for such a purpose, having a large level stretch of open ground and not too much shelter from the wind.

On the first day, Monday 30 March 1903, kites of all sizes were sent up, ranging from the eight-foot kite to the seventeen-foot man-lifter. The wind was very strong and the officer in charge, himself a wireless telegraphy specialist, was greatly impressed by the steadiness and reliability of the kites in a high wind. On the next day, Tuesday, further tests were made on Whale Island, when an actual aerial wire, 600 feet long (180 metres), was sent up.

On Wednesday trials at sea began, *H.M.S. Hector* being used. *Hector* is perhaps best described as a retired first-class cruiser of 6,710 tons, and was normally used as a torpedo repair shop for *H.M.S. Vernon*. The weather was now squally, with rain at times, but the kites continued to behave well. On Thursday and Friday, tests were made from an entirely different kind of ship, *H.M.S. Starfish*, which was a torpedo boat destroyer of 670 tons. On these two days the winds varied considerably from twenty to forty miles per hour (30 to 60 km/hr). Saturday 4 April saw the end of the series, with tests of various kinds of signalling apparatus on Whale Island, in strong winds reaching fifty miles per hour (30 km/hr).

Commander R. Travers-Young in his book, *The House that Jack Built: the Story of H.M.S. Excellent* (1955). Today Whale Island is still the home of *H.M.S. Excellent*, the School of Naval Gunnery.

* *H.M.S. Comet, Conflict, Hero, Hunter, Kite, Mastiff, Narcissus,* and *Skylark.*

The report issued by the Captain of *H.M.S.* Vernon, dated 7 April 1903, was remarkably favourable, especially when it is borne in mind that Captain Egerton had not at first been at all enthusiastic. Given sufficient wind, he said, the kites could readily be flown with the ship sailing in any direction:

These kites are immensely superior to any kites previously tried here and, even as fitted at present, are perfectly suitable for raising an aerial wire. I have no doubt that they could, after some experience, be still further improved. No difficulty was experienced in putting the kites up from a destroyer, either at anchor or under way, and they were kept flying whilst leaving the harbour and steaming in any direction.

There was no delay in preparing and issuing this report, but Prince Louis was even quicker off the mark. He at once interviewed Cody personally, and on the Monday after the trials (6 April 1903) he sent a long note to the First Sea Lord. In this he recommended that negotiations should begin for the purchase of Cody's patents, and for the employment of Cody himself as instructor in kite flying and supervisor of kite construction. He mentioned that Cody had already received offers from foreign governments; and also that the War Office had asked him to assist in the construction of an airship.*

The second stage of the trials, now concerned with man-lifting for aerial observation, began after one week's interval. *H.M.S. Excellent* were now responsible, and it must at once have been realized that man-lifting was a much more difficult proposition than suspending wireless aerials. On Monday 13 April 1903 one of Cody's sons (believed to be Vivian) went up to 500 feet (150 metres) from Whale Island. The wind was moderately strong but very squally. A squall, in fact, occurred with the man 100 feet (30 metres) up, and was accompanied by a six-point (68 degree) change in wind direction. This brought down the whole array, but the carrier kite acted as a parachute and – in the words of the naval officer in charge – 'the man came down quietly'. Cody's son was, to the surprise of them all, completely unhurt and unperturbed. On Tuesday and Wednesday winds were fairly light and variable. The pilot kite and lifters were sent up on both days but man-lifting was not feasible.

On Thursday (16 April 1903) the kiting unit at last went to sea. The ship was *H.M.S. Seahorse*, described in the language of those days as a 'twin-screw special service vessel' of 670 tons. The wind was moderate but there was, of course, the motion of the ship to help. The wind, however, was treacherously squally. The pilot kite and two lifters were safely launched but, just as the carrier kite was about to leave the deck, a squall brought the whole system

* This would be the airship *Nulli Secundus*. Prince Louis's note is probably the only record among surviving documents indicating that Cody was involved in airship construction as early as the year 1903.

down into the water. Subsequent investigation led to the conclusion that the failure was caused by breakage of the bridle of the lower lifter kite.

On Friday (17 April 1903) the kiting unit went out with *H.M.S. Seahorse* again. The wind was firm and steady and conditions near to being ideal. For reasons not officially recorded, but no doubt associated with Thursday's fiasco, only a log of wood weighing 140 lbs (64 kgm) was sent up instead of a man. The ship, however, steamed some eight miles down the Solent, with the full array of kites and the log of wood being sent up and brought down repeatedly. Saturday (18 April 1903) was too calm for flying and so the trials ended.

So far as these trials indicated, the man-lifting kites were only a qualified success; but the week's weather had been particularly unsatisfactory, and the kites were still experimental, especially for naval operations. Nothing could be fairer, however, than the opinions expressed by Captain Percy Scott R.N. who had just taken over command of *H.M.S. Excellent*.* In his report dated 20 April 1903, after commenting favourably on the kites for wireless telegraphy and distant signalling, he said about man-lifting:

At present it cannot be said that they are to be relied on for man-lifting either on land or sea, except in very favourable weather, but as the inventor has only been working at them for two years there seems to be no reason why their efficiency should not eventually justify their use for this purpose.

Meanwhile, consideration was being given to the financial cost of purchasing Cody's patent and of employing him as adviser and instructor. As to the patent, the Admiralty were less concerned with its technical validity than with the merit of the invention as a going concern, but it was decided to have an appraisal made by James Swinburne,† a consulting engineer. On the issue of Cody's employment, Captain Tupper (as mentioned earlier in this History) estimated that Cody's income as a dramatist was about £1,200 per annum. Some tentative plans were therefore made to give Cody adequate compensation on this basis if he should enter the official service as kite instructor, designer, and manufacturing supervisor. It was at the stage that Cody made a grave error of judgement and probably by his own actions wrecked all his immediate prospects.

For some time Cody had been writing at fairly frequent intervals long, verbose and rambling letters to the Admiralty. It is difficult to decide why

* Captain Percy Scott (1853–1924) later became Admiral Sir Percy Scott. As a Captain, he was in command of *H.M.S. Excellent* from 1 April 1903 to 31 March 1905. He was famous for his revolutionary ideas on naval gunnery.
† Later Sir James Swinburne, third baronet.

he did this. Possibly the great respect and attention he had received had gone to his head. Certainly the wise and practical Cody seemed to have disappeared, to be replaced by a temporarily unbalanced person. Matters came to a head when, in a letter dated 21 April 1903, Cody sent his financial terms to the Admiralty:

I should be disposed to accept the sum of £25,000 (twenty-five thousand pounds) as a premium for my patents, and, for my services during my tenure of office, a salary of £1,250 (twelve hundred and fifty pounds) per annum. I to be allowed six weeks vacation in each year at a time most convenient to the Admiralty; then, at the expiration of my stipulated engagement, if my aerial apparatus, or apparatuses are still doing good service, a further premium of £25,000 (twenty-five thousand pounds) to be paid on my discharge.

Rarely can there have been such unanimity of opinion among officers at the Admiralty as that produced by this letter. Among at least a dozen people who were called upon to give an opinion the only differences lay in the choice of words to express universal disapproval. Phrases such as 'excessive terms', 'inordinate value', 'wild exaggeration' and 'exorbitant demands' are only a few examples. From Cody's standpoint the situation could hardly have been worse, when there arrived at the Admiralty an adverse report on the Cody patent from James Swinburne.

Technically the Swinburne report has no value except as a prime example of the danger that lies in allowing an expert to wander outside his own specialized field when expressing an opinion. James Swinburne acquired a high reputation generally as an expert witness on engineering subjects, yet on this occasion his work was as slipshod as it was prejudiced. In his report Swinburne said: 'With some trouble I have found little literature on the subject [of kites].' This was utterly false! There were masses of literature on kites of every conceivable kind in Britain alone, to say nothing of Hargrave's papers in Australia, and countless publications in America. His general display of anti-Cody prejudice reached the high-light of absurdity, however, when he referred in disparaging terms to the combination of wings and box-kite, particularly when he stated: 'There can hardly be any advantage in combining these wings with the box-kite.'

Yet of this very combination, G. Houard, probably the greatest authority on kites of his generation, said in 1911: 'Cody finally used the box-kite with dihedral wings that bears his name, and which, with every justification, is famed for its stability and lifting power.'*

* 'Cody utilisa enfin le cellulaire à ailes dièdres qui porte son nom, et qui est, à juste titre, renommé pour sa stabilité et sa force ascensionnelle.' *Les Ascensions en Cerfs-Volants*, by G. Houard, Librairie Aéronautique, 1911.

On the purely verbal aspects of the patent, Swinburne was on firmer ground. The specification was undoubtedly imperfectly drafted and quite out-of-date in relation to Cody's later and more successful developments. Swinburne's main contention appears to have been that the provisional specification was inconsistent with the final, and that neither had much to do with the system Cody was actually using. The formal summary submitted to the Admiralty read:

This patent is, in my opinion, invalid because there is no invention in what the patentee claims. It is also technically bad because there is disconformity between the provisional and complete specifications. The kite submitted to the Admiralty may have merit apart from this specification.

The result was now a foregone conclusion. Cody somehow or other got wind of the trend of opinion at the Admiralty and pleaded for re-consideration on less costly terms, but the Admiralty was adamant. On 20 May 1903 a letter was sent to Cody that was as firm as it was courteous:

I am commanded by my Lords Commissioners of the Admiralty to acquaint you that, after giving the subject their careful consideration, they regret they are unable to accept your offer. In communicating this decision, I am to add that in view of the ready assistance given by you in explaining your system and the principles and practice of kite flying as applied to Naval purposes, My Lords are prepared to give you (as an act of grace) a sum of one hundred pounds in addition to the out-of-pocket expenses that you have claimed.

The outlook for Cody after this refusal, however, turned out to be not nearly so bleak as might have been expected. He had acquired in a month an amount of experience that in any other way would have taken years; and financially it had cost him practically nothing. As Captain Tupper is known to have said, the Navy taught Cody as much as Cody taught the Navy. All this was most important when Cody came to work for the War Office. They had been in close touch with events at sea and on Whale Island, and were only waiting for the Navy's decision to take action themselves.

Furthermore, the Navy did not intend to drop kiting altogether. An order was placed for four sets of kites, each set comprising a pilot kite, two lifters, and a carrier kite with the basket and controls. These were to be supplied to the following of His Majesty's sea-going ships: *Majestic, Doris, Revenge,* and *Good Hope.**

Finally, Cody rapidly acquired a national and, indeed, an international

* There are grounds for supposing that when delivering the kites Cody took the opportunity for gaining further flying experience at sea, though none of this was recorded officially.

26 *top*. Kite with winch and ground crew (1904/5). A dozen or more sappers were needed to operate a complete array, and they worked to a complicated drill requiring great precision

27 *bottom*. Cody on his white horse inspects his kiting team (1904/5). Cody was a familiar figure on his famous horse, for which he was by the terms of his contract allowed free fodder

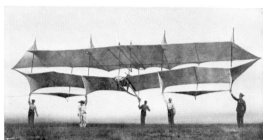

28 *top left*. The glider-kite in the air (1905). Cody not only produced a flyable glider, but one which could be made to go up first as a kite, and change over to gliding in mid-air. Here a Royal Engineer is flying the hybrid machine as a kite

29 *centre left*. The glider-kite held up for inspection. The machine was very modern-looking for its time, and was notable, among other things, for the primitive ailerons which are here to be seen below the bottom wings. This is believed to be the first time ailerons were ever used successfully to control roll

30 *below*. Another view of the glider- kite. Structurally the glider-kite was a weird contraption, with vertical fins 'sprouting everywhere like weeds in a neglected garden'. But it seems to have been just right from the very start – a rare achievement for any new flying machine

31 *facing*. 'Kite on Naval Manoeuvres', an artist's impression in *The Sphere* (1903): it captures the spirit of the time, though not, unfortunately, a true picture of an actual Cody kite

32 *above left*. The motor-kite in 'flight'. This picture shows the motor-kite with forward balancing planes. It has been heavily re-touched by someone in the past but there is no need to doubt its being a genuine representation. The machine 'flew' when arranged to slide along a horizontal wire, and according to Cody it was never allowed to go free

33 *centre left*. Front view of the motor-kite

34 *below*. Cody adjusting his motor-kite (1907?).

Cody's first attempt at powered flight was with a machine not intended to carry a pilot. Although only a qualified success, it taught Cody things that were invaluable when he came to make his full-scale powered aeroplane

reputation as the King of Kiting. He was no longer dependent for his fame upon demonstrations on the sands at Blackpool or at garden parties at Bath and Cheltenham, but had ships upon the high seas bearing witness to his skill. Writers and artists paid him tribute in newspapers and magazines in great variety. The whole atmosphere of the time was captured, for example, by an artist for *The Sphere*, though unfortunately without a true representation of the Cody Kite (see Fig. 31).*

3   The Navy's second venture
1908

Nearly five years have to go by before the story of Naval kiting can be resumed. In that time the Royal Engineers and the Balloon Factory have brought man-lifting kites to an advanced state of development at Farnborough. They are now standard equipment for the Balloon School; and the Balloon Factory has all the necessary resources for both their design and manufacture. With Colonel Capper as both Commandant and Superintendent, Cody is established as Chief Kite Instructor, a post which involves not only training at the School but supervision of kite manufacture in the Factory. The work on kites, however, in all its aspects, has tended to become routine, and the active minds of Capper and Cody are more concerned with the prospects of producing a powered aeroplane. The revival of interest by the Navy in the year 1908 suddenly brings, though only for a brief period, some new life and vitality into kiting work; and introduces new problems that must inevitably shatter routine and technical complacency.

Since 1904 the Navy had maintained a more-or-less continuous interest in the kiting work of the Royal Engineers. Suggestions had even been made that the Army should supply men to train a Naval crew, but hitherto such proposals had come to nothing. The request for help in the year 1908, therefore, may not have come as a great surprise, but it certainly came as a great inconvenience. The Navy not only wanted the loan of some man-lifting kites for testing at sea, but also wanted the loan of Cody's services. At that time he was deeply involved in the construction and flight testing of what was to become the first successful British aeroplane. The diversion

* This impressive picture covered two whole pages of *The Sphere* for 29 August 1903.

of effort might well have wrecked the whole aeroplane project, but in the event, Cody managed to cope with both undertakings with a measure of success that must always seem incredible.

From the standpoint of kiting history, however, we benefit greatly from the work undertaken by the Navy. The Naval Trials of 1908 were performed in a most methodical way, and in the best traditions of scientific experiment. They were, moreover, properly recorded to a standard that has had no parallel in kiting history.* For the all-round satisfactory way in which these experiments were conducted much of the credit must go to an old friend, Captain R. Tupper. He, it will be remembered, was the man who, as an Assistant Director at the Admiralty, witnessed the kiting demonstrations on Woolwich Common in the year 1903, and by his reports inspired the Admiralty to organize the brief Naval experiments that followed on Whale Island and at sea. Now, five years later, Captain Tupper was in command of *H.M.S. Excellent*, the Gunnery Establishment on Whale Island; and it was upon him and the men of *Excellent* that the Admiralty placed the responsibility for re-investigating man-lifting kites for Naval use.

Preliminary negotiations for the 1908 kite experiments actually began on 13 November 1970, when the Admiralty sent Captain Osmond de Brock R.N to Farnborough on what would nowadays be called a fact-finding mission. At the time Captain de Brock was Assistant Director of Naval Intelligence. He was well received and given a full demonstration of man-lifting, conditions being good with a strong breeze blowing. The pilot kite and three lifters were sent up; and there then followed in turn the men of practically an entire Balloon Section. Many of the men, according to de Brock, were obviously novices and in no sense specially trained performers; and no attempt was made to impress the Naval visitor unduly.

Captain de Brock's report on his visit has several points of interest. The men using the kites did not require special skill or knowledge, he thought, and the whole kiting system had been improved considerably from the standard attained on Whale Island in the year 1903. There should be no difficulty in flying the kites from ships. A certain amount of training, however, would be required and he recommended that, if the Admiralty decided to proceed with kites, a few men should be sent to Farnborough for initial training. Captain de Brock made some suggestions for the Naval use of kites and laid emphasis on what he thought would be their value for detecting

---

* It is not intended to imply that the historian's task was reduced to mere reporting. The Naval records for both 1903 and 1908 that had survived were battered and disarranged, and called for diligent searching and sorting, and not a little deciphering and I am grateful to Mr L. G. Seed and others at the Public Record Office for help in this matter.

underwater objects, especially mines and submarines. He estimated that, for operations on land or from stationary ships, a wind of not less than twenty-two knots (25 m.p.h. = 40 km/hr) was desirable but seventeen and a half knots (20 m.p.h. = 32 km/hr) was an acceptable minimum.* In dead calm air (admittedly a rare occurrence at sea) the same result should, he believed, be obtained by the ship's motion at corresponding speeds.†

Captain de Brock's report was sent by the Admiralty to Captain Tupper of *H.M.S. Excellent*, with a request for his comments. In his reply, dated 16 December 1907, Captain Tupper first of all reminded their Lordships that it was he who had first brought kites to their notice. He had been present at the trials made on Whale Island and on various seagoing ships in 1903. He had also used kites in the Mediterranean from a ship under his Command. While in the Mediterranean he had seen two cruisers of the Italian Fleet flying captive observation balloons, and was aware that France and Germany were experimenting on similar lines. He thought, however, that kites were much superior to balloons and very much cheaper.

Tupper's views on the prospects for kites in the Navy, however, were realistic and not prejudiced by his manifest enthusiasm; and he laid stress on the difficulties without being unduly perturbed by them:

> I respectfully beg to point out that experience and knowledge is as necessary for successfully flying kites as for sailing boats; and that the art cannot be acquired in a few hours. . . . I feel confident that if some Officers and Men are instructed in their use kites will be found most useful for Naval purposes, and that the more we know of them the more use we shall be able to make of them.

Captain Tupper ended his letter by seeking authority to experiment with kites in the coming summer, and requested that the War Office be asked to lend Mr Cody whenever he could be spared.

The Admiralty agreed to the plans for tests by *H.M.S. Excellent*, and after some discussion the War Office undertook to lend Cody to the Navy for one month. There were, of course, the inevitable arguments about cost and who should pay. Eventually the Admiralty agreed to pay the War Office the amount of Cody's salary, plus fifteen shillings subsistence allowance for Cody himself. The point is of interest as indicating that the Admiralty were almost

* Captain de Brock's report had a mixture of miles per hour for wind speed and knots for ship speed, apparently a common practice at the time. I find this confusing and in what follows have used knots for all speeds. Note: one knot = 1·15 miles per hour = 1·85 kilometres per hour.

† This was a common and understandable belief at the time, though not strictly accurate. A given *natural* wind speed at ground or sea level is usually indicative of something stronger up above, whereas a *relative* wind caused by the towing ship's motion is the same at all heights.

as tightly controlled financially as the War Office; and the chances of a really large-scale venture were small. In these circumstances it is remarkable how much was achieved by Cody and the Navy for no more than two or three hundred pounds.

On 3 April 1908, Captain Tupper himself visited the Balloon Factory at Farnborough and interviewed Colonel Capper and Cody. He discovered that Colonel Capper and all the men at Farnborough were willing to be helpful in every possible way. It was as though Colonel Capper found in Captain Tupper a kindred spirit in enthusiasm for aerial activity, and intelligent understanding of its operational potentialities. Together they drew up a general plan of action, and made tentative arrangements for the preliminary training at Farnborough of a small contingent from *H.M.S. Excellent*.

Towards the end of May, six men arrived from *H.M.S. Excellent* – two Petty Officers and four Leading Seamen – and they immediately entered upon a course of training under Cody. The precise date of their arrival is uncertain, but a note from Captain Tupper, dated 3 June 1908, indicates that they had then been at Farnborough for some days. Cody himself made day visits to Whale Island on two occasions to make preliminary arrangements for the tests, which were to begin in earnest on Monday, 17 August 1908.

For some unknown reason the tests were planned and carried out under conditions of greatest secrecy. No one at the Balloon Factory seems to have been aware of what was happening, apart from Colonel Capper, and probably his deputy, Captain Carden. Even the family of Cody do not appear to have known what he was doing. Historically, therefore, there has been a gap, which it is now possible to fill from documentary evidence. The only clue that past historians seem to have had is contained in the *R.A.E. Chronicles*:

In July (1908) Mr Cody was lent to R.N. to assist in Naval Experiments.

The date, however, is manifestly wrong, but it is the date that is quoted in most of the histories where the trials are mentioned at all.*

* This is an interesting example of error in the *R.A.E. Chronicles* (see commentary in Note 1 of Appendix A). These records were produced officially from original documents, within a decade or so of the events recorded; and for this reason they have hitherto been regarded as the equivalent of an original documentary source. This particular reference assumes importance when Cody's aeroplane flights are being considered.

4   Description of the kites
1908

Before the trials are considered in detail it is worth-while to take a look first at the kites themselves. As part of the operation they were photographed with skill and thoroughness, and the photographs form a unique collection (see Figs. 35 to 39). Unlike most of the Cody photographs these were taken, not for dramatic effect, but in order to reveal the essential details of design. The prints that have survived have suffered with sixty years of time, but it has been possible to retrieve much that is of value.

Although the pictures were taken as a necessary part of the final report on the Naval experiments, it should be remembered that the kites were designed and made in the Balloon Factory at Farnborough. There may have been minor alterations to meet Naval requirements, or even as a response to Naval advice, but basically they were the latest designs used by the Royal Engineers of the Balloon School. Furthermore, owing to the manner in which interest in kites declined after the year 1908 with the advance of the aeroplane, these pictures represent the most up-to-date designs that have ever existed.

First for consideration is the *pilot kite*, reproduced in Fig. 35. The scene is obviously Whale Island, and although two of the four sailors from *H.M.S. Excellent* are fading away through chemical action, the kite itself is almost perfect. It does not appear very different from the *top lifter kite* of the next picture, Fig. 36, except that it is slightly smaller. The pilot kite does not have, of course, the nose-ring of a lifter kite for sliding along the wire, since it is permanently tethered to the upper end of the main cable (as illustrated earlier in Fig. F, page 108).

The *second lifter kite*, which is reproduced as Fig. 37, appears almost identical with the top lifter, which is now up in the sky. Opportunity has been taken, however, to illustrate what was called a 'save-all', part of which is visible at the back of the kite and nearly touching the ground. In modern terminology this was an airbrake, being simply a flat fabric sheet facing the airstream. Cody had discovered that an array of kites could become unstable and get out of control if some of the intermediate kites became aerodynamically too efficient and edged their way forward into the wind. In Cody's view, the main cable must sag backwards down-wind, and the extra drag of the save-alls was intended to ensure this.

A better view of a save-all appears in a picture taken for an entirely different purpose, and reproduced here as Fig. 38. The save-all is to be seen, darker than the rest, at the back of the kite and roughly in its correct flying position. The same photograph also shows the method of attachment of the nose-ring, which is fixed to the end of a short strut whose other end is lashed to the intersection of the diagonal members.

The original purpose of this photograph, however, was to show how compactly a complete kite could be folded-up, or 'stowed' as the navy described it. By tradition the Navy paid great attention to this, as also to speed of assembling and dismantling. No doubt it was a carry-over from his showman days, but Cody received the highest praise for meeting naval standards in these matters.

Finally, there is the *carrier kite*, reproduced with its basket and towing system in Fig. 39. It is obviously much more robust than the other kites and larger, its span being estimated at about twenty feet (6 metres).* The photographs as a whole illustrate how neatly one end of a diagonal strut slides smoothly into a fabric pocket while the other end projects and has a tautening string attached to it. It will be noted, however, that the carrier kite operates the opposite way to the other kites, having the tautening device on the bottom horns, instead of on the upper horns and wings as on the pilot and lifter kites.

The nose-ring on the carrier kite is seen to be more elaborate than that on a lifter kite, being a kind of slot with pulleys at the upper and lower ends. Presumably this gave easier control in adjusting the inclination of the kite for ascent or descent. The great length of crossbar is another notable feature, with the two half-bridles attached to the extreme ends in order to restrain any swinging tendency in the kite.

The original set of photographs does not include views of the kites being operated at sea. There is available, however, a photograph from elsewhere, reproduced as Fig. 40, showing the carrier kite and the aeronaut just leaving the ship for their aerial voyage. In this particular case the aeronaut is suspended in a breeches buoy, which was used instead of the balloon-type basket on some occasions.

* Dimensions of the kites are only known approximately, as determined mainly from measurements made on the photographs. The estimated spans for the three basic types are:

Pilot kite	14 feet	(4·3 metres)
Lifter kite	17 feet	(5·2 metres)
Carrier kite	20 feet	(6·1 metres)

5   The Naval Trials of 1908

Starting on Monday 17 August 1908, the first series of seagoing tests were made every day, except Saturdays and Sundays, for three weeks, whenever weather conditions permitted. There now follows a day-by-day account of the more important experiments.

Monday, 17 August 1908 (Revenge)

On this very first day the Navy was to learn an important lesson. The kiting unit went out in *H.M.S. Revenge*, which was a twin-screw battleship of 14,150 tons and on the permanent strength of the *H.M.S. Excellent* gunnery school. With the wind at eleven knots the ship steamed straight into it at twelve knots, giving by simple addition a nominally equivalent wind speed of twenty-three knots. The fallacy behind such simple reasoning, however, was soon discovered. With the ship steaming head to wind, the superstructure so screened the quarter-deck and stern of the ship that the kites were reluctant to leave the ship at all. Eventually one kite was got into the air, but proper flying was impracticable.

Tuesday, 18 August 1908 (Fervent)

This time the kiting unit went out in another ship, *H.M.S. Fervent*. She was a torpedo boat destroyer of 310 tons and capable of a fairly high speed. The wind was blowing at about eleven knots and by steaming at twenty-two knots it was possible to get up the full kiting array with a man in the basket. In order to reduce screening by the ship's superstructure, however, it was necessary to steer the ship so that the wind was partly abeam, and to launch the kites at an angle with the ship instead of directly astern.

Thursday, 20 August 1908 (Revenge)

On this day it was decided to try again with the battleship *H.M.S. Revenge*, using the new side-launching technique. This method was rendered more feasible by there being a stronger natural wind, twenty-two knots or so (Force 5); and it was found possible to fly from *Revenge* after all. Cody himself went up after a pilot kite and two lifters.

Monday, 24 August 1908 (Revenge)

Out with the battleship *H.M.S. Revenge* again. The wind was really worth-while, being twenty-six knots (Force 6). An experiment was tried with a modified form of the side-launching technique. As a kite was about to leave the deck the ship would be yawed temporarily to give the desired cross-wind, and after the launching the ship would return to its original course. The method appears to have worked satisfactorily, though obviously success depended largely on the strength of the natural wind.

On this day four men went up in turn: Cody first, then one of the Farnborough-trained Petty Officers, and finally two Lieutenants. Having just about mastered the technique of take-off, however, the kiting unit and the crew of the ship encountered another difficulty: the aeronauts having gone up satisfactorily were finding difficulty in getting down again. Cody, weighing fourteen and a half stones (204 lb = $92\frac{1}{2}$ kg) came down like a bomb, but the more lithesome eleven-stoners would remain suspended.

Conditions up aloft in the basket were described as comfortable, and the final touch-down on to the deck as 'easy'. Behind the various comments, however, it is possible to detect mental reservations, such as 'provided you are a sailor or an acrobat'.

Tuesday, 25 August 1908 (Revenge)

A gale was blowing, forty knots or so (Force 8). This produced a classic example of the paradoxical law that wind above a certain strength decreased the effective lifting power instead of increasing it. In any event, Cody could not get up with the usual two lifters and had to send up three.

The main exercise was 'spotting' shots that were being fired at a target towed by a destroyer. Natural vision was good until smoke from the firing got in the way; but it was not practical to use glasses, presumably owing to the motion of the basket.

All were pleased with the way the kites and kiting gear stood up to a combined wind of about fifty-two knots; but again the aeronauts had difficulty in getting down, even when the ship changed course to bring the relative wind right across the beam.

Wednesday, 26 August 1908 (Revenge)

Wind was again strong, forty knots (Force 8), but flying was becoming routine, and it is clear that sailors in general had a natural aptitude for the work. Cody and three lieutenants went up in turn.

Cody was still working on the problem of the resisted descent. He had decided that the difficulty encountered by the flyers was attributable not so much to insufficient body weight as to a tendency for the men to pull down the nose of the carrier kite too far.

Friday, 28 August 1908 (Recruit)

A full gale was blowing, over forty knots (Force 8/9). This time the kiting unit went out in another ship: *H.M.S. Recruit*, a torpedo boat destroyer of 385 tons, temporarily attached to *H.M.S. Excellent*. Only the pilot kite was got up, and the wire snapped; but the kite was recovered undamaged.

Monday, 31 August 1908 (Recruit)

This was the most exciting day of all. The wind varied from eleven to twenty-one knots, and was blowing almost directly from the south. The weather was dull and squally as *H.M.S. Recruit* steamed up the Solent in an easterly direction at a speed of eighteen knots. With the wind on the starboard beam, Cody was up at a height of 800 feet (240 metres) with a kiting array that included as many as four lifters. The intention was to look for submerged mines just outside St Helen's Bay. When the ship had just passed Noman's Fort (three or four miles east of Ryde) on its easterly course, it left the partial shelter provided by the Isle of Wight and suddenly met the full force of a strong wind from the south.

The basket (with Cody) was seen to shake and shudder. Then the pilot kite dived vigorously to the right. Next the lifter kites dived to the right also and almost turned completely over. They all recovered, but only to begin the process all over again. According to eye witnesses there were two such recoveries, with the whole array descending all the time. It is not difficult to imagine what Cody felt like in the basket, but his problems were solved when the basket hit the water with a smack and overturned. It is not clear whether Cody climbed out or was tipped out, but he was unhurt and hung on to the basket, which stayed afloat.

On board ship, action was quickly taken: engines were reversed and someone had the presence of mind to cut the cable. Whether this did any good or not is uncertain, for the cable was found to have snapped near the carrier kite anyway, presumably as the basket and kite were dragged through the water, and a thousand feet or so of cable were never recovered. Cody was readily picked up, and apart from a thorough soaking was little the worse for his experience.*

* This incident is curiously like the absurd story told in a number of history books, usually as having happened in the year 1903, though not appearing in any official records. According to this story, the ship was steaming head-to-wind under control of a captain who either forgot he was towing some kites or who did not know that their support was largely dependent on the ship's forward motion. Without any warning the ship was turned down-wind, thus bringing the kites down. Cody, who was supposed to have been flying at the time, had his life saved (so the story goes) only by the presence of mind of a sailor who cut the cable with a knife.

Wednesday, 2 September 1908 (Recruit)

Work was still proceeding with repairs after Monday's adventures, but the damage was not serious. Cody attributed the enforced descent to lack of truth of the pilot kite. He therefore went out with *H.M.S. Recruit* in order to make the necessary adjustments. For these he believed a very strong wind was necessary. *Recruit* was therefore made to steam at twenty-three knots against a wind of seventeen knots.

In view of Cody's immersion on Monday, the opportunity was taken to test the seaworthiness of a breeches buoy (see Fig. 40), as a possible alternative to the basket. A sailor was put overboard in one, and it was found to keep him afloat and well up in the water. It was liable to overturn, however; but putting some lead weights in the feet was tried and proved effective in keeping the man upright.

An interesting experiment was also made with a kite towing a whaler. It was found that in a wind of eighteen knots the whaler could be made to travel at four knots in a direction as much as fifty degrees away from the wind. The Navy, however, did not seem to be impressed by this performance.

Thursday, 3 September 1908 (Recruit).

Cody went up from *Recruit* to try to see some mines in the neighbourhood of the Nab Rock, and also a submerged submarine. The Admiralty placed great emphasis on the value of being able to see beneath the surface of the sea, and there were hopes that this would be possible from a kite. The tests made on 31 August had proved this to be possible under somewhat ideal conditions of good light and clear water. On this particular day (3 September) the weather was dull, misty and overcast; and under these conditions Cody saw nothing at all beneath the surface.

The wind blew from the south with strength increasing during the experiments up to twenty-one knots. A pilot kite and three lifters were used on this occasion, but the whole array was very unsteady, swinging from side to side through about 200 feet (60 metres). Cody attributed this to the absence of save-alls on the lifter kites. As already described, a save-all was a flat sheet acting as an airbrake (see Figs. 37 and 38), and its purpose was to make the main cable sag down-wind, a condition – Cody believed – conducive to stability.

Friday, 4 September 1908 (Recruit)

Trouble was again experienced through oscillatory instability. This was attributed by Cody to the pilot kite having got out of adjustment while being repaired. The day was spent experimenting with the pilot kite, and on this anticlimax there ended the first stage of the Naval Trials of 1908.

The tests were now stopped for some weeks and Cody went home. They did not begin again until Monday, 28 September 1908, but they have become too humdrum for day-to-day reporting in the present History. The dates of operation, however, and the names of the ships were as follows:

Monday, 28 September	1908	*H.M.S. Grafton*
Tuesday, 29 September	,,	,, ,,
Wednesday, 30 September	,,	,, ,,
Thursday, 1 October	,,	*H.M.S. Recruit*
Friday, 2 October	,,	,, ,,
Monday, 5 October	,,	,, ,,
Tuesday, 6 October	,,	,, ,,
Wednesday, 7 October	,,	,, ,,

The new ship introduced to kiting experiments, *H.M.S. Grafton*, was described as a twin-screw protected cruiser, first class, of 7,350 tons. After three days, however, a return was made to the torpedo boat destroyer, *H.M.S. Recruit*, presumably for economy of operation.

There was now a tendency for the Naval contingent to become less and less dependent on Cody, in anticipation of the day when the Navy would have to operate on their own. Nevertheless, he stayed active, although he did not attend on the first two days (28 and 29 September), being much preoccupied in testing the first Farnborough aeroplane.

Cody finished finally on 7 October 1908, although the Navy continued for a time with some not very successful experiments in which magnesium flares were suspended from kites at night. Reporting for 7 October 1908, Lieutenant Usborne, who was in charge of the Naval Party, wrote:

This completes Mr Cody's time on Whale Island and, with the exception of the experiments with magnesium lights, which will be carried out without him, completes the series of experiments.

6   The final verdict

1908

Captain Tupper sent to the Admiralty the full day-by-day report of the trials under cover of a letter dated 22 October 1908. He added a long report of his own in which he analysed the advantages and limitations of kites for

Naval use. As would have been expected, he was enthusiastic; but he was also factual and restrained in his comments. He recommended the purchase of two kiting outfits, each comprising two complete sets of kites and one winch. He considered that Scouts and fast cruisers were the best ships to use. Destroyers, under all but ideal conditions, were unsuitable owing to the cramped space and excessive motion. Captain Tupper rightly insisted, however, that kites would be virtually useless unless the men operating them were fully trained and experienced. He offered to provide the training at *H.M.S. Excellent*.

The Commander-in-Chief at Portsmouth, Admiral Fanshawe,* gave Captain Tupper his full support. In a covering note of the same date he said:

After having read this report with great interest, I am strongly of the opinion that Captain Tupper's recommendation, that complete outfits should be supplied to a Cruiser of the *Invincible* type and a Scout for further tests, should be adopted.

The Admiralty did not share this enthusiasm, and men of *H.M.S. Excellent* must have been shocked by their attitude to what all regarded as a fine piece of work.† From what transpired it is difficult to imagine that it had ever been the intention of the Admiralty to adopt the kites, whatever the result of the trials. Nevertheless, a reasoned case against them was prepared and argued, though apparently minor arguments were set alongside the more substantial ones.

The Admiralty regarded it as a great disadvantage that destroyers could not be used. It was also considered a great disadvantage that, in order to be sure of operating in all weathers, a ship capable of twenty-five knots was required. Manoeuvring, moreover, would be seriously impeded in or near a naval action. In addition, the hoped-for advantage of being able to see mines and submarines under the sea did not normally exist in waters around the British Isles. All these arguments carried weight; but it was perhaps only indicative of the economic policy of the time that the cost of a complete outfit being £1,000 should be included as an important adverse factor, which would seem a small price to pay if kites proved to be a major technical advance in naval warfare.

There were other arguments more controversial. As regards target spotting for gun laying (aiming), smoke would obscure vision:

It is unlikely that this method will be of value for Naval actions on account of smoke obscuring the vision.

* Later, Admiral of the Fleet, Sir Arthur D. Fanshawe.
† In his autobiography, *Reminiscences*, published in 1929, Admiral Sir Reginald Tupper makes no mention of his kiting work.

No reason was given why vision should not also be obscured in other methods of observation, or why the altitude of the kite should not actually be helpful to visual penetration. In any event, the fact was ignored that *H.M.S. Excellent* had carried out tests and had found that kites improved accuracy of fire.

As a further point it was conceded that kites gave a better angle of vision for seeing over fortifications, hills, and other obstacles, but at the same time it was claimed that the improvement was too small to be significant. The angle of downward vision at 8,000 yards (four nautical miles), it was rightly maintained, could not exceed seven or eight degrees. As things turned out, the value of the extra angle of vision was never ascertained in actual naval operations. Balloons operating at similar heights had been highly successful from this standpoint in South Africa during the war, but probably the objectives were much nearer than would be likely for ships at sea.*

The one undisputed advantage for the kites was the increased range of vision in clear weather and the more distant horizon. This point was conceded by the Director of Naval Ordnance, Captain R.H.S. Bacon,† when he ended his own personal assessment, which was unfavourable in every other way:

> The only practical use at present of kites therefore appears to lie in obtaining a larger horizon for scouting purposes; and the possibility of obtaining this is limited by the necessity of having sufficient force of wind more or less in a desired direction.

While all these various operational items were listed and argued, very little discussion seems to have taken place regarding the technical reliability of the kites themselves. Possibly the officers of the Admiralty felt that this was outside their own professional domain. On the evidence of the tests, however, there were clearly grounds for some concern at the number of occasions in which the kiting array had got out of control by swinging violently from side to side. The phenomenon was known to the Royal Engineers at Farnborough, but occurred more frequently at sea. Cody's tentative explanations of a badly adjusted pilot kite or absence of a save-all are not entirely convincing, and there was clearly a need for a more scientific

---

* Seven or eight degrees as the angle of downward vision was a generous estimate. It was based on a height of 3,000 feet (900 metres) assumed to have been reached at Farnborough. If this height was actually attained there, it was a freak result, and 2,000 feet (600 metres) was the normal optimum. In the Naval Trials 1,600 feet (490 metres) was the highest altitude reached, corresponding to a downward angle of approximately four degrees at the specified distance.

† Later, Admiral Sir Reginald H. S. Bacon.

study of the stability of a kiting array, similar to that study so freely given to aeroplane stability a few years later.

Nevertheless, the Admiralty must have had some underlying uneasiness about the control of the kites. When they came to give their reasons for turning down the proposals, they did not produce their own serious professional arguments but merely referred to the *difficulties* and *risks* associated with flying kites at sea. Reasons were a minor matter, however, compared with the actual decision, and this was a definite *No*!

On 24 December 1908, the Admiralty wrote to the Commander-in-Chief of His Majesty's Ships and Vessels at Portsmouth:

With reference to your letter of 22nd October and later correspondence in regard to experiments with Cody Kites carried out by *H.M.S. Excellent*, I am commanded by My Lords Commissioners of the Admiralty to acquaint you that, in view of the difficulties and risks at present attaching to the use of these kites, they consider it is premature to supply them to sea-going ships, but *H.M.S. Excellent* should be directed to keep in touch with any further developments in kites and kite-flying.

7 Templer's Airship - Nulli Secundus I 1901-7

1   An introduction to Templer's great experiment

History has not done justice to Templer's pioneer work on airships. Rarely can an achievement such as Templer's original airship have been supported by so little published information. Although we have records of the flights of the airship,* which became known as *Nulli Secundus I*, very little has been made known about how it was made, and even less about the creative thought that lay behind it. In the course of investigation for the present History much additional information has been discovered, including descriptions of the finished airship published in the newspapers and periodicals of the day. The result is a fuller picture of Templer's creative work, and greater recognition of his scientific contribution to lighter-than-air principles.

One of the main reasons for the lack of authorative information about the first British military airship was the political climate of the time.† There are grounds for believing that for some years after Templer's retirement in 1906 any mention of Templer's contribution to airship development was officially frowned upon. Not only the War Office but also the Government of the day were placed in an awkward situation. The achievements of France and Germany in airship construction, and especially the work of Count Zeppelin‡ in Germany, produced lively topics for the British Press. 'What has Britain done in the airship world?' could well have been asked. 'Got rid of Britain's greatest authority on airships and the acknowledged world authority on military balloons,' could well have been the derisive answer.

Lest the possible consequences of the manifest neglect of airship development in general, and of Templer in particular, seem to be exaggerated, it is necessary only to reflect upon the furore that arose when aeroplanes were in

* Reproduced in the *Extracts from the Proceedings of the Royal Engineer Committee*, referred to here for brevity as the *R.E.C. Extracts*. See Note 2 of Appendix A.
† As described in Chapter 3 – 'The last years of Colonel Templer'.
‡ Strictly, we should speak of Count (Ferdinand) *von* Zeppelin (1838–1917) but I am adopting the British practice of referring to him simply as Count Zeppelin.

a similar situation a few years later. The flight across the English Channel by the Frenchman, Louis Blériot, from Calais to Dover on 25 July 1909, stunned the whole British people and forced an apathetic Government to take some action. As it happened, nothing so drastic occurred over the airship situation, partly because airship designers abroad encountered a number of setbacks, and partly owing to the air of competent efficiency which emanated from Colonel Capper in his new role of Superintendent of the Balloon Factory.

Templer's entry into the airship field was fraught with difficulty from the start, and conditions compared most unfavourably with those of his rivals abroad. Although there had been some successes earlier,* it was about the year 1899 that airships were becoming recognized as having future possibilities beyond mere scientific experiment. This was the year, however, that Templer had to go to war in South Africa, while his rivals abroad were free to go ahead with airship development. It was not until 1902 that there was some return to normality in Britain, and the War Office became aware that airships might be about to enter the military field. In the period from 1899 to 1902, however, considerable advances had been made in both France and Germany. Alberto Santos-Dumont made history by his spectacular flight round the Eiffel Tower in Paris on 19 October 1901. Work also proceeded in France on the famous airship, *Lebaudy*, which first flew on 13 November 1902 and made the world's first cross-country flight of 38 miles (62 km) on 12 November 1903.† As for Germany, Count Zeppelin completed his first airship in the year 1900. This was a monster, 420 feet (128 metres) long, and was first launched from Lake Constance on 2 July 1900.

Handicapped as he was by a late start, Templer was still further impeded, when work on the airship did begin, by the inadequacy of the money that the War Office could allow, mainly owing to a policy of financial stringency over which they had little control. Airships cost much more than other forms of flying machine – balloons, kites, gliders, and aeroplanes. They were ordinarily outside the scope of individual pioneers, and even large public companies were faced with certain financial loss in days when airships were almost entirely experimental. In France, Santos-Dumont was a wealthy man who paid for his tiny airships out of his own private resources. Soon, more-

---

* As early as 1884 the French pioneers, Charles Renard and Captain A. C. Krebs had flown what has been described as the first practical airship, *La France*. This was powered by a primitive electric motor run from batteries. More contemporaneous was the flight by Santos-Dumont in his first airship in 1898, which had a small petrol motor.

† Forerunner of the Lebaudy-built airship that was bought by the readers of the *Morning Post* in 1910, and presented to the Balloon Factory. It was later wrecked over Farnborough, on 4 May 1911.

over, the French Government showed more than a casual interest in airships and, much to Colonel Templer's chagrin, made munificent grants to the official aeronautical establishment at Chalais-Meudon, and even found it possible to be generous to individual pioneers as well. In Germany, Count Zeppelin first used up his considerable private fortune, then borrowed from his friends and, finally, when still short of funds, showed ingenuity in raising money by lotteries and public subscriptions from an enthusiastic German people.* Templer, unfortunately, had no other source of financial strength than the apathetic British Government, having spent all his own private fortune on military balloons in the eighties of the previous century.

The final and most serious handicap was the personal treatment of Templer himself. While men like Santos-Dumont and Count Zeppelin were national heroes, Templer was subjected to every conceivable humiliation, as already described in this History (Chapter 3). The climax came when, having been led to believe that he would be retained as Superintendent until March 1909, he was retired on 27 May 1906. This must have been a serious set-back in the design and construction of the airship, which had then reached a critical stage. It was, however, completed fifteen months later, with Templer employed as an adviser on a part-time basis.

In all these circumstances it seems remarkable that a flyable airship was ever completed; and this brings us to what is perhaps the most crucial issue of all – how successful was the first British airship that came to be known as *Nulli Secundus I*? Unfortunately, it became the practice to disparage the value of this airship. Modern historians as a rule do not speak highly of it; and there has been a tendency to forget that it was the first of its line in Britain, and devised at a time when airships abroad were not being conspicuously successful.

So far as is known, Colonel Capper never gave an overall assessment of Templer's airship during his active life, and always confined himself to factual comments on its performance. He was singularly reticent about Templer's contribution, and this may have misled many people. It was not until some forty years after the events here recorded that he relaxed a little to comment on the first British airship. In a letter to R.A.E. dated 2 June 1946, and written in response to an R.A.E. request, he commented most dismally about the airship: 'It was a horrible unmanageable balloon, built by Colonel Templer, with a speed of only 14 miles per hour [22½ km/hr].'

* It was somewhat later that the German Government began to show interest to the extent of financial support. Then, as is well known, they went beyond all other nations in developing airships.

While the speed is perhaps only slightly understated, the airship according to the best evidence was neither horrible nor unmanageable.

Ironically, evidence of refutation comes from Capper himself. The reports on the flight trials of the airship, reproduced in the *R.E.C. Extracts*, were the responsibility of Capper in the threefold role of Superintendent of the Establishment, Captain of the Airship, and associate member of the Royal Engineer Committee. There were indeed the usual teething troubles, expected for any new design of vehicle for land, sea or air; but the report on the third trial flight included the following:

> The control was excellent – the ship keeping on a horizontal keel, no pitching, no rolling, and the helm was duly answered. A little difficult to keep on a straight course.

It is indeed hardly conceivable that any new design of airship anywhere and at any time has had such a good report on its third time out.

In mitigation of Capper's unfortunate appraisal in 1946 it should be recorded that when he wrote the letter he was then in his eighty-fifth year. On his own admission his memory was very poor, and all his papers had been destroyed.*

The story that now follows is presented on the premise that Templer knew what he was about and that his airship was truly a great experiment. On this basis his plans and methods (so far as they are known or can be deduced) are examined a little more closely than seems to have been possible hitherto.

2   The expandable airship (a technical appraisal)

The history of the early airships loses much of its interest when their basic technicalities are neglected. The story of *Nulli Secundus*, especially, is hardly worth telling unless some account is taken of the more important principles that were embodied in its design. There is an accumulation of evidence to show that the original *Nulli Secundus* was the product of much thought and study, and in its way a masterpiece of originality. To Colonel Templer, the design of an airship at the beginning of the present century was a problem of

* Major-General Sir John Capper, as he had then become, sent all his papers for salvage during the Second World War. How valuable they would have been to historians today!

the greatest fascination; and to us it is especially interesting because his solution was not the same as anybody else's.

Templer's airship had several unique features, but most important was the embodiment of a concept that may conveniently be described as the *expandable airship*. This is essentially an airship made of flexible sheet material that not only recovers its original size and shape after stretching but also stretches very easily in the first place. In other words, the material behaves very much as would be expected of an ordinary piece of elastic; and a toy balloon made of rubber provides a good illustration of the overall principle – by the way it expands or contracts as the blowing-up pressure is increased or decreased.

In 1903 the War Office Committee of Inquiry into Military Aeronautics referred to this conceptual device as the *elastic airship*, a term which some people might prefer even today. Unfortunately the rigorous technical definition of *elastic* – and also the primary meaning given in most dictionaries – merely denotes the power of recovery of size and shape after stretching, without any regard to the ease with which the stretching may be effected. The term *expandable airship* should remove any ambiguity, but it needs to be borne in mind that the envelope may contract as well as expand appreciably, according to circumstances, and by a repeatable process that requires the material to be truly elastic. In what now follows some of the more important principles of general airship design are reviewed, so that the *expandable airship* may be given its proper place in the general pattern.

*The non-rigid airship.** An airship is essentially a balloon, but it is a balloon provided with the means of horizontal travel, not with the wind, but at the command of the pilot and in the direction he chooses. It follows, therefore, that in addition to having the power of levitation like a balloon it must also meet certain other requirements. First of all, it must be approximately cylindrical in shape or preferably – by modern standards – streamlined, so that it can travel through the air with the least practicable resistance. Next, it must have the means of propulsion, which is normally provided by the engine–propeller system. Third, it must be steerable, not only horizontally like an ordinary sea-going ship, but also, within reasonable limits, along an upward or downward path.

These rather obvious characteristics seem at first sight to constitute the

---

* For the present purpose the so-called *semi-rigid* airship is included in the *non-rigid* category since, although it has some structure incorporated within the envelope, it depends upon internal pressure to maintain its shape completely. Sometimes the term *pressure ship* is used to comprehend all types requiring internal pressure.

main essentials of airship design, but they did not impose upon the designer of a non-rigid airship his most difficult problem in the early days. The envelope of the non-rigid airship maintains its shape through internal pressure. It is blown up like the tyre of an automobile but to pressures, of course, very much lower. Unfortunately, while the airship is in operation there are natural agencies at work trying to burst it, and there are other agencies trying to do the opposite by turning it into a flabby shapeless thing, quite unsuitable for motion through the air. The task of a designer of a non-rigid airship is thus quite clear: he has to ensure reasonable tautness of the envelope without risk of either bursting or flabbiness.

Differential pressure. When we speak of 'pressure' inside the envelope being required to maintain its shape, we have in mind what is more correctly described as 'differential pressure'. This is simply the *excess* of pressure inside the envelope over that of the atmosphere outside.* Thus it is the differential pressure which determines whether a non-rigid airship's envelope will be flabby, reasonably taut, or on the point of bursting. The word 'pressure' alone, however, is often used instead of 'differential pressure' when the meaning is thought to be clear; but misunderstandings have arisen at times through this practice, and special care is necessary when dealing with *Nulli Secundus.*

On *Nulli Secundus* and later British airships it was usual to express differential pressure in terms of inches of water. This was readily indicated by water in a U-tube, with one end connected by tubing to the bottom of the envelope and the other to the open air. The differential pressure was then taken as the difference between the two levels.†

The water-scale was also convenient numerically, about half an inch being the acceptable minimum, with one inch preferable, for maintaining a firm envelope. Higher values could be tolerated for *Nulli Secundus*, however, in circumstances yet to be discussed, but three inches seems usually to have been taken as the allowable maximum.

Climb and descent. The first threat to maintenance of the correct differential pressure comes about immediately the airship begins to climb. The differential pressure tends to rise owing to the reduced pressure of the outside

* The term 'superpressure' is given in the *British Standards Aeronautical Glossary* (B.S.185 Section 7) instead of 'differential pressure' as used here. 'Differential pressure', however, is normally used for aeroplane pressure cabins.

† The relation between the water scale and other methods of expressing pressure is given approximately by the simple rule:

One inch of water = five pounds per square foot = twenty-five kilogrammes per square metre.

atmosphere with increased height, so that unless precautions are taken the envelope will burst.

Immediate relief from increasing differential pressure could be obtained, of course, by release of hydrogen, but this would reduce the original buoyancy and necessitate discharge of ballast, since the hydrogen needs to expand freely inside the envelope if there is to be direct compensation for the reduced lifting power of the more rarefied atmosphere outside.

The need to maintain a taut envelope, however, is an entirely different and in many respects a more important consideration than the saving of hydrogen and ballast. It has to be borne in mind that after climbing to altitude the airship will eventually have to come down again. If hydrogen has been released, therefore, there is a danger that contraction of the remaining hydrogen during descent will produce a flabby shapeless envelope.

Ballonet versus the expandable envelope. The most widely recognized method of coping with this problem of expansion and contraction of the hydrogen is by use of the *ballonet*. This is a collapsible air-bag that is totally enclosed inside the airship envelope. It is so arranged that when the hydrogen seeks to expand it does so by squeezing the ballonet and forcing air from it into the outer atmosphere. Conversely, if the hydrogen needs to contract, air can be pumped into the ballonet in order to maintain the correct differential pressure for tautness of the envelope.*

Templer worked on an entirely different principle. He did not use a ballonet at all, but made use of the natural elastic stretchability of goldbeater's skin. If the hydrogen needed to expand, it could do so by stretching the material of the envelope, to give only a small increase of differential pressure. Conversely, if the hydrogen needed to contract afterwards, so also would the envelope, and back to its original condition. Goldbeater's skin, moreover, being exceptionally strong material, had adequate strength to deal with the limited expansive stresses thus imposed upon it.

The relative merits of the expandable goldbeater's-skin envelope *without* a ballonet, and the almost unstretchable fabric envelope *with* a ballonet, are difficult to decide for the period under discussion. Although nowadays a

---

* *Ballonet* is now pronounced bal-on-nett and is spelt as shown. In the past there have been a few alternative pronunciations and several spellings. The ballonet is essentially an *air-bag*, but some dictionaries give it a secondary meaning of *reserve gas-bag*. Such is a misuse of language, since the two meanings are the antithesis of each other, and the distinction must be preserved. Misunderstandings have arisen through this practice, and *Nulli Secundus* has not been exempt.

For simplicity, a single ballonet is here assumed in discussion of principles, though there can be several smaller ones instead. Ballonets placed respectively forward and aft have also been used for trimming an airship.

ballonet would be considered essential, Templer probably made the correct decision at the time, with due regard to the resources and skills at the Balloon Factory. Other designers scarcely had a free choice, since only the Balloon Factory had the full technique for manipulation of goldbeater's skin at its disposal. Many of the difficulties encountered in the design, construction, and operation of *Nulli Secundus*, it should be noted, were common to all non-rigid airships. This was not always properly appreciated in Britain, and among the initiated there was probably more enlightened recognition of the merits of *Nulli Secundus* in France.*

Numerical Values. Generalizations about the elastic expansion of the envelope of *Nulli Secundus*, and of its being a workable alternative to the ballonet, are not very convincing without the support of some actual figures. Unfortunately, virtually no direct quatitative information about the elastic properties of *Nulli Secundus* has survived – if any was ever formally recorded, which is doubtful. For the purpose of this History, however, it has been possible to make some rough calculations based upon the reports of the flight trials of 1907 as reported in the *R.E.C. Extracts*. To these there is to be added the substance of a lecture given by Colonel Capper to the School of Military Engineering at Chatham on 12 March 1908.†

The figures which follow relate primarily to the effect of climb and descent as already discussed, but may also be used as a general guide to the other effects still to be dealt with. It is estimated that a rise in differential pressure of about ten pounds per square foot (50 kg/sq metre), or two inches of water, would accommodate a climb from the ground up to a height of 1,500 feet (450 metres). The corresponding rise in differential pressure for an unstretchable envelope – assuming it did not burst – would be about ten times as great. This gives a good indication of the effectiveness of the goldbeater's skin. The actual increase in volume of *Nulli Secundus* for these conditions works out at about five per cent.‡

A maximum operational height of 1,500 feet (450 metres) seems very low by modern standards. The early pioneers in the airship world, however, were all preoccupied with forward travel, and to them this figure would seem more than adequate. It is indeed doubtful whether *Nulli Secundus I* ever reached this height.

* See, for example: 'Le dirigeable militaire anglais *Nulli Secundus*'; *l'Aérophile*, September 1907.
† See 'Dirigible Balloons' by Brevet Colonel J. E. Capper, *Royal Engineers' Journal*, Vol. VII, 1908.
‡ The standard atmospheric pressure at sea-level is 2,116 lb/sq ft (10,300 kg/sq metre). At 1,500 feet (450 metres) it is reduced by 112 lb/sq ft (550 kg/sq metre).

Sunshine and Shade. A somewhat similar cycle of expansion and contraction can be produced by changes of temperature of the hydrogen. There is expansion when the airship passes from the shade into the sunshine, and contraction when the process is reversed. The circumstances differ from those produced by climb and descent, however, in one important respect. When the airship *climbs*, expansion needs to be accommodated within the envelope in order to maintain buoyancy in the more rarified atmosphere. When the sun shines directly on the airship, on the other hand, the expansion caused by rise in temperature *must* be corrected by discharge of hydrogen; for, in order to maintain the original buoyancy, the volume of hydrogen in the envelope must remain unchanged. The adverse effects of this hydrogen loss are not felt until the external conditions are reversed, and the airship passes from sunshine to shadow, and so cools down. There is then contraction and danger of the envelope becoming flabby.

For an airship with the conventional fabric envelope, a ballonet is used to compensate for this contraction by air being pumped into it. For the expandable *Nulli Secundus* type of envelope, on the other hand, there must be an initial reserve of differential pressure so that some remains after hydrogen release and subsequent elastic contraction of the envelope. Calculations are difficult because the temperature changes are so unpredictable, and there are a great many complications which cannot be gone into in a general treatment.

In practice, the pilot of an expandable airship would have scope for ingenuity in avoiding the simultaneous occurrence of adverse conditions. With an airship temporarily overheated on the ground, for example, he might delay climbing after take-off until it had cooled down. Unfortunately, neither version of *Nulli Secundus* lasted long enough for proper experiment, but there are some figures on record. On one occasion Colonel Capper left the ground with a pressure of one inch of water (5 lb/sq ft = 25 kg/sq metre) and, on another, with a pressure of twice this. Another time the hot sun raised the pressure while the airship was still on the ground until hydrogen was forced out of the safety valve at a differential of just under three inches of water.

The goldbeater's-skin envelope was, of course, protected by an automatic safety valve; and so far as is known this was never set higher than three inches of water (15 lb/sq ft = 75 kg/sq metre). In general, airships with ordinary fabric envelopes and ballonets inside did not have pressures higher than one inch of water, although lower values have been suggested as feasible.

Leakage of Hydrogen. In principle, another contributor towards flabbiness is leakage of hydrogen through the material of the envelope. Hydrogen is the most penetrating of all substances; and all the known fabrics with the best known treatments were vulnerable. It is doubtful, however, whether the effect was very significant on a single journey, although the leakage between flights could add greatly to the cost of maintaining an airship. In any event, the goldbeater's-skin envelope was in this particular respect supreme. It has been claimed that throughout the lives of both *Nulli Secundus I* and *Nulli Secundus II* there was never any measurable loss of hydrogen after manufacturing errors had been corrected, apart from what was released deliberately.*

Goldbeater's skin had the further advantage that if a hole was formed through accidental penetration it never formed a running crack or tear as most other materials were liable to do. On the other hand, it has been said that goldbeater's skin had two counterbalancing disadvantages: there was difficulty in attaching lines or making other forms of connection to it; and it was liable to absorb an excessive weight of water when left out in the rain.

The rigid airship. Passing mention may usefully be made of the rigid airship, if only to explain why this was not chosen for the Balloon Factory's first venture. Although often regarded as an entirely different species, it fits into the same general pattern of principles as the two types of non-rigid airship here considered. Essentially, the functions of maintaining external tautness and gas-holding are kept separate. Thus the outer fabric envelope is stretched over a self-contained and comparatively rigid structure, while the hydrogen is held in special bags inside. These bags are normally incompletely filled so that expansion or contraction of the hydrogen can take place freely as required.

When Templer first made his plans for an airship the prospects for a non-rigid were much brighter than for a rigid type. Success with the rigid airship in Germany was eventually attained only through the many years of patient work by Count Zeppelin, carried out with almost superhuman determination to overcome repeated setbacks.† It is not known whether Templer even

* The original success of goldbeater's skin was largely responsible for Britain falling behind France and Germany in the manufacture and treatment of balloon and airship fabrics when goldbeater's skin was eventually superseded. The situation was more than put right, however, in 1913 when J. E. Ramsbottom invented the highly successful 'Delta dope' that was applied to the envelope of the Royal Aircraft Factory's airship *Delta* in the same year. He had then only recently joined the Royal Aircraft Factory (the contemporary name for the original Balloon Factory) – in March 1913. I am indebted to Dr Ramsbottom for help on several matters of history, and regret to have to record his death on 26 November 1967 while we were still corresponding.

† It seems ironical that when Colonel Templer was forced to retire on his *sixtieth* birthday (27 May 1906), Count Zeppelin was approaching his *sixty-eighth* birthday (8 July 1906), and did not achieve real success until he was seventy.

considered building a rigid airship but, in any event, there could never have been the slightest hope that the British Government would have allocated more than a fraction of the money required for what was inevitably an expensive venture.*

Fuel Consumption. On most types of vehicle, fuel consumption is considered mainly in respect of cost of replenishment and the risk of running dry before a journey is ended. For an airship of any kind, however, these are almost secondary considerations. The airship is steadily losing weight, and if equilibrium-buoyancy is to be maintained then hydrogen must be released. This can become a major economic issue if long journeys are contemplated, but for a non-rigid airship there is again the more important consideration – the risk of losing tautness of the envelope.

Rough calculations indicate that a non-rigid airship, roughly comparable with *Nulli Secundus* but having a ballonet with one sixth the total volume of the envelope, should have been able to cope with a journey of one hundred miles (160 km), with a reasonable margin for safety. This might well have been too much for *Nulli Secundus*, however, if allowance had also to be made for adverse conditions of altitude and for heating by the direct rays of the sun.

The 50-horsepower *Antoinette* engine consumed about ten imperial gallons (45 litres) of petrol in three hours, in which time *Nulli Secundus I* would travel about forty-five miles (72 km) in still air. To balance this about one thousand cubic feet (34 cubic metres) of hydrogen would need to be released; and according to the earlier calculations this would require an extra initial pressure of about four pounds per square foot (20 kg/sq metre). Greater distance would carry penalties in proportion. *Nulli Secundus I* had tankage for thirty gallons of petrol, but no more than half of this was ever used.†

For several decades attempts were made by designers of airships of all kinds to circumvent this problem of unwanted buoyancy by capturing weight from the engine exhaust. Since burning fuel combines with oxygen from the atmosphere there is a decided increase in weight. The water vapour alone is appreciably heavier than the original fuel, and in principle can be condensed and used as ballast. Templer was aware of this possibility, and in anticipation of buoyancy difficulties he designed an engine with a weight-recovery plant.

* Lord Ventry reached the same conclusion when writing in 1950: 'The small balloon shed at Farnborough and the available money would not have allowed of the building of a rigid airship of the Zeppelin type.' See 'The History of British Army Airships', *The Army Quarterly*, July 1950.

† Shell-Mex and B.P. Ltd inform me that petrol for *Nulli Secundus* would probably weigh about seven pounds per imperial gallon or a little under. Modern aviation petrol, it is noted, is somewhat heavier ($7\frac{1}{4}$ lb/gall), and jet-engine fuel is still heavier (8 lb/gall).

Unfortunately the engine did not work satisfactorily and, like his successors for over a generation, he failed to turn a theoretical ideal into a practical proposition.*

Dynamic lift. There was one method – now universally recognized – of compensating for excessive buoyancy without loss of hydrogen, by producing what came to be known as 'dynamic lift'. If the airship was tilted upwards, say to an angle of ten degrees, without climbing taking place, the envelope would produce lift aerodynamically, acting like a rather inefficient aeroplane wing. The reverse effect would result from a downward tilt, a downward force being produced. Paradoxically, the two opposite effects could be made to achieve the same purpose by appropriate adjustment of ballast before take-off. The airship in a heavy condition at the beginning of the flight could make use of the upward dynamic lift for as long as necessary. As fuel was used up this force would be allowed to decline until the lightened airship had ultimately to be *held down* by dynamic lift.

The method had its disadvantages. The reliance upon the engine was not at all good in days when engines were notoriously unreliable. Furthermore, there were disadvantages and even dangers in depending upon forward motion near the ground during take-off and landing. Nevertheless, Colonel Capper made use of the method for *Nulli Secundus* during some of the flight trials. Templer's design, moreover, had one feature which rendered reliance upon dynamic lift rather less objectionable than it probably was for most other non-rigid airships, and this comes next for consideration.

Descent of Nulli Secundus. When all the factors so far mentioned are taken into consideration there clearly remains the possibility that the commander of the airship might be able to keep the envelope taut during a journey, provided that he is allowed to make the final descent in a flabby state. Templer anticipated this in his design by ensuring that his airship could come down with a slack envelope like a balloon, in good order, and still be capable of a fair degree of motion as an airship if required.

When a free balloon descends it is always incompletely filled with buoyant gas, yet the upward force of the gas causes the upper portion of the envelope to maintain its original spherical form by pressing it against the upper rigging network. Templer's system was to produce the nearest possible airship equivalent. First of all, the concentrated weight of the car and its heavy contents – crew, engine, fuel, etc. – was distributed over the whole length of the enve-

* The British Airship *R-101*, which was wrecked at Beauvais, France, on 5 October 1930, was originally intended to have a condensation plant; but this had to be abandoned, which left the airship significantly heavier than it need have been.

lope by a robust framework. This is to be seen in many photographs of the airship, e.g. Fig. 41. The framework thus prevented the airship from sagging or 'jack-knifing' in the middle. In addition, Templer provided an intricate network to hold the slackening envelope in position. Colonel Capper, perhaps not without some justification, thought the system over-elaborate and inefficient. For an untried venture, however, few would regard Templer's caution as unwise. We can almost hear the great balloonist arguing: 'Well, if something does go wrong with the airship it can at least be brought down safely as a balloon.'

When the design of Templer's airship *Nulli Secundus I* is analysed, as it is here, in terms of principles, it clearly appears as a technical achievement irrespective of its immediate operational value. The fact that his methods were not ultimately adopted does not detract from our appreciation. We do not think any the worse of the Montgolfier Brothers as the inventors of the first man-carrying balloon because hydrogen soon replaced hot air. Templer's achievement was that he did something real and practical for airship development in a country that had had very little success before.

Furthermore, when he got his flyable airship into the air, Templer not only inspired his fellow countrymen, but ensured that the later breed of airships in Britain were to have built into them the kind of knowledge that can be acquired only by actual operation of an airship – in this case the first practicable British airship ever to be constructed.

3   Templer's early efforts

1901-3

There is no doubt that it was his visit to Paris in December 1901 which convinced Colonel Templer that the time had come for Britain to build a military airship.* Britain was, he thought, in the lead with design and operation of military balloons; but Santos-Dumont had now demonstrated in France that airships (or 'dirigible balloons' as they were then called) had at last become a practical proposition, and it was imperative that we should seek to maintain our place with them also.

* See Chapter 3, Section 2 – 'Templer's visit to Paris'.

In his report to the War Office, dated 2 January 1902, Templer concluded with the words:

I am of the opinion that we are well ahead of them in all matters apertaining to captive balloon work. At the same time, the *dirigible* balloon has now, by the prowess of M. Santos-Dumont, been so advanced that I shall [shortly] be in a position to recommend that certain experiments be carried out in dirigible balloon work by this Department.

These few words go a long way to explain the task which Templer was undertaking, and to clear away some of the misunderstandings that arose thereafter. The men at the War Office were not in any sense scientists, and few could fairly be described as trained engineers. But they were practical-minded men who were trying to equip an army, though with grossly inadequate funds at their disposal. To them, if you wanted a piece of equipment, even a novel thing like an airship, you either *built* it or *bought* it: research and experiment had no place in the War Office vocabulary. Templer, by contrast, was deeply conscious of all the uncertainties in the path of the new venture, and the limitations of his own knowledge. He wanted the opportunity to do research and make experiments before accepting heavy commitments for construction; but expediency demanded that such tenuous work be attached to a specific project, or he would not be able to obtain the money for it.

Unfortunately, almost immediately following Templer's report on his visit to Paris an extremely difficult situation developed for the Balloon Factory. On 11 November of the preceding year (1901) Templer had submitted to the Inspector-General of Fortifications his financial estimates for the financial year 1902/3.* The total came to £12,000, being divided between labour and material as follows:

Labour	6,960
Material	5,040
Total for thirty spherical balloons	£12,000

Before Templer had had time to submit his plans for dirigible experiments, a devastating reply was received to these modest estimates. In a letter dated 14 January 1902, the War Office instructed him to reduce his estimates by one half, i.e. to a total of £6,000.

In his letter asking for authority to go ahead with his dirigible experiments, Templer somewhat naïvely attempted to take this latest development into account. Accepting the reduction in principle, he asked for a supplementary

* 1 April 1902 to 31 March 1903.

grant of £5,000 for the proposed dirigible work. If this could be agreed, he maintained, then a number of skilled men could still be kept in employment who otherwise would have to be discharged. The letter from Templer to the Inspector-General of Fortifications, dated 27 January 1902, contains the following:

To enable us to retain all skilled hands and specialists in balloon manufacture, I am now in a position to build in this Factory a satisfactory dirigible balloon. My plans are elaborated and tested for this purpose and, as there is an enormous amount of energy being put into this work in Paris, I am of the strongest opinion that we should make these experiments here.

I therefore ask that, in addition to the £6,000 provided for the next year, you should give a supplementary estimate for £5,000 for the erection of a dirigible captive balloon. I may say that I am prepared to take all responsibility in recommending you to pursue this course.

Such a letter was not at all likely to impress the War Office. Templer seems to have had as little understanding of the workings of Whitehall as the War Office had of the difficulties of the head of a research organization. Concern at the prospects of his compact but efficient technical organization being wrecked, together with more than a trace of human feeling for the men who were to be discharged, caused Templer to put things the wrong way round. The letter could be interpreted as an attempt primarily at finding work for his men, with airship work merely as the best solution. He should, of course, have made first of all the strongest possible case for the airship, and then added a rider that his proposal would incidentally solve some difficult staff problems occasioned by the recent decision to retrench on ordinary balloon construction. The War Office (and the Treasury) obviously had to decide their airship policy on the long-term merits of the case.

In any event, the War Office do not appear to have been greatly impressed by this letter, for we find in a further letter, dated 29 May 1902, a direct request for £2,500 for the construction of an *elongated captive balloon*. This reference to an 'elongated captive balloon' confirms the belief that Templer wanted to do no more than experiment in the first instance, and was especially interested in the design, construction, and testing of an airship envelope. Templer appears to have received some money,* if not all that he asked for, since on 3 January 1903 he wrote to the War Office asking for a *further* £500 for completing special rigging for the elongated balloon. In this letter he stated that the balloon was nearly finished, and expressed his own intense satisfaction with the progress that had been made.

* I regret not having found more direct evidence of this.

The additional expenditure of £500 was authorized on 16 January 1903, that is only thirteen days after being requested – a remarkably short time for official action and an unmistakable indication of mounting interest in airships on the part of the War Office and the Government. Templer's own enthusiasm was increasing also, for on 7 February 1903 he wrote again to the War Office, and once again said how well things were going. This time, however, he made a definite offer to produce a 'navigable balloon' – as an airship was often called – the work to begin on 1 April 1903.

Construction of the airship envelope had already been completed by this time,* the work having been carried out in the 'Balloon House' at Aldershot. As indicated on the plan (page 68), the Balloon House was part of the more extensive building usually referred to as the 'Balloon Shed'. Photographs taken after this had been moved to Farnborough are reproduced in Figs 14 and 15.† It seems absurd that the Balloon House could ever have been used for housing the complete envelope during construction, but a study of dimensions shows that it would just be adequate provided it had not to accommodate the understructure, the propulsion system and the control surfaces as well. As already discussed, only a new and properly-designed airship shed could take the complete airship.

Templer's early experimental work was by no means confined to the envelope, but apart from the engine there is not a great deal of detailed information on record. For the engine work we have Templer's own testimony in the letter he wrote to the Inspector-General of Fortifications on 22 January 1904:‡

With regard to the elongated and dirigible balloons, the whole scheme was thoroughly thought out. The engines have been made, and a compound petrol engine has been invented and manufactured in order to avoid having to take up an engine with inflammable exhaust gases; this I consider necessary before sending men into the air. The engines promise to be thoroughly satisfactory and are in the course of construction, and the balloon itself can be elaborated directly we get the new erecting house [airship shed] of such dimensions as are requisite for this service.

Colonel Templer was clearly gravely concerned at what he regarded as a major fire hazard through hot exhaust gases passing near an envelope filled with hydrogen. He sought to contain these gases and cool them before release. He does not mention his parallel scheme for condensation of part of the gases to compensate for weight loss through fuel consumption. A detailed descrip-

* As things turned out this envelope was never used on the actual airship, but was superseded by a later one. See Section 6 of the present chapter.
† For more details of the Balloon Shed see Chapter 2, Section 5.
‡ See Chapter 3, Section 3 – 'Templer's Appeal'.

tion of this, however, was given by Colonel Capper in his Chatham lecture delivered on 12 March 1908.* The two projects – flame suppression and weight reclamation – would appear to be basically one and the same.

In the light of later knowledge we are today more interested in Templer's attempt to produce a successful engine *per se*, with or without any of these refinements. Templer thought he had succeeded, but it is now obvious that he had failed completely; and, as will be seen, Britain had to call upon France for the 50 h.p. *Antoinette*.

4   The policy decisions of 1903

From the rather scattered information we now possess, it would appear that by April 1903 Templer had more or less completed his preliminary experiments. The next stage was the manufacture of a complete and fully-operational airship. For this, of course, he required a new mandate from the War Office, backed by adequate funds. It was at this point that there entered the entirely new factor – the appointment of the Special Committee on Military Ballooning of 1903, which has already been discussed in the wider connotation of all forms of aerial activity.†

It is possible that the prospects of this Committee being created held back decisions in the first instance, as committees of inquiry often do; but in the long run it gave what could have been a tremendous impetus to airship design and construction. The Committee was first authorized on 8 June 1903. So important did the Committee regard British entry into the airship field that it dealt at once with the airship question, in advance of all other subjects. In about six weeks, namely on 24 July 1903, it issued its interim report dealing with balloons and airships exclusively.‡

The requirements laid down by the Committee for an airship included

* See 'Dirigible Balloons' by Brevet Colonel J. E. Capper, *Royal Engineers Journal*, Vol. VII, 1908.
† See Chapter 2, Section 2: 'The Inquiry of 1903'.
‡ The term 'interim report', although used by the Committee, could be misleading. There was nothing tentative or provisional about it, and it was, in fact, the final report on the subjects it covered, i.e., balloons and airships. It was eventually reproduced *en bloc* as an appendix to the main report dated 4 January 1904.

ability to steer, to proceed against such head winds as may be encountered on 300 days in the year, and to maintain its shape when proceeding against these winds. These requirements were, of course, little more than a rather crude definition of an airship. Another requirement was ability to hold gas for long periods, and in this connection it was stated that a goldbeater's-skin balloon had held gas for three months without leakage. This statement is thought to refer to the airship envelope produced by the Balloon Factory.

The last, and technically most important requirement was ability to climb to 5,000 feet (1,500 metres) without prejudice to the airship's effectiveness subsequently at lower altitudes:

> Ability to rise at will to such heights as may practically secure it from danger whilst over an enemy's country (say 5,000 feet), and to descend to earth when necessary to do so, without having lost gas, and so its power to float in the air at all.

Even more interesting than this ambitious requirement in itself is the comment that followed, by which an *elastic envelope* was stipulated as the only solution to the problem of hydrogen expansion during a climb:

> This condition can only be completely fulfilled by a balloon [airship] having an elastic envelope, which by its expansion relieves the enormous internal pressure brought on a closed balloon at high altitudes, without its being necessary to let out gas. A skin balloon expands to a considerable extent without being damaged. A silk balloon is practically non-elastic.

It seems strange that no mention was made of the ballonet as an alternative to elastic expansion of the envelope, which on the lowest assessment was worthy of consideration even if it were ultimately to be rejected. It was, moreover, not a new idea, having been proposed as early as 1783 by the French Lieutenant (later General) J. B. M. Meusnier, who did not live to see his aeronautical ambitions fulfilled. After two or three cases of application by different experimenters to unsuccessful airships, the ballonet became an essential feature of the first practical airship, *La France*, designed by Charles Renard and Arthur Krebs, and first flown on 8 August 1884.*

Perhaps it is less strange that no mention was made of the effects of temperature changes, which could have repercussions on buoyancy and fabric tautness just as changes in altitude had. It has to be remembered that the members of the Committee were soldiers, and even though some were Royal Engineers, this kind of knowledge of basic physics would not come within their scope. It is inconceivable that Templer was not aware of the full

* A useful account of the early airships (up to the year 1903), with information about the ballonet, is given in *The Aeronauts*, by L.T.C. Rolt, 1966.

magnitude of the problem, but neither Templer nor anyone with comparable knowledge was on the Committee.

The report provides also some valuable evidence on the work that was proceeding at the Balloon Factory at this time, and indicates that Templer's airship envelope already existed:

We find that there is already in the Balloon Factory at Aldershot the envelope of an elongated balloon constructed last year [i.e., 1902], which is suitable for use as a body of a dirigible balloon.

This clear statement is regarded as tantamount to recognition that Templer's work had to date been exploratory and of a research character, and primarily concerned with design and testing of the envelope.

The various references to an *elastic envelope* clearly indicated that Templer had experimented with blowing-up the envelope and had been successful in establishing its elastic expansion. It seems likely that he had tested to differential pressures adequate for any reasonable altitude. Whether he would have been happy to operate as high as 5,000 feet (1,500 metres), however, is somewhat doubtful; but there is no real discrepancy here since a forward-looking committee would naturally set a standard for the future somewhat higher than what was thought to be immediately attainable.

In this connection it is appropriate to mention that one authority, Wing Commander C. M. Waterlow, has stated that the final airship was tested to a pressure of thirty pounds per square foot (150 kg/sq metre), or the equivalent to six inches of water. It was intended, however, that this should be associated with operations at only half this pressure to give what was thought to be a desirable margin of safety.*

Perhaps the most important thing the Committee did, however, was to make a specific recommendation for financial allotment. It was noted that there had already been provisional cover for £2,000 in the budget for 1903/4, and it was recommended that this should be given to the Superintendent of the Balloon Factory without delay. The actual words were:

We recommend that authority be now given to the Superintendent of the Balloon Factory to proceed with experiments for producing a dirigible balloon, the £2,000 already voted being placed at his disposal for the purpose.

There then followed what now seems an absurdly optimistic item concerning the time required for completion:

* Wing Commander C. M. Waterlow, R.N. served initially as a 2nd-Lieutenant in the Balloon School from 18 October 1906. He spent the rest of his life on airships until killed by one on 25 July 1917. Some of his records were published in *The Airship*, 1948. His testimony is discussed in Note 9 of Appendix A.

If this authority is promptly given, there is every reason to hope that the balloon will be ready for trial early next year.

The War Office did not waste any time in acting upon the Committee's financial recommendations. In a letter dated 4 August 1903 the Superintendent was told that he had authority to spend £2,000 on the construction of a dirigible balloon. Thus for the first time Templer had a clear mandate to build an airship; and so a new stage was entered in the creation of *Nulli Secundus I*.

The initial impetus, however, soon lost momentum. There were too many obstacles in the way of effective airship development. The most important was the absence of an airship shed, without which no worth-while airship could be built: the airship shed at Farnborough was not completed until April 1905. There was also the move to Farnborough, with its inevitable consumption of time and dislocation spreading over much of 1905 and 1906. Finally, there was the change of leaders and Templer's retirement, as Capper became Superintendent on 27 May 1906.

Nevertheless, progress though slow was definite and the first flight was made in September 1907. Before we trace progress through the intervening years, however, it is useful to have before us a mental picture of the finished work, for it is easier to trace a path when the end is in sight.

5 A description of the finished airship

1907

Nulli Secundus I probably reached its peak of efficiency on 3 October 1907, when alterations to the control and stabilizing surfaces – indicated as desirable by behaviour in earlier trials – had been completed. The airship is shown in flight in Fig. 48, and the same basic picture is reproduced in Fig. 41 with annotations to show the various component parts.

On board are Colonel Capper, in command; Cody, in charge of the engine; and Captain King as third crew member.* For a journey of any appreciable length a crew of two was the normal complement; but for a short flight under favourable conditions three men could be carried.

---

* Captain W. A. de C. King R.E. was Chief Instructor in Ballooning at the Balloon School corresponding to Cody as Chief Instructor in kiting.

The envelope comes up first for consideration as being the most unique component of the ship. Its dimensions have in the past been the subject of much speculation, some twenty or so different sets of figures having been produced by various authors. The actual dimensions are now deemed to lie between the limits (a) and (b) of the following table:

Dimensions of envelope of Nulli Secundus I

	(a)	(b)
Length	122 feet	122 feet
	(37·2 metres)	(37·2 metres)
Diameter	25 feet	26 feet
	(7·6 metres)	(7·9 metres)
Volume	50,000 cubic feet	55,000 cubic feet
	(1,420 cubic metres)	(1,560 cubic metres)
Nominal Volume	56,000 cubic feet	60,000 cubic feet
	(1,590 cubic metres)	(1,700 cubic metres)

Apart from the item referred to as 'nominal volume', the first set of figures agree with those given by Lord Ventry for *Nulli Secundus I*.* The second set are those given by Observer Officer A. F. Insoll who in 1919 was commissioned by the Air Historical Branch of the then newly formed Air Ministry to collect data about all Farnborough airships.† Ordinarily, any argument about a foot difference in diameter for something so difficult to measure accurately would not be justified, but it happens to correspond roughly to the difference of 5,000 cubic feet (142 cubic metres) in volume, which may be significant. According to Colonel Capper, writing in the *R.E.C. Extracts*, the envelope was actually growing larger with use, and Insoll may have been referring to the same envelope when it had become part of *Nulli Secundus II*. In any event, precision is not possible since the dimensions obviously depended to a noticeable degree upon the differential pressure to which the envelope was subjected at any given time.

The 'nominal volume' comes from a calculation made on the assumption that the envelope was a simple cylinder with hemispherical ends, as it has often been described, although in reality it was somewhat more pointed at the ends. The calculation is a useful check, though only an approximate one, upon the consistency between the specified linear dimensions and the volume

* 'The History of Army Airships – Part IV', *The Army Quarterly*, April 1961.
† The status of A. F. Insoll as a contributor to airship history is discussed in Note 8 of Appendix A.

– a test, incidentally, which most published sets of figures, unlike those of Ventry and Insoll, fail to pass by a considerable margin.*

The envelope was unique in being made entirely of goldbeater's skin. The average size of each piece is believed to have been roughly twenty-four inches long (60 cm) and ten inches wide (25 cm).† The task of covering nearly ten thousand square feet (930 sq metres) of surface, therefore, must have been rather like papering a large room with postage stamps. The Balloon Factory, of course, had long experience in working with goldbeater's skin, having by this time made some hundreds of spherical balloons. The finished envelope had a neat appearance, as is shown in close-up view in Fig. 43.

There were many superposed layers of goldbeater's skin to give the required strength, though the precise number has been somewhat controversial in the past. It is now reasonably certain that, apart from local reinforcement, there were twelve such layers – a figure supported by the two authorities, Wing Commander C. M. Waterlow and Observer Officer A. F. Insoll. This was five more layers than the seven provided for the stronger makes of spherical balloon.

The arrangement of the main controls for pressure and buoyancy are shown in the annotated photograph reproduced as Fig. 41. There were two controlled escape valves on top of the envelope, one well forward and the other symmetrically placed aft. They were operated by cords which passed straight down through the hydrogen and out through flexible snouts at the bottom, these being specially designed to prevent unwanted leakage. In the middle of the ship, underneath, was the main filler neck. To the rear, also underneath, was a spring-operated safety-valve, sometimes known as a 'Mallett' valve, which released pressure automatically if the internal pressure showed signs of becoming excessive.

The main understructure is clearly to be seen in most photographs of *Nulli Secundus I*, though more detail is revealed in Fig. 43.‡ Here the frame-

* Basil Clarke, however, in *The History of Airships* (1961) gives reasonable figures identical with those of A. F. Insoll.
† Writing in 1930, H. Roxbee Cox (now Lord Kings Norton) and T. S. D. Collins stated that goldbeater's skin pieces varied in size from 27 inches by 6 inches (70 cm × 15 cm) to 40 inches by 10 inches (100 cm × 25 cm). See the chapter, 'Airship Design', in *Handbook of Aeronautics*, 1931 edition. Templer had scope for a good deal of selectivity, however, since in his day the Balloon Factory was virtually the only user engaged in aeronautical work.
‡ The presence of Cody in this photograph and in some others is of interest. There are few surviving photographs taken from *inside* the Balloon Factory during this period (1906 to 1908), and Cody appears in almost all of them. It is thought that they were taken on Cody's instructions and that, in some cases, negatives were retained by him.
When Cody was killed flying in 1913, no will was found, and his effects were sold by the

work is shown during construction in the airship shed, which dates the photo-graph as being taken during the latter half of the year 1906 or early in 1907. The long framework consisted of steel tubes with screwed ends, connected to each other by aluminium joint-fittings. In end-view the structure was four-sided, but with the lower horizontal members about half the length of the upper ones. The canoe-shaped car fitted in remarkably well with the general structural scheme.

With the airship in this incomplete state, it will be noted, the filled envelope is held down by bags of sand; and to those unfamiliar with balloons and airships it takes time to acquire an instinctive realization that gravity is being defeated and that part of the system is more likely to disappear through the roof of the building than descend through the floor.

The method of supporting the understructure is of particular interest. Goldbeater's skin does not lend itself to sewn connections or sticky patches, and the whole envelope was harnessed like a horse. The four broad saddle-bands supporting the understructure, four feet ($1\frac{1}{4}$ metres) wide and made of silk, are the most distinguishing feature of *Nulli Secundus I*. A net was spread over the envelope in addition, and was arranged to prevent the bands from sliding along the envelope. The net was also attached along the length of the understructure and appears to have carried an appreciable share of the suspended load.

In addition to acting as a distributor of the weight of car, engines, and crew, the understructure provided a base for the attachment of the control and stabilizing surfaces. The actual envelope had no control or stabilizing surface attached directly to it, in which respect *Nulli Secundus* differed from the great majority of non-rigid and semi-rigid airships.

The control and stabilizing surfaces are indicated in Fig. 41. The forward surfaces were known as 'aeroplanes', and consisted of two pairs of horizontal surfaces with vertical fins at their ends. They were hinged and aerodynami-cally balanced to rotate as elevators. Situated aft was a large vertical rudder, and there was also a horizontal tailplane backed by a projecting hinged surface to act as an elevator.

Finally, there was the propulsion system and engine-installation designed by Cody. The engine was the 50 h.p. *Antoinette*, which had eight cylinders arranged as four Vs in line. The actual engine, which was later used in the

---

legally appointed executor for the intestacy. It is believed that Cody's negatives were purchased by the firm of photographers and printers, William May and Co. Ltd of Aldershot, and added to their own extensive collection. Eventually, the whole of May's collection of historic photographs of early aviation at Farnborough were, as mentioned in the Introduction, presented to the R.A.E.

first successful Farnborough aeroplane, has been preserved and is to be seen in the Science Museum, South Kensington, London: Fig. 42 is taken from a photograph the museum has supplied.

The engine was mounted in an unorthodox but typically 'Codian' way, being suspended on wires that were tightened by turnbuckles. Crude though the system may now appear to have been, it seems to have worked better as a vibration damper than many of the more sophisticated systems of a later age. The cooling system was less satisfactory, and involved an excessive weight of water piping augmented by a honeycomb radiator, the whole system producing an unduly high air-resistance to forward motion. There was here, however, a universal problem of the times: it was no easy task to cool an engine working continuously at near-maximum power, for many hours, and at a forward speed of only about sixteen miles per hour (26 km/hr).

The most ingenious part of the propulsion installation was the propeller and power-transmission system. A wire-braced frame of ash carried the bearings of the two propellers on projecting arms. The unit comprising engine, propellers and belt-drive was first tested on a temporary mounting just inside the airship shed, and two photographs which were taken at the time have survived. In one (Fig. 44), Cody is just about to start the engine and, in the other (Fig. 45) he has just succeeded in doing so, while in the background looms the ghostly shape of the now fully-inflated envelope.

The stationary picture shows the shape of the blades of the propellers, which were adjustable for pitch while stationary on the ground. The drive was by twin V-belts for each propeller, with the port belts (right-hand of picture) crossed to give contra-rotation and so eliminate any overall twisting action. The pulleys were also arranged to give a speed reduction from engine to propeller (probably three to two), which was an unusual feature at the time but which contributed appreciably to propulsive efficiency.

A minor but rather fascinating feature was the combined fly-wheel and starting-wheel on the main engine shaft. This comprised a heavy rim that had been roughly forged and turned to truth on a lathe in the Balloon Factory workshops, and then fitted with ordinary bicycle spokes. Tradition says that Cody, who many believed had almost superhuman physical strength, was the only man who could turn it and so start the engine.

6 The years of frustration
1903–6

Following the recommendations of the special Committee of Inquiry of 1903, the War Office had written to the Superintendent of the Balloon Factory on 4 August 1903 authorizing the expenditure of £2,000 for the construction of a dirigible balloon. One of the first actions Templer then took was to arrange a visit to Colonel Charles Renard, the corresponding head of the French Balloon Establishment at Chalais-Meudon. On 17 October 1903 Templer sent a report of his visit to the Inspector-General of Fortifications. The report has regrettably been destroyed, but there has survived a brief comment by the writer of the *R.A.E. Chronicles*. Apparently the French Government were allocating between £25,000 and £30,000 per annum to their Aeronautical Establishment. The British allocation had been reduced to less than one quarter of this, and Templer pleaded for more.

According to the *R.A.E. Chronicles*, miscellaneous work in great variety was undertaken by the Balloon Factory during 1904. Templer's list sent to the War Office on 2 November 1904 comprised:

> Man-lifting kites
> Special photography for balloons
> Signalling balloons and equipment
> Petrol motors
> Elongated balloons
> Mechanical hauling-down gear
> (for balloons and kites)

An interesting reflection on this list, which follows closely the recommendations of the 1903 Committee of Inquiry,* is the way in which the Balloon Companies and the Balloon Factory were obviously working together despite their nominal independence and separate leaders in Capper and Templer. Thus, for example, both organizations were concerned with Cody kites, although Cody himself was working specifically for Colonel Capper's Balloon Companies. The two organizations, in fact, were dependent upon each other, and neither at that stage was capable of an entirely separate existence.

* See Chapter 2, Section 2, Item – *The Balloon Factory*.

The elongated balloons referred to in this list were the forerunners of what became kite-balloons and not airship envelopes. Templer had been working on these for some years, even before he went to war in South Africa in 1899. He never had much success, however, with his kite balloons, which were intended as a more stable replacement of the captive spherical balloons. Germany was more successful but it was a great struggle and the German kite-balloons at this time were unduly heavy and difficult to handle.

Another responsibility of Templer and the Balloon Factory was the examination of work done privately in the way of airship development. Any major success would have had a great effect on Government policy since there was a general predilection for private ventures, mainly in order to economize in research and development. In the year 1903 the Balloon Factory was asked to assess two particular designs – the 'Beedle' and the 'Spencer'. Furthermore, the allocation of £2,000 to the Balloon Factory had actually been withheld pending a decision on a third private design, known as the 'Barton'. All three were deemed to be unacceptable, as also was another but later design – the 'Welford' – which was examined and reported upon unfavourably in 1905. Thus, as things turned out, Templer had virtually no competition in his own country.

In the light of all the known circumstances, the Balloon Factory would appear to have been well occupied without having to build an airship, especially as the miscellaneous demands had to be met while the move to Farnborough was being planned and then implemented. This does not entirely explain, however, the extreme slowness of the airship work following the allocation of £2,000 in August 1903, as recommended by the Committee of Inquiry of 1903. The root cause of all the trouble, of course, was the delay in producing the airship shed, without which construction of the airship could not proceed to anything like a conclusion.

No doubt this delay was influential in deciding Templer in 1904 to construct a second airship envelope following that already made in 1902. Construction of an envelope was just possible using the old Balloon House, although there was insufficient room for building the understructure and installing the propulsion system. There were several advantages to be gained from having a new envelope. The first envelope had been admittedly experimental, and there were lessons learnt that could only be applied in new construction. Perhaps overriding, however, was the value of an existing envelope as a mould for a new one. In this case, the new envelope was built up piece by piece over the inflated old one, which was then deflated and pulled out through the nose of its successor.

Policy decisions concerning these two envelopes do not appear ever to have been properly recorded. No doubt Templer was granted considerable technical discretion, provided he kept within the agreed financial limits. This has led to several conflicting stories. The *R.A.E. Chronicles*, for example, state that there was only one envelope which took from 1902 to 1904 to make. The Waterlow *Memoirs*, on the other hand, state that there were two envelopes, but both were made in 1904. The only account consistent with all the known facts is that given here – one envelope was made in 1902, and a second, using the first as a mould, in 1904.

The new airship shed was completed, apart from the doors, in April 1905 (see Chapter 2, Section 4), and Templer at once took full advantage of the new shed for working on the airship under realistic conditions. Records, however, are few; and historians have been inclined to leave this year 1905 a blank so far as airship development is concerned. The whole Factory team were obsessed with the move to Farnborough of the complete organization, which began in earnest in October. The *R.A.E. Chronicles* however, produced just a few works of guidance:

1905. An experimental elongated balloon was rigged out for trial runs in the summer.

Quite what is meant by 'trial runs' is uncertain. The airship could not have been taken out with a worth-while engine, since the *Antoinette* did not arrive until early 1907. On the other hand, it is unlikely that such a description referred to mere testing of the envelope for buoyancy and expansion. It is difficult to believe that the airship did not have some kind of understructure, ballasted to represent engine weight.

The year 1906 brought still more organizational changes, with Colonel Capper becoming Commandant of the newly-named Balloon School on 1 April 1906, and Superintendent of the Balloon Factory on 27 May 1906, the day Templer retired. The new responsibilities thus placed upon Capper must have imposed a great strain upon him since the transfer of the Balloon Factory had barely been completed and there had not been time for a settling-down of the workshops. The military side had complications also since the hundred men or so of the old Balloon Companies had been re-quartered in North Camp, Farnborough; and offices for the new School Headquarters had to be found within the new Factory grounds. Fortunately, Templer was still retained as a part-time adviser on airship design and construction; and for several months after his so-called retirement he seems to have worked harder than ever on his masterpiece.

Apart from his organizational problems, however, Capper had technical interests of other kinds than airships during most of the year 1906. These interests lay mainly with gliders, which were regarded essentially as prototypes of the powered aeroplanes that were still to come. Both Cody and Lieutenant Dunne* were encouraged to interest themselves in this work. The Royal Engineer Committee were behind him in the course he was taking, and went so far as to authorize, on 18 June 1906, the expenditure of £600 for construction of gliders, first as models and later as full-size machines. By one of the strangest pieces of irony, this diversion of interest away from the air-

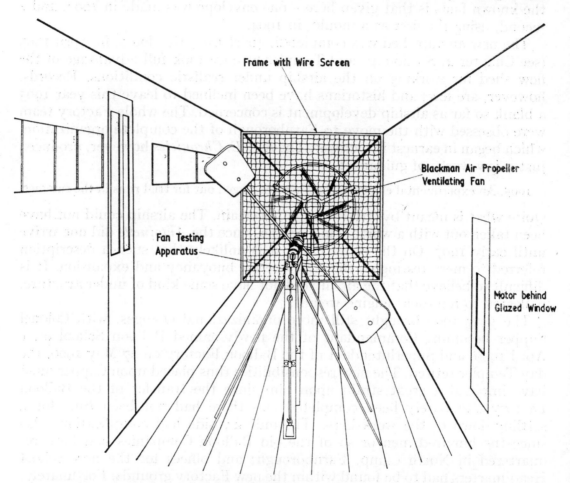

Frame with Wire Screen

Blackman Air Propeller Ventilating Fan

Fan Testing Apparatus

Motor behind Glazed Window

(H) Farnborough's first wind-tunnel (1906).

This curious diagram represents Farnborough's first attempt at wind-tunnel design, forerunner of a series that was in time to cost millions of pounds. The tunnel is here being used to test a propeller, in those days called a 'fan'

* John William Dunne (1875–1949) joined the Balloon Factory as a Lieutenant in 1906. His pioneer work on aeroplanes, and that of S. F. Cody, are dealt with in Volume II of this History.

ship ultimately contributed to its success, for the engine purchased for glider work (the *Antoinette*) was first used to propel *Nulli Secundus I*.

Capper also undertook many other tasks in 1906. Among these were such things as aerial photography and telescopic observation from balloons, and experiments with guns firing at balloons in order to assess their vulnerability. From the standpoint of aviation history, however, the most important of these miscellaneous activities was the construction of one of the earliest wind-tunnels. Thus in the *R.E.C. Extracts* we read:

On June 18th 1906, at the request of the Commandant of the Balloon School, £50 was allotted for apparatus for testing air resistances.

and again:

On December 14th 1906, the Commandant of the Balloon School reported completion of the tunnel and forwarded a description of the apparatus.

A diagram of the wind-tunnel – then called an 'air-tunnel' – was given in the *R.E.C. Extracts* together with a description. The diagram is reproduced here as Fig. H, and extracts from the description are given in Appendix D. Ostensibly designed for testing the air resistance of bodies of different shapes, the wind-tunnel appears to have been first used for testing propellers – then usually called 'fans'. It thus contributed to both the early Farnborough airships as well as the early aeroplanes. By modern standards, of course, it was unbelievably crude, but it was the first of a series that was eventually to cost millions of pounds.

Thus, up to the end of 1906 Capper had had little to do with the airship. For Templer, the long years of frustration were drawing to a close, and he was soon to see the results of his tireless industry. The year 1907 was to produce intense activity to finish the airship and get it into the air.

7   Completion of *Nulli Secundus I*

1907

It was probably in January 1907 that Colonel Capper was first told to finish the airship as quickly as possible. The date is uncertain: it could have been a little earlier and it could have been a little later. This is not so much a case of lost documents, as of decisions and instructions being conveyed by word of mouth. Capper seems to have worked well with his main contact in the Directorate of Fortifications and Works, Major Baker Brown,* and such were the political overtones at that time that much more was accomplished by friendly discussion than was possible in any other way. Capper was definitely promised, however, an allotment of £2,000 in the coming financial year, which began on 1 April 1907. By that time there had already been spent on the airship a total sum of £6,679 4s. 9d, mostly under Templer's control.†

When this policy of intensification of work on the airship was decided upon, Templer had only recently handed over to Capper the direct responsibility for the airship. He had done so in a personal letter dated 5 November 1906:

My dear Capper,

I can come down any day you want me. I am thinking of going to Paris next week, and to Swansea on Wednesday, when I fancy they will be starting to make tubes.

I have worked on the dirigible and will come and explain to you when you are ready. I shall be in London again on 4th December.

I have taken, or nearly taken, a house here. We are only waiting for agreement.

With best regards to you both from the wife and myself.

Yours sincerely,
James Templer.

This letter, together with Capper's reply, is quoted earlier in this History (Chapter 3, Section 6) in order to destroy the myth that Capper and Templer were unfriendly or, as has been suggested, even enemies. It is quoted here again to destroy another myth: that Capper designed *Nulli Secundus I* almost *ab initio*, making use incidentally of one of Templer's envelopes that happened to be available. This letter alone is evidence of continuity in the work on *Nulli Secundus I*, with one leader handing over the prime responsibility to another; and, even so, Capper insisted on Templer being *re-engaged* as Adviser from 1 April 1907 to ensure completion of the airship. The letter is also a clear indication that up to November 1906 Capper had not greatly concerned himself with the airship, since Templer had to explain to him what had so far been done.

* Major William Baker Brown (1864–1947), who later became Brigadier-General, served in the Directorate of Fortifications and Works for about four years (1904–8). With the curious title of 'Inspector of Electric Lights' he was head of a section responsible for detail headquarters administration of several of the more scientific and technical activities of the Army, including electrical engineering and the work of the Balloon Factory. He had previously been Inspector of Submarine Mines. In later life he produced Volume IV of *The History of the Corps of Royal Engineers*, which was published postumously in 1952.

† See *Aeronautical Journal*, April 1908.

In Capper's opinion the airship was always 'Templer's airship', and he never claimed to have been the designer of *Nulli Secundus I*. This was the official view also, and it went even further by recognizing that the *design* of the airship was virtually completed when Capper took over. Thus, in connection with Templer's retention as Adviser, the Finance Branch of the War Office said in a letter to the Treasury, dated 11 September 1906:

Among reasons for Colonel Templer's retention was that the Department might have advantage of his advice in connection with the dirigible balloon *which he designed*.*

In a later letter, dated February 12th 1907, the Finance Branch asked for renewal of Templer's engagement as Adviser, and supported their case by the statement:

The trials of the dirigible balloon designed by Colonel Templer will be continued for some time longer, and *Colonel Templer's advice and assistance will be indispensible.*

Thus we are led to the conclusion that Capper's main task was to finish the *construction* of an airship already *designed*, making such use of Templer's advisory service as he thought desirable. This task Capper accomplished in about eight months in a remarkably effective way. The work was not entirely straightforward: there were difficulties in construction of the understructure, and there was still no usable engine when Templer handed over. The envelope with its controls for pressure and buoyancy, however, was probably in a most satisfactory state as regards completion, and Capper almost certainly left this aspect of the work to Templer entirely.

The incorporation of Cody into the airship team proved to be a masterstroke since he had a genius for mechanical engineering that was unsurpassed within the Factory. He took over almost entire responsibility for the engine and its installation in the airship; and appears to have been able to cooperate well with the Works Manager, Mr F. McWade.† The control and stabilizing surfaces of the airship, moreover, showed more than a trace of Cody's influence, with many features suggestive of man-lifting kites. Exactly when

* The italics in this quotation and the next are mine.
† F. McWade, the Works Manager, was not such a glamorous character as Cody, but he appears to have made a useful contribution to the work of the Balloon Factory in his time. He was primarily a balloon and airship man; and when the Navy took over the Farnborough airships in 1914 he went with them.

McWade's name became familiar to many people in Britain through the Public Inquiry into the *R-101* airship disaster of 5 October 1930. Some time before the fatal flight he had expressed his views – in writing – about the excessive leakage of hydrogen, and it was suggested at the Inquiry that the document had been partially suppressed, though not entirely ignored.

Cody first became involved is uncertain, and he may well have been helping Templer before Capper had completed the take-over.

In any event Cody was the man who obtained the *Antoinette* engine (illustrated in Fig. 42), though he did so originally with the intention of using it for an aeroplane. The Royal Engineer Committee had already, on 18 June 1906, authorized £600 for expenditure on gliders. Early in December of the same year they authorized a further £550 for an *Antoinette* engine to put into a glider, or in other words to produce a powered aeroplane. Thus the *R.E.C. Extracts* record:

The experiments with gliders were continued throughout 1906, and by the end of the year sufficient progress had been made to warrant the purchase of a motor. £550 was allotted for a 50 h.p. *Antoinette* motor in December.

Cody was sent to France in December (1906) to purchase the *Antoinette* engine, and while he was there Capper wrote him a letter:

To: From:
S. F. Cody Esq.   H.M. Balloon Factory
Hotel Westminster,   South Farnborough.
Paris   17th December 1906

Dear Mr Cody,
  You will have been hearing that we have got the money for the motor all right and it is lodged to your credit at the Credit Lyonnais. If there is any hitch at all, wire me.
  As regards your movements: if necessary you can stay in Paris to bring the motor back with you. I know you will not be wasting your time; but if you think it is unnecessary, of course, you must come home. Let me have a note to say shortly what you are doing.

                               Yours sincerely
                    [Signed]   J. E. Capper.*

The *Antoinette* engine was handed over to Cody when it arrived, for installation in the airship. By chance there have survived a few letters passed between private industry and the Balloon Factory in February and March 1907, and these reveal the tremendous energy of Cody in obtaining what was required. Oil for the engine, ball bearings for the propellers, belts and pulleys for the transmission, are among subjects he dealt with. As little as possible was made inside the Factory whenever standard mechanical parts could be purchased outside. Most difficulty was experienced in obtaining the belts and

---

* Surviving records do not reveal who read Cody's incoming letters for him while abroad, or helped generally with his correspondence. It is probable that Mrs Cody (Lela) accompanied him on this visit to France.

pulleys. Cody was asking for what he described as a motor cycle belt wheel to take a seven-eighths inch 'watawata' belt. One firm after another declined to supply until the Rex Hallé Agency offered a twenty-inch diameter wheel.*

The letter of acceptance is of interest as illustrating a curious streak in Capper's make-up:

To: From:
Rex Hallé Agency   H.M. Balloon Factory
Store Street   Farnborough
Tottenham Court Road   Hants
                                              15th March 1907

Gentlemen,

With reference to your letter of the 14th instant regarding a belt rim:

Please despatch one as early as possible, for which I enclose a formal order (No. 2407).

In your letter above quoted you refer to a telegram which you state was despatched by you yesterday: it was not received here until about 11.20 this morning, in fact, after receipt of your letter.

I would also point out that on your memo forms your telegraphic address is shown as 'Autolatory, London'. A telegram sent you with that address was however returned by the Post Office stating that the address was 'insufficient and not now registered'. A further telegram had therefore to be sent you with your full address thereon.

In the circumstances I shall be glad if you will kindly remit me the sum of tenpence (10d), the cost of the original telegram which could not be delivered.

> (Signed)   R. Friar. Lieutenant.
>   for Superintendent Balloon Factory.†

It is not known whether Colonel Capper ever got his tenpence. Such petulant behaviour was regrettably not untypical, if surviving records are anything to go by; and the interests of the Balloon Factory must have suffered on this account.

By March 1907 the War Office showed signs of wanting to know what was happening to the airship; and on 1 May 1907 a letter of inquiry was sent by Major Baker Brown:

---

* According to Waterlow (*The Airship*, Summer 1948) *Nulli Secundus I* had each propeller driven by a pair of 'watta-watta' belts, those on the port side being crossed for contrarotation. Friends at the Patent Office tell me that this type of belt, designed primarily for motor cycles, was produced by O. and W. Omerod of Rochdale in 1903 and improved in 1906. It was a V-belt made up of laminations of leather bolted together in an unusual way to give adequate flexibility. The joint was a simple hook and eye. Details of the belt are to be found in *Motor Cycling*, 24 January 1910.

† This letter was presumably dictated by Colonel Capper and signed on his behalf by Lieutenant R. Friar, who acted as deputy for Balloon Factory affairs until the appointment of Captain A. D. Carden R.E. as Assistant-Superintendent on 8 May 1907.

Will you please say when you expect to be able to carry out trials this Summer with the dirigible balloon. This information is required in connection with the question of Colonel Templer's services during 1908/9.

While it was obviously reasonable for the War Office to wish to be informed of progress, it is not immediately clear why the request had to be linked with Templer's possible re-engagement so far ahead, i.e. for the year 1908/9, Templer only recently having been re-engaged for the year 1907/8 in a letter dated 15 February 1907. A likely explanation is that the War Office had some special reason for not wanting to appear to be badgering Colonel Capper; and his obvious irritation in reply gives support to this contention.

In a letter dated 2 May 1907 Colonel Capper said:

I have reported that I hope to have the dirigible balloon out this Summer, about July. I am very unwilling to fix an exact date, as there has been so much work in connection with kite fittings at the Factory that the whole of my tools and shop staff have practically been employed on this. There are also some special joints which I cannot make up myself and a firm has undertaken for me, and it is always difficult to make sure of delivery of special work. I will let you know when I can fix a date with greater certainty.

The comments about the special joints are a tit-bit of information of no great interest to the War Office, though significant to anyone concerned technically. These were machined drop-forgings made in aluminium, and they had tapped holes to take the screwed ends of the tubes comprising the understructure. According to Waterlow they were highly satisfactory in operational use, although difficult to make by the standards of the time.

It is the reference to kite fittings, however, that is truly significant, since it gives a clue to official policy about which very little has hitherto been known. The kites referred to were manifestly not the Cody man-lifters, which had become a piece of routine equipment that could hardly have been making heavy demands on the Factory at this late stage, and could never have been given precedence over the airship. It is almost certain that the fittings were required for the future aeroplanes of Cody and Dunne. The implications are that Capper regarded work on aeroplanes as of prime importance, even to the extent of prejudicing the airship. There is more to it than this, however: the general tenor of Capper's letter indicates prior knowledge of this policy by the War Office, and their agreement to it.* Thus Capper had

* This interpretation may be more readily acceptable to the reader when the *true* facts are known about the negotiations between Colonel Capper, the Wright Brothers, and the British War Office. See Volume II of the present History.

convinced senior men in Whitehall that neglect of the aeroplane could be disastrous in view of what was happening in France, and still more in view of what had been achieved by the Wright Brothers in America. The official policy, however, was to work quietly in secret for the time being; and the public, who would not have understood, were to be kept in the dark.

Despite these distracting political overtones, however, the Director of Fortifications and Works genuinely wished to know what was happening to the airship, and for a definite reason: the British public were growing anxious and soon the Government would have to do some explaining. For a number of reasons, achievements in the airship world had been much more widely publicized than the corresponding achievements with aeroplanes. Nothing could now satisfy the British people than to have a British airship flying around for all to see.

The concern of the people of Britain was expressed in Parliament by Major Anstruther-Gray M.P., who on 5 August 1907 asked the Secretary of State for War:

Whether, in view of the progress made by Foreign Powers in the solution of the problems of aerial flight, he will consider the desirability of increasing the grant of research on this subject.

At that time, 'aerial flight' referred primarily to work on airships; and the Secretary of State for War, R. B. Haldane, in a written reply commented:

The importance of this subject is recognized and experiments are in progress. It is not considered necessary or desirable to increase the grant of money available this year for this subject. My advisers are fully aware of the work that is being done elsewhere [i.e. in France and Germany].

This reply was remarkably non-committal in view of the airship work in hand, but if temporizing was disconcerting, an unfulfilled promise could have been disastrous. The Secretary of State, however, need not have been worried. The Balloon Factory had made good progress in the few months preceding, and the airship was nearly ready. On 10 September 1907 *Nulli Secundus* was seen to come out of the airship shed and take to the air.

8 The Flights and Adventures of Nulli Secundus I 1907

1   Capper the balloonist

     1906–7

The most anxious time for the designers of an aircraft of any kind comes just before the first flight takes place. There are always last-minute doubts and fears. Perhaps an airship has the advantage over the aeroplane at such a time, but even so there is the additional factor that instantaneous and critical judgement may be required from the ground-handling crew as well as from the men on board. *Nulli Secundus I*, of course, had more than the usual disadvantages associated with any new and untried airship: not only had both she and her pilot never flown before, but the whole design and construction had been carried out by a team that had never produced an airship before.

In these circumstances the obvious course was to reduce the uncertainties by making sure that the pilot was at least a skilled balloonist, and this Colonel Capper set out to be. The Balloon School, of course, operated captive balloons as a routine, but this was not quite what was wanted. Free-ballooning was obviously more relevant, and scope for this at the Balloon School was somewhat restricted. Colonel Capper therefore went further and sought outside experience by taking part in balloon events and competitions of an entirely non-military character.

Thus it comes about that we find Colonel Capper taking part in the very first race of the world-renowned series of international Gordon Bennett balloon races. These races normally took place every year from 1906 to 1938, with an obvious break for the First World War, the first race starting from Paris in 1906.

Sixteen balloons took off from the Tuileries Gardens on 30 September 1906, the winner to be the one who flew furthest irrespective of direction. Colonel Capper acted as assistant to the well-known balloonist C. S. Rolls, in Rolls's own balloon *Britannia*, which had a capacity of 78,000 cubic feet

(2,200 cubic metres).* Seven of the balloons were blown over to England, *Britannia* being one of them. After an interesting trip, in which they trailed a rope on the sea all the way across the English Channel,† Rolls and Capper came down near Sandringham in Norfolk. They were only third in the race, however, being beaten by Frank P. Lahm (U.S.A.) who reached Fylingdale in Yorkshire and by Alfred Vonwiller (Italy) who came down just south of the River Humber.‡

For Colonel Capper, the Gordon Bennett race, in which he was acting only as assistant, was somewhat exceptional. He had his own private balloon *Pegasus*, a vessel of about 45,000 cubic feet (1,270 cubic metres) capacity. With this he took part in numerous races and competitions in Britain, which were usually organized by the Aero Club of Great Britain. An interesting example was the ballooning competition that took place on 26 May 1907 from the Ranelagh club in London, in which the Colonel had Mrs Capper with him as a passenger.§ Some interesting photographs were taken on this originally very fine day, one by the *Illustrated London News* being a good specimen (see Fig. 46) and as fascinating for the show of Edwardian costume as for the balloons.

The balloons on these occasions were filled with coal gas produced in ordinary town gas-works, and this gas was about seven times heavier than hydrogen and had only about half the lifting power. For the load they had to carry, therefore, the balloons were considerably larger than the corresponding hydrogen balloons. They had the advantage, however, that they could be filled up in any large town having its own gas-works, the local gas engineer usually cooperating by producing a special light-weight brew for the occasion.

* The Honourable Charles Stewart Rolls (1877–1910), third son of Lord Llangattock, was one of the most courageous and most glamorous of aeronauts, being equally interested in both ballons and aeroplanes. He was also reputed to be one of the most wealthy, but financially one of the meanest, among his colleagues. He was an exhibitionist in a not unattractive way, and did much to rouse and maintain interest in aviation in Britain. He was killed during a demonstration at an air display in Bournemouth on 12 July 1910, while flying a modified Wright Brothers' aeroplane. Rolls was also a pioneer motorist and co-founder of the firm of Rolls-Royce Limited.

† The trail rope had been specially treated to make it float on the sea and cause the balloon to fly steadily close to the surface. The purpose of a trail rope is discussed more fully in Section 3 of the present chapter.

‡ Colonel Capper published an account of the race in the *Aeronautical Journal* January 1907. An account by a member of l'Aéro Club de France is also given in the *Aeronautical Journal* for October 1906.

§ Ranelagh, situated at Barn Elms, Barnes, London, was – and still is – a famous polo ground. It should not be confused with the historic Ranelagh Gardens of eighteenth-century Chelsea, which were closed in 1804.

The object of this particular race was to land as near Goring Railway Station as possible.* Colonel and Mrs Capper in *Pegasus* were second in the race, coming down only a few yards from the winner. Other ladies besides Mrs Capper took part, but not all those who originally intended to do so, since some thought it advisable to retire when it became known that the balloons would have to pass through a thunderstorm on the way.

This social and sporting interest in ballooning had a much greater influence on official policy than might be supposed. It gave the public a lively interest in balloons and hence in airships as a natural corollary. The garden-party atmosphere, however, must not be allowed to obscure the dangers that lay in ballooning. Only three days after the Ranelagh outing just described, there occurred a disaster that was to disturb the people at Farnborough profoundly.

At this time Prince Fushimi of Japan was on a visit to Britain, and on Tuesday 25 May 1907 King Edward VII brought him to Aldershot, where various military demonstrations had been specially arranged. In the afternoon the Royal Party visited the Balloon Factory at Farnborough to witness a demonstration of free ballooning. Lieutenants T. E. Martin-Leake and W. T. McC. Caulfield, both Royal Engineers, took off in the balloon *Thrasher* in front of the King and his guest. *Thrasher* disappeared from view in the south-west and was last seen close to Abbotsbury, near Weymouth, on the Dorsetshire coast. The balloon was then at a height of about 40 feet (12 metres), and one of the aeronauts shouted to a farmer to catch hold of the trail rope, but this he failed to do. The two Royal Engineers were never seen again, though next day the trawler *Skylark*, sailing off the coast near Exmouth, picked up a tangled mass of fabric and cordage, which was all that was left of the *Thrasher*.

King Edward and his party, of course, could have no knowledge of what was going to happen, and it is believed that they ended their visit by going to look at the new but still nameless airship nearing completion in her shed. The sensation produced by the disaster to *Thrasher* later caused some lack of interest in the rest of the day's events at the Balloon Factory and, in any case, there was a high degree of secrecy being maintained about the airship at this time. This is almost certainly the occasion, however, when the King personally named her *Nulli Secundus* or 'second-to-none'.

She was indeed a most impressive sight, her blunt ends giving an effect of solidity not possessed by more streamlined and possibly more efficient designs; and her being inside a shed would give an impression of enormous size to anyone who had not seen an airship before. Thus, from the first

* Goring-on-Thames, in Oxfordshire, and about ten miles north-west of Reading.

moment she appeared in public – in September 1907 – the new airship was known by her royal title: *Nulli Secundus*.

There has always been a mystery about the naming of *Nulli Secundus*, but I am convinced that the explanation here given is the true one, and I would indeed like to endorse the **view** of the great French aeronautical periodical, *l'Aérophile*:

Nulli Secundus, such is the name, we are assured, which has been given to the new British dirigible at the request of King Edward VII. It is enough to show that England does not intend remaining behind continental nations in development of the navigable balloon.*

2   The airship's first day out

10 September 1907

Early on Tuesday morning, 10 September 1907, a large crowd of Farnborough residents gathered on Farnborough Common to peer through the iron railings that formed the boundary of the Balloon Factory.† For some days, perhaps weeks, the first appearance of the first British military airship had been expected. It was said that the airship had been ready for some time and that Colonel Capper had only been waiting for suitable weather conditions for the first flight. Exactly what the ideal conditions were has never been laid down, but they obviously could not be better than a fine and clear September morning and, from what transpired later, a steady gentle breeze in preference to a complete calm. On this particular morning it was obvious that the Royal Engineers meant business, for the staff of the Balloon Factory had been allowed to come out and watch.

The spectators first of all saw a number of small balloons released to check

* 'Nulli Secundus, tel serait, assure-t-on, le nom donné, sur le désir du roi Edouard VII, au nouveau dirigible anglais; il suffit à indiquer que l'Angleterre entend bien ne pas demeurer en arrière des nations continentales dans les applications du ballon automobile.' – *l'Aérophile*, September 1907.

† A view of the crowd looking through the railings is shown in Fig. 57. This might easily have been the first appearance of *Nulli Secundus I* but was actually a similar event a year later for *Nulli Secundus II*.

the strength and direction of the wind. Then, at ten o'clock in the morning, things began to happen. In the words of the contributor to the *Automotor Journal*, 'the great doors slid open and the huge caged monster was brought blinking into the sunlight.' Lieutenant Waterlow had a photograph taken of this historic event, and it has been possible to reproduce this as Fig. 47.

From this illustration, and from another photograph of the airship in flight (Fig. 49), it is seen at once that she has quite a different appearance from the final form described earlier (Chapter 7, Section 5). The two sets of 'aeroplanes', i.e. the biplane systems recognizable by their diamond-shaped fins, are well separated by being placed respectively fore and aft instead of close together in the forward position of the final form illustrated in Fig. 48. Although there is a large rudder at the rear, moreover, there is no sign of the large tailplane and elevator that was ultimately installed. The most striking feature of all, however, is the pair of enormous wings amidships. These were raised and lowered like a drawbridge: raised when the airship had to enter the shed, and lowered for flight in the (mistaken) belief that they were necessary to prevent the ship from rolling.

Twenty-five sappers walked the ship out on to the Common, which was by no means an ideal place for testing an airship since it was strewn with clumps of gorse and shrubs. Once out in the open, the airship was first ballasted carefully to obtain true balance. This process proved to be not quite so straightforward as had been expected. When inside the airship shed the envelope had been blown up to a differential pressure of five pounds per square foot (25 kg/sq metre), or one inch on the water scale.* In the sunshine, however, the pressure rose to nearly three times this, which was about the limit set for the blow-off safety valve.

It had originally been intended that only Capper and Cody should go on board, but the extra buoyancy associated with the high differential pressure permitted Captain King (Chief Instructor in Ballooning) to join them, and all three are to be seen in Fig. 49.

For the first operation the airship was allowed to rise vertically to a height of about 150 feet (45 metres). It was held by ropes attached to the ends of the broad silk bands passing over the envelope, these ropes being paid out by the sappers down below. The ship was then pulled down again; and the up-and-down sequence was repeated two or three times until confidence in the buoyancy of the airship and in the skill of the ground crew had been established. Then, with the ship at full stretch of the ropes, an attempt was made to start the engine.

To the surprise of many – for engines were wilful and obstinate in those

* Measured by the head of water in a simple U-tube, as described in Chapter 7, Section 2.

days – the engine responded at once to Cody's persuasion. The airship then proceeded to fly head to wind, which so far as can be deduced was blowing from the south-east. The wind had freshened somewhat since the ship had left the shed, and the ship flew dead against it at a speed through the air of about fifteen miles per hour (25 km/hr). In consequence, the sappers, by running like men possessed, were able to keep pace and still hang on to the ropes. After five breath-taking minutes or so the ship was released to have her first taste of freedom. Her behaviour at first was remarkably good for a new and untried machine. Climbing to 400 feet (120 metres) she continued on her course for a few minutes and then made a complete turn so as to fly downwind and return to the starting point. She did not quite reach home when things went wrong, not through incorrect application of the profounder laws of levitation and aerodynamics, but through simple mechanical trouble which was the curse of the pioneering days of flying: the belt driving the cooling fan of the engine came off and the engine had to be stopped. Here the significance of the gentle breeze became manifest, for the ship drifted downwind to its starting point as a free balloon, and the sappers took hold of the ropes and walked her back to her shed.

The amount of flying that had been accomplished was just sufficient to establish that the ship was steady and steerable left and right in a horizontal plane; but she was inclined to pitch somewhat irresponsibly nose-up and nose-down, rather like a bucking bronco. The 'aeroplanes' were quite inadequate to control or suppress this tendency, which obviously required a large horizontal surface in the rear of the ship. For a start, however, the flight could only be regarded as successful and encouraging. The envelope and the whole system of pressure control, moreover, were reported as working perfectly.

This performance was watched by many people – men, women, and children – on Farnborough Common. Many photographs were taken, among these being one for the *Illustrated London News*, which is reproduced here as Fig. 49. Thus the original excessive secrecy under which the airship had been constructed had perforce to be abandoned, with a swing to the other extreme of full publicity.

Testing for the day had not ended, however. While the main protagonists were having lunch the wings amidships were removed completely, never to appear again. In the afternoon another flight was undertaken. Capper and Cody went on board as before, but Captain King was replaced by McWade, the Works Manager of the Balloon Factory. Colonel Templer, who had not been present in the morning, arrived in time to see the take-off in the afternoon.

The wind had now freshened still more, and as the airship flew into wind the men holding the ropes hardly needed even to walk in order to keep pace with her. The ship was released, but almost immediately afterwards trouble began; and in the excitement which followed no one seems to have known exactly what happened. It would appear, however, that the engine stopped without warning. Then the wind seems to have taken charge and dashed the ship to the ground. According to observers on the ground, whose views were expressed by the contributor of the *Automotor Journal* – a man never guilty of intentional exaggeration – the affair looked like a terrible disaster. The men on board, however, were only aware of a slight bump. In any event no one was hurt and the ship was scarcely damaged: there were only a few bent tubes in the understructure, and these were easily put right.

3　The second day out

30 September 1907

After the successful trials of 10 September 1907, intensive flying would normally have been expected. The summer was passing; and October winds, which could be fatal to an untried airship, were approaching. Furthermore, British prestige in the air was being threatened. Count Zeppelin was making rapid progress with his rigid airship in Germany, and the Lebaudy firm in France had produced what looked like being a really successful airship, appropriately named *La Patrie*.

Every consideration, therefore, stressed the need to press on with the trials of *Nulli Secundus*, but plans had already been made for the Balloon School to take part in the autumn manoeuvres of Aldershot Command. So away on manoeuvres the men had to go, taking with them their kites and balloons, and leaving behind the airship in her shed. As things turned out, however, the time was not entirely wasted. The opportunity was taken to make several alterations, some of which were vital; and the airship attained her final configuration, as illustrated in Fig. 48.

Most important was the introduction of a large tailplane. In the construction of this some use was made of the original 'drawbridge' wings that had been removed for the afternoon trials of 10 September 1907, but the size of the new tailplane was greater than these alone. A new central portion was incorporated and carried backwards for a considerable distance. The rear portion, moreover, was hinged to produce a controllable elevator. The original rear set of 'aeroplanes', which would now have been shielding the new tailplane, were moved to the extreme forward end of the airship's understructure, so that there were now two sets of 'aeroplanes' ahead of the control car.

The Balloon School returned from manoeuvres and the modifications were completed in time for a trial flight on 30 September 1907. At five minutes past four in the afternoon the airship rose from Farnborough Common when only a slight wind was blowing. The envelope had been blown up to a pressure of two inches of water (10 lb/sq ft = 50 kg/sq metre). The lifting capacity was judged to be poor, so that there were only two men on board: Capper and Cody. There were twelve gallons of fuel in the tank, and the ship carried a two-hundred foot (60 metres) trail rope weighing fifty pounds (23 kg).

The use of a trail rope is specially interesting, being more often associated with a balloon than an airship. Skilled balloonists made a trail rope serve a multiplicity of purposes. Perhaps its main function was to enable a balloon to fly steadily close to the ground without risk of striking it. Thus, if the balloon rose while there was some rope still on the ground, it would pick up extra weight automatically; and if it descended, it would lose weight automatically. The trail rope also acted as an arresting device if a descending balloon was approaching the ground faster than the balloonist had intended, and in this way a violent bump might be avoided. Colonel Capper probably had this arresting function primarily in mind for normal operation of the airship; but he must also have been concerned at the possibility of engine failure, and having to treat the airship as a balloon, in which case the trail rope would be useful in several ways. It was also, as a last resort, a form of reserve ballast, since it could be thrown overboard in an emergency.

In the flight now under consideration, the airship first rose to a height of 400 feet (120 metres), and then proceeded to traverse a complete circle about three quarters of a mile (1·2 km) in diameter. She then climbed steadily to 600 feet (180 metres) while proceeding roughly southwards to Government House, the official residence of the Commander-in-Chief, Sir John French. According to the *Automotor Journal* (5 October 1907) the airship paused there for Sir John to see. She then proceeded roughly south-westerly, crossing the Basingstoke Canal west of Wharf Bridge. She then made a wide turn eastwards, recrossing the canal at Iron Bridge and proceeding across Queen's Parade back to Farnborough Common.

The airship did not stop here, however, but after performing a stiff figure of eight proceeded northerly to Frimley. At about this time, a climb was made to 800 feet (240 metres) with a descent after some minutes, to 600 feet (180 metres) again. The turn was made over the outskirts of Camberley, probably within sight of the main London Road along which the airship was later to travel on her historic journey to St Paul's Cathedral on 5 October 1907. On the home stretch back to Farnborough Common the airship descended to 400 feet (120 metres), and on reaching home came down vertically like a balloon after a small quantity of hydrogen had been released. The entire journey had lasted fifty minutes during which it was estimated that a total distance of twelve miles (20 km) had been covered.

Even the restrained and colourless account of the flight given in the *R.E.C. Extracts* could not conceal the astonishing success of the airship on its second day out. C. M. Waterlow* was less restrained, and rightly described the flight as a 'grand success'. There had been little attempt to spare the airship, moreover, or to break it in by gentle treatment. The *Automotor Journal* (5 October 1907) described how the airship appeared to an observer on the ground to be continually turning first to the left and then to the right, and alternately climbing and descending as she was put through her paces.

It is clear from the reports that the new tail plane and elevator gave nearly perfect stability and control in pitch. This was truly remarkable since, with the trial-and-error methods in use at the time, it could easily have taken a year or more of experimenting to obtain such good results. Despite continual climbing and descending, moreover, no ballast had to be discharged, and no hydrogen had to be released except in the few hundred feet of final descent. Horizontal steering was not quite so good, and there was a tendency to overshoot when turning. In the light of later knowledge, however, the trend was not at all serious, or even abnormal; and it could be explained in part by inexperience on the part of the pilot. The engine appears to have behaved almost perfectly on this occasion, although it was never allowed to develop full power – thirty horse-power being estimated as against a possible maximum of forty or fifty. According to the *R.E.C. Extracts* the reduced horse-power of thirty produced an airspeed of fourteen miles per hour (23 km/hr).

* See *The Airship*, Vol. 7, No. 5, Autumn 1948.

4   The third day out

3 October 1907

The day was fine on Thursday 3 October 1907, and according to *R.E.C. Extracts* 'the lift was greater than on the previous trial owing to the drier atmosphere.' In consequence it was possible to take up three men instead of two, the extra man additional to Colonel Capper and Cody presumably being Captain King, Chief Instructor in Ballooning (see Fig. 48).

The airship took off from Farnborough Common at half past four in the afternoon. The wind was blowing at about eleven miles per hour (18 km/hr) at a height of about 500 feet (150 metres); and probably from the south-east, though the direction is not recorded. At ground level, however, the wind was very changeable, being sometimes a complete calm.

Variation of wind speed with height – a not unusual phenomenon at Farnborough – seems to have been partly responsible for trouble at the start.* A guy rope† fouled the propellers, and the blades were bent. Repair was unbelievably crude: the blades were simply hammered back roughly to their original shape, and the airship took off again.

She then proceeded south over Queen's Parade, Aldershot, and turned eastwards towards Guildford. At Wanborough Railway Station, however, heavy rain clouds appeared, and the airship showed signs of serious loss of lift, although no rain actually fell. The airship was turned about, and she rapidly made for home like a horse returning to her stable.

It took ten minutes to cover the odd five miles (8 km) or so, this being indicative of a following wind from the south-east. The total distance covered during the flight was about twelve miles (15 km).

This was, strictly speaking, the last trial flight of *Nulli Secundus I*. The next flight, premature though it may have been, was in the nature of a major operation, involving an attempt to fly to London and return. Before this

* Farnborough Common (as it then was) and, in fact, the whole of the modern Farnborough airfield, including the original Laffan's Plain, lie in a kind of flat-bottomed bowl inside which the wind at times plays many tricks. Both airships and the early slow-speed aeroplanes were susceptible, and even pilots of modern high-speed aircraft have been not unaware of some inconvenience upon occasion.
† This would be one of several light ropes hanging down for holding by the ground-handling crew.

next flight is considered, however, it is desirable to take a more detailed look at the flight records for enlightenment on the way research and development in the airship field was being conducted at the Balloon School and Factory.

5   Interlude – The airship flight reports
       September/October 1907

To anyone expecting a story of continuing success, the detailed study of the flight records is a disappointment. The tests were not at all well-conducted; and there was a grave lack of knowledge of basic scientific principles that is essential for success in research and development. In the pioneer work of Colonel Templer there had been cause for legitimate pride in Britain's scientific achievement in lighter-than-air activities, but the Templer influence was on the wane, and whatever replaced it, however neat, tidy and efficient by purely military standards, did not produce the sound original work that was required.

The flight reports on the airship trials during Colonel Capper's term of office were issued as appendices to the *Extracts from the Proceedings of the Royal Engineer Committee*. It is almost certain that they were written by Capper himself, but in any event they were his responsibility as Commandant of the Balloon School and Captain of the airship. He was, moreover, personally responsible for submitting the reports to the Royal Engineer Committee as an ex-officio Associate-Member of that Committee.

The reports make difficult reading. They contain many minor textual errors that would normally be corrected by a careful person in the proof-reading stage, if not before. These mistakes are annoying to the reader, but their main significance lies in the implications of carelessness on the part of the writer and a suggestion of indifference. Occasionally, however, real difficulties are caused. No date is given, for example, for the second day's outing of *Nulli Secundus I*, and this has to be obtained from contemporary periodicals. Later, for *Nulli Secundus II*, a wrong date is given for one of its flights, 24 June 1907 instead of 24 July 1907, and this obviously entails much investigation to obtain overwhelming proof that the official date is wrong.

More serious than mere textual errors, however, is the random way in which information is presented. No attempt is made to set out the essential test data systematically or consistently. Sometimes the time of the day is given, sometimes it is not; sometimes the wind direction is given, sometimes it is not; sometimes the air temperature is given, and again sometimes it is not; and so on with all the variables that were vital to these scientific experiments. *Nulli Secundus I* survived long enough to fly on only four separate days; yet full reports, even for such a limited period, would have been invaluable in deciding what was right and what was wrong with the first airship and, above all, in determining the next step to take in airship development.

It is not until the reports are studied in detail, however, and compared with information obtained from other sources, that their deficiencies can be fully realized. It then becomes clear how little basic scientific knowledge Colonel Capper possessed. In particular, despite his lectures to Army organizations and learned societies – and some of his lectures had great merit from the military standpoint – he did not understand how the expandable airship was supposed to work. Military commanders of experimental stations have been known to cope with a similar situation by creating their own team of qualified and experienced men, and heeding their advice. Colonel Capper does not appear to have had such a team, or even to have wanted one: he was a man with his own ideas and happily confident that he was right.

It is not proposed to enter into all the technicalities of the expandable airship as already discussed in Section 2 of Chapter 7, but to mention only two of the more important technical errors that jeopardized the flight experiments. First, there is the all-important differential pressure required to maintain the shape of the envelope. This is mentioned only casually or not at all in the reports, as though it were a piece of perhaps interesting information but of minor consequence. In actual fact it determined the volume of the envelope and hence its lifting power. In this connection, it has to be remembered, *Nulli Secundus* flew with a very small margin of lift. When she left for London, for example, she had only sixty pounds (27 kg) reserve of ballast. In such circumstances the initial differential pressure for the expandable goldbeater's-skin envelope was a paramount consideration, but it is not even mentioned in the accounts of the London flight.*

* Rough calculations show that an increase of one inch (25 mm) in differential pressure on the water scale (within the prescribed upper limit of three inches) would give an extra lift of about seventy-five pounds (34 kg). This is based on the assumption that differential pressure would rise by two inches in a climb to 1,500 feet – which is believed to have been a design objective.

The second technicality is the barometric pressure of the atmosphere at ground level, which Capper rarely, if ever, mentions at any time. Yet a fall in the barometer could drastically reduce lifting power.*

This ignorance of the effect of barometric pressure led to considerable misunderstanding when *Nulli Secundus I* encountered rain. Loss of lift was then invariably attributed to water soaking into the goldbeater's-skin envelope and literally pulling the airship down. The effect cannot be denied in principle, but how significant it was in reality is uncertain. What is certain is that rain must always have been accompanied by a low barometer reading. The water-soaking theory became particularly strained, moreover, when loss of lift occurred with only the *threat* of rain, and none actually coming down. Then they were satisfied with the specious explanation that the air was damp and made the goldbeater's skin heavy.

There is one other matter that needs to be mentioned concerning the flight reports. Anyone reading the *R.E.C. Extracts* must soon find difficulty in reconciling conflicting accounts of wind direction. Investigation has revealed that more is involved than casual error or mere carelessness. Colonel Capper was utterly confused between east and west, and probably had the two exactly reversed in his mind most of the time. Lest this explanation appear fantastic, it is worth noting that the same difficulty arises with Capper's own account of the first Gordon Bennett Balloon race, in which he took an active part.† Among a number of examples in his published article, the following is perhaps the most striking:

The contest was fixed for September 30th, the hope being that the strong easterly winds usual at that time of the year would give a long course westwards over Europe, and thus permit a record run being made.*

There is, of course, no telling what misunderstandings this idiosyncrasy has occasioned. It would appear, however, that one potential cause of trouble

* A fall of one inch (25 mm) of mercury as indicated by a conventional barometer would reduce the lifting power of *Nulli Secundus I* by as much as 120 pounds (55 kg). Yet such a fall is not outside everyday experience in England as between fine and rainy weather.

† See *Aeronautical Journal*, January 1907, and also Section 1 of the present chapter.

‡ There are, of course, only about 150 miles (240 km) of land *westward* of Paris, and then about 2,000 miles (3,200 km) of sea further westward to Newfoundland. The great land mass lies *eastward*, extending more than 5,000 miles (8,000 km).

Now that the reader has been warned of the unreliability of the *R.E.C. Extracts* when reporting direction, especially wind direction, I shall give my own best estimates using the various sources of information that are available. It is usually necessary merely to interchange east and west in the *Extracts*, without altering north and south; thus, for example, north-east becomes north-west, and south-west becomes south-east.

can be eliminated, namely, difficulty in using a compass: according to Waterlow, all the early Farnborough airships flew without one.

We can now return to the main story, less happy but more critical about what is happening. At first, events are encouraging, with accounts of the sensational flight to London. Then there is disaster, and this is followed by an unbroken series of mistakes and failures with Farnborough airships until Colonel Capper ceases to be Superintendent of the Balloon Factory.

6 The flight round St Paul's Cathedral

5 October 1907

It must always be a matter of opinion whether Colonel Capper's flight to London was an act of courage or of rashness. The airship had flown for a total time of only about three hours. Two days before (3 October 1907), moreover, the engine had given trouble and generally proved itself unreliable. Even the ground crew had revealed their lack of skill by allowing the trail rope to become entangled with the propellers. Finally, London lay roughly in the direction followed by the prevailing south-west wind, and in October it was not unlikely that a return journey against the wind would prove impossible with an airship that could fly at not more than sixteen miles per hour (25 km/hr).

On the other hand, a successful British flight was a tonic which the airminded among the British public sorely needed. In France, the Lebaudy airship, *La Patrie*, was much in the news, while Count Zeppelin in Germany was going from strength to strength with his enormous rigid airships. As regards the element of risk, moreover, it has to be noted that Colonel Capper proceeded very tentatively. When the flight began, the wind came near to absolute calm; and he believed that in all likelihood the conditions would persist long enough for the return journey to be accomplished.

As things turned out, Colonel Capper became for a day one of the greatest of showmen. The timing from a publicity standpoint was perfect, and the London flight must have been witnessed by more than a million people, practically none of whom had seen an airship before.

Nulli Secundus I was out on Farnborough Common, ready for her journey, at about half past ten on the morning of Saturday, 5 October 1907. According to the *R.E.C. Extracts* the wind was then blowing at a very gentle four miles per hour (6½ km/hr) from the *south-east*, although it had increased in force to fourteen miles per hour (23 km/hr) by the afternoon and was then said to be blowing from *east-south-east*. This is interpreted as a gentle breeze from the *south-west*, strengthening as the day proceeded and veering round towards the *west*. London lies almost exactly east-north-east of Bagshot, Surrey; and all accounts of the flight, including that given in the *R.E.C. Extracts*, indicate a following wind of increasing force for most of the journey from Bagshot to London.

On board the airship were Colonel Capper and S. F. Cody. There was no third member of the crew, although *The Times* reported that Lieutenant C. M. Waterlow was on board also, a story that has got into many histories but is entirely incorrect. The airship was heavily laden without a third member anyway, having on board thirty gallons of petrol, weighing approximately 210 lb (95 kg), and 100 lb (45 kg) of ballast. There was also a trail rope 200 feet (60 metres) long and weighing about 50 lb (23 kg).

Colonel Capper took her off at about 10.40 a.m., flying initially against the wind. In order to get into the air he used – or so he claimed – dynamic lift. This meant that, flying against the wind in a south-westerly direction, he had the whole of the Common and Laffan's Plain in which to gain height.

The ship then turned eastwards over Farnborough, and by about 10.50 a.m. headed north for Frimley. The margin of lift was not over-generous, however, and the dangling trail rope, just missing Farnborough's chimney pots, became such an embarrassment that 40 lb (18 kg) of ballast had to be released. In all probability it was not until the airship reached Frimley that Colonel Capper finally committed himself to the London journey. The ground crew had certainly been warned that a long journey was contemplated, but the destination up to this point had been uncertain. Everything seemed to be going well, however, and the decision to proceed was almost inevitable. Lieutenant C. M. Waterlow was in charge of the ground crew, and they followed the airship on the roads as best they could. According to Waterlow,* no official motor-car was provided and they had to make use of Cody's own.

From Frimley the airship made its way to Bagshot, and there turned eastwards to follow the road to London. This is the now well-known A30 that runs from London to Land's End. The journey was not entirely uneventful. Capper reported a tendency for the nose of the airship to go up and down of its own accord. This was not, however, attributed by him to any peculiarities

* *The Airship*, Vol. 7, No. 5, Autumn 1948.

35 *left*. Pilot kite for the Naval array of 1908. The disappearing act by the two sailors on the right is the result of sixty years of chemical action upon an old photograph

36 *below*. Top lifter kite for the Naval trials (1908).

The naval gunnery school *H.M.S. Excellent*, situated on Whale Island near Portsmouth, was the base for the sea-going trials; and to provide a systematic record the kites were photographed on the green in front of the naval barracks. In this picture the top lifter kite is waiting to be released, with the pilot kite already up aloft

37 *above*. Second lifter kite for the Naval trials (1908). Usually only two lifter kites were used for naval work, though more were sometimes required in abnormal weather. Here the second lifter is seen with its nose-ring already threaded on the line, and ready to follow the first lifter skywards

38 *facing top*. Lifter kites 'spread' and 'stowed'. The dark patch at the back of the kite in the picture is an airbrake, called a 'save-all', which Cody thought necessary on some occasions

39 *facing bottom*. Carrier kite with basket and trolley (1908).
The carrier kite, which towed the aeronaut in his car or basket, was the largest and most elaborate of all the kites in the array. Standing behind the basket in this picture is a sailor holding up to view the trolley or 'traveller' that is to run up the line

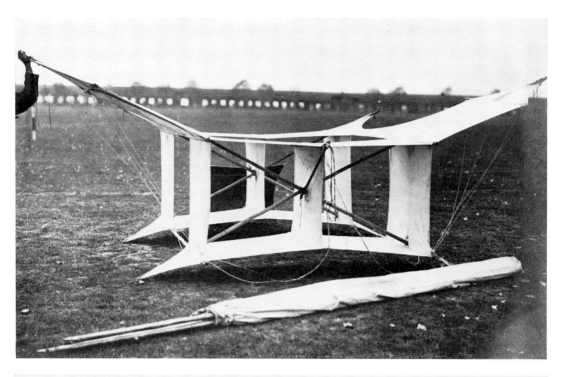

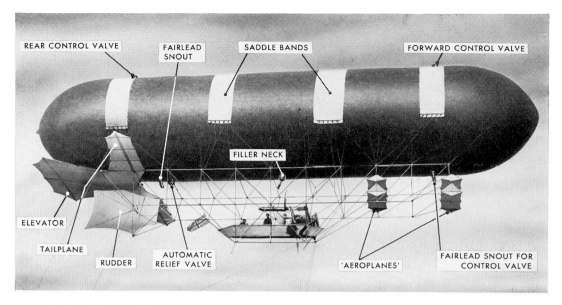

REAR CONTROL VALVE   FAIRLEAD SNOUT   SADDLE BANDS   FORWARD CONTROL VALVE

FILLER NECK

ELEVATOR

TAILPLANE   RUDDER   AUTOMATIC RELIEF VALVE   'AEROPLANES'   FAIRLEAD SNOUT FOR CONTROL VALVE

40 *facing*. Carrier kite and aeronaut leaving the ship. In this experiment a breeches buoy is being used instead of a basket: a precaution in the event of an accidental descent into the sea, such as happened to Cody on one occasion

41 *above*. Principal features of *Nulli Secundus I*.
This illustration indicates the pressure and buoyancy control system for the envelope, and also the aerodynamic stabilizing and control system for the airship's forward motion

42. The famous 50 H.P. *Antoinette* engine. It propelled not only the first Farnborough airship, but also the first Farnborough aeroplane, and is now on view at the Science Museum, South Kensington, London

43 *facing. Nulli Secundus I* in the course of construction (1907). Beneath the hydrogen-filled envelope is the tubular framework and the canoe-shaped car, with Cody standing by

44 *above (top)*. Cody about to start the engine of *Nulli Secundus I*, on test before installation in the airship. Note the crossed belt for the propeller on the right

45 *above (bottom)*. Cody with the engine running.
The whole installation including the twin outriggers was Cody's own design, and it was said that he was the only man strong enough to start the engine

46 *top*. The balloon race from Ranelagh (26 May 1907). Colonel Capper took part in several balloon races in his balloon *Pegasus,* in anticipation of having to pilot the new airship (*Nulli Secundus I*). Mrs Capper went with him as passenger on this occasion

47 *bottom*. The launching of *Nulli Secundus I* (10 September 1907)

of the airship but to up-and-down air currents of a kind not experienced in earlier flights. There were also side gusts, which pushed the nose to the right and to the left, and made steering an onerous task.

The wind, blowing almost directly towards London, increased in force; and it was estimated that the average speed over the ground for the outward journey was about twenty-four miles per hour (40 km/hr). Most of the journey was made at a height of 750 feet (230 metres) according to the more reliable accounts, but the greatest height reached was 1,300 feet (430 metres).

In this way the airship passed over Sunningdale, and crossed the River Thames near Staines at about 11.30 a.m. According to the *Automotor Journal* she was then at a height of 1,300 feet (430 metres). She was later seen to pass over Hounslow and Brentford, reaching Kensington Palace about noon.

It was from Hyde Park that Capper began what was more like a conducted tour of London for an overseas visitor than the flight of an airship. Turning into a south-easterly direction, *Nulli Secundus* first went to the extensive lawns of Buckingham Palace to show herself to the Royal Family. She then proceeded in an easterly direction to visit what was then described as the 'New War Office' in Whitehall.* Several members of the Army Council came out to watch and, according to several newspaper accounts, Capper put the airship through a few simple manoeuvres for them to see.

Flying at a few hundred feet and watched by vast crowds of people, the airship proceeded along Whitehall to Trafalgar Square, then along the Strand and Fleet Street. She then went round the dome of St Paul's Cathedral, a magnificent sight; and among many photographs taken was one published in *The Illustrated London News* (12 October 1907) and reproduced here as Fig. 50.

The turn around St Paul's, clockwise as viewed from above, was made at about 12.20 p.m. The airship did not at first make direct for home but, crossing the river at Blackfriars Bridge, proceeded almost due south to Kennington Oval, which was passed over at 12.30 p.m. The temperature was now falling and the adverse wind was rapidly increasing in strength. Somehow Clapham Common was reached at about 1.10 p.m., but forward speed against the wind was now reduced to practically zero. Here was a possible place to descend, but there was some natural hesitation in making the irrevocable decision. The airship remained practically stationary over the Common for forty minutes, and then descended to a height of about 200 feet (60 metres). In the time that had elapsed, however, a crowd had collected so that Colonel Capper would not even attempt a landing and hazard the lives of the people

* Now the 'Old War Office', part of the Ministry of Defence. The building had only just been completed earlier in the year 1907.

below. He therefore eased the ship partially into the wind and proceeded south-east towards the Crystal Palace at Sydenham.*

In order to get down to 200 feet at Clapham Common, Colonel Capper had been obliged to release some hydrogen. As a consequence, he found the trail rope scraping the telegraph wires, and ten pounds of ballast had to be discharged to clear them. The airship passed over the Crystal Palace at almost exactly two o'clock in the afternoon and then turned back into wind for a final descent (see Fig. 51). After some more hydrogen had been released, the airship came down almost vertically into the Crystal Palace grounds seven minutes later. She seems to have landed very neatly, straight into the arms, as it were, of the ground-handling party who had arrived on the scene with perfect timing. Travelling in their motor-car, they had lost contact with the airship in London but had picked up the trail again at Clapham Common, and the rest of the journey had been easy.

It seems more than pure coincidence that the Crystal Palace was chosen for a landing, even though it was conveniently at hand when the situation was becoming desperate. Cody had had his workshop there when working on his kites in 1903 and 1904 (see Chapter 4), and had used the grounds for his kiting experiments. He therefore knew the terrain well, both from the ground and from the air. In any event, it was a good place for an emergency landing, the cycle racing track providing a roomy space, well sheltered from the prevailing south-west wind.

At the time of landing, *Nulli Secundus* had been in the air for three hours and twenty minutes, and had travelled a total distance (over the ground) of approximately fifty miles (80 km). There was still, according to *R.E.C. Extracts*, enough petrol left in the tank for four or five hours flying. Hence, even with an adverse wind of eight miles per hour, which was twice as strong as that at the beginning of the journey, a safe return would have been a likely prospect. But with an adverse wind reported to be roughly equal to the airship's own speed through the air there was, of course, no hope at all.

* The Crystal Palace was originally built in Hyde Park, London, to house the Great Exhibition of 1851. It was afterwards re-erected (1852) in the extensive grounds at Sydenham, South London; and both the building and the grounds were used for public entertainment of various kinds for many years. The Palace was destroyed by fire in 1936.

7 Fame and disaster

5–10 October 1907

The enthusiasm generated by the flight round St Paul's has only on rare occasions been surpassed in British history. There had been an unpleasant ring in the ears of the British people at the stories of success in France and Germany; and now, it would appear, Britain was being put back into what they deemed her rightful place among progressive nations. The British Press did full justice to the achievement, and the pictorial magazines had unique opportunities for first-rate photography. For the weeklies the timing was excellent since, the flight having taken place on a Saturday, there was time to gather a detailed story and numerous pictures for the weekend following.

The *Illustrated London News* (12 October 1907) is a typical example:

AERIAL NAVIGATION SOLVED
THE AIR-SHIP'S VISIT TO LONDON

On October 5th the British military air-ship sent London wild with delight by its appearance above the Metropolis. The vessel started from Farnborough about eleven o'clock under the direction of Colonel Capper, Mr Cody, and Lieutenant Waterlow. The aeronauts expected to reach London about one o'clock, but before half-past twelve they were over Trafalgar Square, travelling at the rate of twenty-five miles an hour. Travelling eastward by way of the Strand and Fleet Street, attracting enthusiastic attention, the air-ship rounded the dome of St Paul's within the compass of the church-yard, and then headed westward against a stiff breeze. The course was set for the Crystal Palace, and when the machine was over the football ground, the aeronauts decided to descend, as the supply of petrol was running low. The manager of the Palace shouted through a megaphone an invitation to lunch, and Colonel Capper accepted, bringing his balloon skillfully to anchor. The whole trip was a gratifying success.*

Other papers told a similar story, one going so far as to say: 'England Mistress of the Air', which was a parody of the well-known adage: 'England Mistress of the Sea'. Here, however, enthusiasm was becoming fantasy. As recently as the Monday preceding the Saturday flight of *Nulli Secundus*, Count Zeppelin's latest airship had travelled 200 miles (320 km), making a

---

* In order to avoid misunderstanding, a few minor errors should be noted: Lieutenant Waterlow was not on board; the landing was made on the cycle track, not the football ground; and there was no shortage of fuel, less than half having been consumed.

complete circuit round Lake Constance in a flight lasting nine and a quarter hours.

Nevertheless, *Nulli Secundus* had flown further and longer than any other airship apart from Count Zeppelin's. The journey, unfortunately, did not end at the starting base, and a journey made mainly with a following wind loses much of its significance as a record. The French airship *La Patrie*, on the other hand, had made a closed loop of forty miles (65 km) from Chalais-Meudon on 12 July 1907, at an average speed of twenty-two miles per hour (35 km/hr).*

None of these comparative considerations could damp the enthusiasm of the British public; but this very enthusiasm produced a shocking anti-climax when the airship was smashed-up at the Crystal Palace and had to be brought home to Farnborough in pieces by road. After being tethered to the ground on the evening of the great flight, *Nulli Secundus* stayed on the cycle track at the Crystal Palace until early on the following Thursday. She then began to break loose in the wind, and had to be deflated by slitting of the envelope with a knife.

The full story of what happened has never been entirely clear and there still remain elements of mystery. The main reason for this state of affairs is the determined efforts made by all who were concerned in the disaster to make light of the consequences and to conceal the negligence which gave rise to it. The story that now follows is derived from all the available sources, including the contemporary newspapers. The British Press as a whole was remarkably factual, and deserving of the highest praise for refusing to make a sensation out of what was regarded as a national disaster.

8 The end of *Nulli Secundus I*

5–10 October 1907

The account of the last days of *Nulli Secundus* at the Crystal Palace, given by Colonel Capper in the *R.E.C. Extracts*, is brief and incomplete; and it disagrees in several particulars from information derived from other sources. Failure to take to the air is attributed to constant strong winds and rainy

* Chalais-Meudon – the French national aeronautical establishment just outside Paris, and the nearest French equivalent to the Balloon Factory at Farnborough. See also Chapter 3, Section 2.

weather. Rain there was in plenty but the records of the Meteorological Office for the period show only light winds up to the night preceding Thursday's disaster. The strongest winds recorded are Force 2 on the Beaufort Scale, which is interpreted as four to seven miles per hour (6½ to 11 km/hr) – 'wind felt on face and leaves rustle'.*

The ultimate disaster is explained in the *Extracts* by a sudden gale that was entirely unforeseen,† and which tore loose the holding-down pickets. No explanation is given as to why the holding-down pickets were so insecure that they succumbed at once on the first sign of a strong wind. Above all, no explanation is given why this valuable airship was left in charge of a corporal instead of a commissioned officer with rank appropriate to the responsibility; and why he was supported by the absurdedly small handling crew comprising only six men.

For the full story we begin with the Sunday following Saturday's great flight. The airship had been picketed on the cycle track, as shown in Fig. 52. The day was spent checking the airship for signs of wear-and-tear and possible damage in the forced landing. Hydrogen had to be brought from Farnborough to replace that released at Clapham Common and during the final descent at the Crystal Palace. During the night it had rained very heavily and rain continued through much of the morning. The airship, it was said, was weighed down with water, which had soaked into the goldbeater's skin and had saturated the nets and ropes. The rain does not appear to have deterred the crowds of onlookers, however, some of whom are seen in Fig. 52 with umbrellas, though some apparently preferred the shelter of the airship herself.

Monday was a most unsatisfactory day. It had rained all through the night and continued during much of the morning. The airship was deemed to be too heavy for flight, and an attempt to take off does not appear even to have been considered.

Tuesday was more promising, although there was some rain in the morning. The weather cleared in the afternoon and hopes ran high. Not until about half past four in the afternoon did Colonel Capper decide not to make the attempt that day. This was a great disappointment to the crowds who had waited expectantly for many hours.

* I am indebted to the Meteorological Office for use of their weather records for the period under consideration, but these relate specifically to their recording station at St James's Park, which was six miles north-west of the Crystal Palace.
† The wind when the airship met with disaster was undoubtedly stronger than predicted in the official weather forecast but, so far as I can ascertain, nothing approaching gale force was experienced.

On Wednesday conditions changed considerably. Up to then the winds had had an unfavourable westerly component. On this day, however, the wind came squarely from the east, of strength Force 2 according to the records of the Meteorological Office. A flight home was obviously considered seriously. The airship was turned round to face the wind from the east and re-tethered, and Cody gave the engine a trial run. Drizzle came along at noon, however, and was blamed for failure to achieve buoyancy and take to the air.

Insufficient buoyancy would also be attributable in part to the low barometric pressure associated with the rain, as already discussed. It is estimated that at least sixty pounds (27 kg) of lift was lost in this way compared with conditions at Farnborough when the airship began her flight.* It is almost certain, moreover, that Colonel Capper failed to take advantage of the maximum allowable differential pressure in order to get clear. Sunshine would have helped by raising the pressure artificially, but instead there was a dull overcast sky when it was not actually raining, with the hydrogen already chilled by all-night exposure out of doors.

In this connection it is interesting to record an interview that Colonel Templer gave to a newspaper correspondent after the final disaster to *Nulli Secundus*. By this time Colonel Templer had virtually severed his connection with the Balloon Factory, but he lived in London and called to see the airship, as did many other distinguished people. During the interview, which was reported in the New York *Tribune* for Friday, 11 October 1907, Colonel Templer said: 'The three circumstances against her flight on Wednesday were a low barometer, cold gas [hydrogen], and the weight of water absorbed.' There does not appear to have been much wrong with the old balloonist's knowledge and understanding!

It was on this Wednesday night that, unsuspected by all, events were approaching a climax. After the disaster, Colonel Capper said that he could at this stage have dismantled the airship and brought her home by road none the worse for her adventures. He did not do this but, in the belief that the weather next day would be much the same, he went home, leaving his airship in charge of Corporal Ramsay and six sappers.

The disastrous Thursday (10 October 1907) began with every sign of being a good day. The sun rose at about quarter past six and the weather was fine and clear. The wind was not unduly strong at first and came roughly from the east. What happened next is to some extent uncertain, but towards eight o'clock the wind appears to have increased in strength and veered to the south-east. It does not seem to have even approached gale force generally

* Based on the contemporary weather reports of the Meteorological Office.

at this time of the day, but there were almost certainly local effects with some channelling of the wind through a gap in the surrounding trees. In any event, a fairly severe gust struck *Nulli Secundus* on the nose. The picketing stakes do not appear to have been at all secure, and the front ones were pulled out almost immediately. Thereafter there was hell let loose, with the airship tossing this way and that in her efforts to get completely free.

According to the American Press, five of the six sappers were away at breakfast at the time. They came running out, apparently, and were joined by several civilians working in the grounds of the Crystal Palace and round about. It soon became clear, however, that *Nulli Secundus* was winning and would soon be free, so Corporal Ramsay thereupon opened the escape valves to release the hydrogen. This was too slow, unfortunately, and he decided to slit the nose of the envelope, using, it is said, a knife tied to the end of a long pole.

In the event, *Nulli Secundus* did not escape, but she took some time to become quiescent. There was indeed time for many spectators to arrive, and many photographs were taken of the struggling airship. A photograph published by *The Automotor* is reproduced in Fig. 53,* and gives some idea how difficult it is to deflate an airship, even when the envelope is ripped open with a knife. By strange chance the unusual attitude produced the best view ever recorded of the tail surfaces. The final process of disruption at the rear end has only been deferred, however, and already the rudder has been forced upwards hard against the tail plane. At the front end of the airship, of course, the understructure is completely mangled at this stage.

It is not difficult to imagine the dilemma with which Corporal Ramsay had been faced. For a man of his rank it must have been a terrible decision to have to make: first to release the precious hydrogen by the valves, and then, in desperation, to slit open the envelope with a knife. So far as is known, moreover, there had been no practice drill, and he had not even been told what to do in such an emergency. According to Lieutenant Waterlow, he was at once promoted to sergeant in recognition of his presence of mind; and in all published accounts he is referred to as Sergeant Ramsay.

Immediately after the disaster, every attempt was made to soften the blow to the British public, even to the extent of perverting the truth. The Aeronautical Society at once came to the rescue with a masterpiece of euphemism and understatement:

Just on going to the press a report was circulated in London that the British military airship had been wrecked in a gale of wind at Crystal Palace. The report, however, was

---

* This photograph is reproduced for its great historic interest; and the imperfections, though regrettable, are unavoidable.

a much exaggerated one. The incident which occurred to the Government Balloon on October 10th was one very likely to happen to a navigable balloon anchored in our uncertain climate.

It appears that the airship was caught in a squall between eight and nine in the morning, and a number of stakes to which she was attached were pulled out, with a result that the contrivance heeled over.

The most fitting comment to make on the accident would seem to be a commendation of the efficiency of the sappers in charge of the airship, who speedily accomplished the necessary deflation, and thus saved the envelope and motors from threatened damage.*

It was entirely wrong to accuse the Press of exaggeration. The envelope was repairable and the solid part of the engine could be used again, but the rest was just a mangled mass of wreckage. This conclusion is the only one that can be drawn after examination of the many photographs that were published; and few people could disagree with the choice of words by *The Scotsman* (11 October 1907) – 'a hopeless confusion of wreckage'.†

Colonel Capper's own description in the *R.E.C. Extracts* 'played down' the damage to some extent but did not entirely evade the issue. His words were:

The damage done to the balloon consists only in the breaking up of the steel tubing used in the framework, together with one or two aluminium joints and the arms of one of the screw propellers.

In any event this was the last of *Nulli Secundus I*. She never flew again. She was indeed resurrected as *Nulli Secundus II*, with most of the original envelope and engine; but in both appearance and behaviour the new airship bore little resemblance to her predecessor.

Although *Nulli Secundus I* suffered severe damage, it was indeed remarkable that she did not free herself altogether, and eventually meet with total destruction. For this the presence of mind of Corporal Ramsay – and his sharp knife – must be given the credit. *Nulli Secundus*, however, was not the only airship to become a victim of the winds about this time. Only six weeks later her great French counterpart, *La Patrie*, not only suffered damage but disappeared for ever.‡

Early in the afternoon of Friday, 29 November, *La Patrie* left Verdun with a crew of seven. Almost immediately trouble with the engine was encoun-

* *Aeronautical Journal* for October 1907.
† In the British newspaper extracts examined by me I have not found any mention of the five sappers having breakfast at the critical time. I accept the story, however, and think that the British Press deliberately refrained from using it, out of regard for the national interest. The American Press were, naturally and justifiably, less inhibited.
‡ See *Automotor Journal*, 14 December 1907; and *l'Aérophile*, December 1907.

tered through a mechanic getting his clothing caught up in the mechanism. Repairs in the air were unsuccessful and the airship had to make a forced landing for the night. Repairs then took up the whole of the next day also, and during this time the wind increased in force. By eight o'clock on Saturday evening *La Patrie* was being held down in a gale by 150 men. Attempts to operate the valves by the lieutenant in charge were unsuccessful and there was no Corporal Ramsay to slit the envelope. The men were eventually unable to hold the airship and she escaped with no one on board.

La Patrie then made a fascinating journey on her own. She proceeded through the night over Northern France, crossed the English Channel, and passed over Cornwall. At eight o'clock on Sunday morning she was observed when passing over Wales. She then crossed the Irish Sea to Ireland where, at Ballydavey in County Down, she showed signs of coming down to rest. This was not to be, however, for after striking a hill, tearing up a field, and knocking down a wall, she took off again, having lightened herself by leaving behind a propeller and a collection of miscellaneous debris.

La Patrie was eventually seen, still travelling fast, by a trawler off the Isle of Islay, Western Scotland, at about five o'clock on Sunday evening. She has not been seen or heard of since.

9 Nulli Secundus II
1908

1   Plans for the new airship

     Early 1908

It is not at all certain exactly when serious work on *Nulli Secundus II* began, but there are indications that preliminary work was undertaken by the end of 1907, with the concurrence of the War Office. Two or three periodicals, in fact, with their somewhat roundabout methods of finding things out despite the barrier of secrecy, implied that work was well under way in January 1908.

Absence of clear-cut records and definite dates is understandable in the light of methods in use at the Balloon Factory. The nearest approach to a working drawing would be a rough pencil sketch, and practically all instructions were conveyed by word of mouth. The minutes of meetings, the works-order forms, and the blue prints of a later age were entirely non-existent.

With this period particularly in mind, the writer of the *R.A.E. Chronicles* put his own conclusions on record:

> At this period there was no drawing office at the Balloon Factory. Jobs were not given out to the trade [i.e. private industry] and the factory was so small that Superintendent, Works Manager, and men worked together on a verbal [i.e., oral] basis. It is no doubt partly owing to this fact that detailed records are so few.

It has already been commented in the present History that communications between Colonel Capper (as Superintendent of the Balloon Factory) and the Directorate at the War Office were mostly informal, perhaps more so than in Colonel Templer's day, so that documentary records are rare. The *R.A.E. Chronicles* contain interesting remarks on this also, for, in continuation, it is said:

> The same remark applies to broader [i.e., policy] questions: the Superintendent of the Balloon Factory took his instructions verbally at War Office interviews and conferences, and as a consequence these notes [i.e., the *R.A.E. Chronicles*] are made up mostly from accidental references in later correspondence to what had been done months before.

218

Nevertheless, it is possible to gather from various sources a firm impression of careful planning in the *re-design* of *Nulli Secundus*. All pretence of mere repair of the old airship was, so far as internal discussions were concerned, completely abandoned; and major re-design was accepted as the official policy. In this way there was avoided the difficulty of explaining to the financial branches how much damage had been done at the Crystal Palace, since financial allocation was set against re-design of *Nulli Secundus* instead of repair. There are no grounds for supposing, however, that this was in any sense a prime motive with Colonel Capper, who clearly believed that here was an opportunity to introduce what he considered to be improvements at little extra cost.

The case for re-design of *Nulli Secundus* was based on an assessment of the qualities of the original, which were put on record in the *R.E.C. Extracts*. In Colonel Capper's opinion the original design had only one point in its favour: its remarkable retention of gas within the goldbeater's-skin envelope. 'There is no dirigible balloon in the World,' he said, 'that can compare with ours in this respect.' But he did not like the way in which the goldbeater's skin absorbed water and became, in his view, unduly heavy in wet weather.

The netting, which gave the principal support to the understructure, was objected to on the grounds of excessive air resistance through the rough surface it presented to the airstream. The understructure itself was also criticized on the grounds that the uncovered tubes had excessive air resistance. Objection was raised against the shape of the envelope, with its near hemispherical ends, again on the grounds of air resistance. In point of fact, a modern view is that, for the speeds at which this airship could hope to fly, a proper streamline shape would not produce a significant improvement, but the men of the Balloon Factory could not rightly be expected to know this in 1907.

Colonel Capper was most concerned about the smallness of the airship and the absence of a ballonet. Thus he says in the *R.E.C. Extracts*:

The balloon is too small for serious work and long distance runs. It does not allow of the provision of a ballonet and blower, which are necessary for non-rigid balloons which have to rise above 1,200 to 1,500 feet, nor does it allow of a sufficient crew, or of the carriage of ballast to any considerable extent.

He also laid down, as a minimum requirement, accommodation and lifting power to carry three men:

The crew should consist of at least three persons. One to look after the engine; one to watch the aneroid [altimeter], to work the aeroplanes for altitude, to watch the pressure gauge, and to work the valves and ballast; and one to steer and watch the map.

There were, in addition, a number of miscellaneous comments, one of the more important being a demand for more responsive aerodynamic control of ascent and descent.

Colonel Capper did end his remarks, however, with some words of praise for what was largely the handiwork of his predecessor:

> On the whole the experiments, which were almost on a model scale, were satisfactory, considering the shape of the envelope which had to be used.

The policy of re-designing the original airship is open to question. *Nulli Secundus I* was, indeed, too small and too slow; but, despite his final comments, Colonel Capper did not realize how good she was. She had, moreover, made only three flights, if we discount the first day's efforts which were little more than buoyancy tests. It would have been better to restore the airship exactly to her original condition, and continue the experiments which were the main justification for her ever having existed. With more data available, consideration could then have been given to making a completely new airship. As things turned out, however, while *Nulli Secundus I* may have had faults, *Nulli Secundus II* was never any use at all.

2　　Design and construction of *Nulli Secundus II*
　　　1908

It is in many ways remarkable how different in appearance was *Nulli Secundus II* (see Fig. 54) from her predecessor, especially when we bear in mind that the same envelope was used for both. For the rest, it would appear that everything that could be altered, was altered; and even the original engine, which had to be used, had most of its ancillary gear re-designed. Perhaps the most conspicuous change was the widespread use of silk sheeting, which covered virtually everything. This was a rather complicated innovation, and is best considered in progressive stages.

First of all, the entire envelope, except the rounded ends, was clothed in a thin jacket made of varnished silk. This was usually referred to as a 'chemise', but the word is inappropriate. Dictionaries define 'chemise' as a woman's undergarment, but on *Nulli Secundus II* it was essentially an outer covering

designed to be impervious to moisture and resistant to both wind and rain.*
Its ostensible purpose was to prevent the goldbeater's skin becoming saturated with rain-water, and the airship thereby rendered unduly heavy. There
was clearly behind this a vigorous and possibly costly reaction to the failure
to fly *Nulli Secundus I* out of the grounds of the Crystal Palace in the
previous October.

The introduction of the silk covering, however, was based on a number of
misconceptions. As mentioned earlier, rain was normally accompanied by a
fall in the barometer; and this could in itself reduce lifting power appreciably,
for which the goldbeater's skin could clearly not be blamed. Secondly,
during and immediately after rain, most materials cling to a certain amount
of water without requiring any special sponge-like properties with which
goldbeater's skin had been credited. Thus, on these two counts alone, the
disadvantages of goldbeater's skin had been exaggerated.

Another misconception was that goldbeater's skin, unlike silk, could not
be directly protected by varnish. It is clear that the technical problem was
not properly investigated, since all subsequent airships using goldbeater's
skin were adequately protected and rendered reasonably waterproof by a
varnish made up of linseed oil and copal, or an equivalent in the form of a
proprietary product which men at the Balloon Factory referred to as
'Pegamoid'. According to the *R.E.C. Extracts*, Pegamoid varnish was applied
to the silk cover of *Nulli Secundus II*.†

According to a weight analysis given in the *R.E.C. Extracts* (see Appendix
E), the silk cover weighed 332 lb (150 kg). Although some allowance
should be made for the other purposes which the silk cover was made to
serve, this weight was a terrible price to pay for surface protection, and it
would seem to have been much cheaper from the standpoint of weight economy
to have allowed the goldbeater's skin to get wet.

The main additional function of the silk cover was as a replacement for
the original netting that assisted the saddle-bands in providing support for
the understructure and hence for the useful load in the way of crew, engine,
fuel, control and stabilizing surfaces. It did so, it was claimed, with less
air-resistance as well as less tendency to absorb water. The four saddle-

* Readers may suspect here a rather crude soldierly pun – a chemise being often defined as 'a
garment worn next to the skin'.

† Strictly speaking Pegamoid was a complete covering material or cloth, not just a varnish;
and it is still defined in many dictionaries as a proprietary form of imitation leather. An
exhaustive search made by the Patent Office has not revealed the name as ever having been
applied to a varnish or other paint-like substance in ordinary commercial practice. It seems
likely that the airship varnish was supplied by the makers of Pegamoid and the name conveniently used to identify it.

bands might appear at first sight to be the same as before, but they were narrower and placed outside the silk cover. They did not, moreover, now help to support the understructure, but were used solely to provide anchorage attachments.

The main understructure itself was a fairly radical re-design, although the same basic type of tubular construction was used as for *Nulli Secundus I*. Some of the old tubes salvaged from the Crystal Palace wreckage, in fact, were straightened and used again. In order to reduce weight, however, the four-sided beam construction of *Nulli Secundus I* (see earlier Fig. 43) was replaced by a triangular section. Unfortunately, photographs do not appear to have survived to show the skeleton structure before it was covered by silk fabric, but the external form can be seen in a head-on photograph, reproduced as Fig. 55.

The silk covering for the understructure was introduced in the first instance because the air-resistance of the exposed tubes was thought to be unduly high. The covering was regarded as an improvement aerodynamically, and an attempt was made to produce an overall boat-like and streamline shape. The length of the 'boat' was about seventy-five feet (23 metres).

It should perhaps be remarked that Colonel Capper and his Royal Engineers were skilled at this kind of structural engineering, and were much more at home with it than with corresponding work in the mechanical engineering field. It is salutary to note, however, that Colonel Capper's successor as Superintendent, Mervyn O'Gorman, once said that Colonel Capper had no one who could work out stresses and calculate structural strength. Everything had to be decided by eye and intuition.

The understructure was suspended from the silk cover of the envelope by further silk sheeting expanding upwards to give a snug fit into the circular form of the envelope (see Fig. 55 again). The three sides of the triangular section were each seven feet (2·1 metres) in length, and the two upper longitudinal members were suspended two feet (0·6 metres) below the lowest point of the envelope.

This suspension system produced a covered-in space that was used for introducing a remarkable innovation. Inside was a reserve gas-bag having a capacity for holding one thousand cubic feet of hydrogen (28 cubic metres). The declared purpose of this was to provide compensation for loss of weight through fuel consumption, without interference with the differential pressure in the main envelope. Its lifting power of about seventy pounds (32 kg) would allow consumption of ten gallons (45 litres) of petrol, equivalent to a cruising flight of about fifty miles (80 km). According to Colonel Capper's records the reserve gas-bag weighed thirty-three pounds (15 kg), and from a weight-economy standpoint seems to have been scarcely worth-while. Colonel Capper himself was never greatly impressed with the idea, but it was an interesting experiment.*

As might be expected, however, this novel and unorthodox feature has caused misunderstanding in the past. It has been confused at times with a ballonet, which it certainly was not. C. M. Waterlow regarded it as a kind of alternative to a ballonet, in acting as a relief storage chamber for gas during climb. Thus, he commented: 'The idea was that this [the auxiliary gas-bag] should take the excess of gas as the airship rose and so avoid having to let out gas from the valves.'† This is absurd, since for an operation of this kind there would have to be interconnection between the main envelope and the subsidiary bag, with pumps in operation to effect the hydrogen transfer. This would entail a system far too elaborate for practical application, and one which was obviously not used in this case.

The various control and stabilizing surfaces were modified considerably, some with a new purpose and others necessitated by the new covered-in structure. The original single rudder, which would now have been shielded by the silk-covered understructure, was replaced by two rudders set outboard on port and starboard respectively. The rear elevator appears to have remained roughly as before, but the large span tailplane was removed. There was introduced in its place a row of quaint projecting planes resembling arrow feathers. These can be seen in Fig. 54 and are shown up in rather odd perspective in Fig. 55.

The most controversial and most drastic change of all, however, was the introduction of a large elevator in front. If any single thing can be blamed for ruining the new airship it is this. Colonel Capper had always been obsessed by what he thought was inadequate control in pitch, and wanted more power to put the nose of the airship up or down at will. He certainly got this, but so also did the airship herself, for she would toss her nose up or down in the random fashion associated with extreme instability. It is ironical that Colonel Capper always referred to this forward elevator as a 'stabilizer'.

We next pass on to the control and engine car. In *Nulli Secundus I* the car had been integrally built into the main framework of the understructure. For reasons not entirely clear, Colonel Capper did not like this arrangement and, in any case, the main understructure was now completely covered with silk fabric. The car, therefore, was slung by wires well below the rest of the airship. It was made mostly of hickory wood, one of the most resilient of

* Approximate calculations indicate that the reserve gas-bag was equivalent in capacity to an extra one inch of differential pressure, on the water scale, in the main envelope.
† From *The Airship*, Winter 1948/9.

materials, and calculated to be resistant to the battering it might receive when the airship was tethered on a windy day. Here again was evidence of design being influenced by what had happened at the Crystal Palace.

A new development was the pointed structure underneath the car, which was little more than a vertical spike suitably braced to resist side forces (see Fig. 54 and, for more detail, Fig. 56). The basic idea was an acknowledged copy of the spike used on the French airship *La Patrie*, and its main purpose was to provide a pivot about which the airship could be turned more easily by the ground-handling crew. The scheme appears to have been, on the best assessment, unhandy. The crew had difficulty in both embarkation and disembarkation; and detachment of the car from the understructure was a major task, since it could not stand up by itself on one leg.

The installation of the engine-propeller system was basically the same as on *Nulli Secundus I*, but there were detail alterations. The old *Antoinette* engine was used, and the propeller shafts were still mounted on the projecting arms of Cody's design, but the drive was different. A single belt-and-pulley system was used with each propeller, instead of the previous twin-belt drive.* Furthermore, neither belt was crossed, so that both propellers now revolved in the same direction. Why this was so does not appear on record, but it is not unlikely that the heavy type of belt used (see Fig. 56) could not be twisted without causing trouble. The propeller blades were spoon-shaped, being hammered out of aluminium sheet, and are thought to have been somewhat larger than those on *Nulli Secundus I*.

Finally we come to the actual engine. This has been the subject of much misunderstanding and even controversy in the past over which engine was used and when it was available. C. M. Waterlow said categorically that a new *Antoinette* engine was provided. Thus there appears in his memoirs:

The power plant complete in its wooden frame, was utilized from the previous ship [*Nulli Secundus I*], though a new engine of identical pattern was fitted.†

The *R.E.C. Extracts*, however, leave no room for doubt that the old *Antoinette* engine of *Nulli Secundus I* was used. This view is borne out by the *R.A.E. Chronicles*. The writer had before him what he described as:

A letter dated June 11th 1908, and written by the Officer Commanding the Balloon School to the President of the Royal Engineer Committee.

In commenting the chronicler says:

* From photographs it would appear that 'Whittle' belts were used, made by Thomas Whittle & Co. Ltd of Warrington. See *Motor Cycling*, 24 January 1910.
† From *The Airship*, Winter 1948/9.

The great difficulty experienced by the Superintendent of the Balloon Factory in his aeroplane experiments was want of powerful and reliable engines. A fifty horse-power *Panhard-Levassor* engine was delivered in March and broke down under test. He had been counting on this engine for Cody's flying machine. He could not get another. 'The *Antoinette* might be suitable,' he writes, 'but this is in the dirigible balloon.' He did not buy a second *Antoinette* last year, as he had hoped that British makers might have produced an engine.

The ultimate fate of the *Panhard-Levassor* engine is one of Farnborough's mysteries, since it appears never to have been heard of again, but the facts about the *Antoinette* are clear: there was only one *Antoinette* and this was in the airship. Furthermore, the airship had priority over aeroplane work; and, in particular, Cody's aeroplane would have to wait until the flight tests on *Nulli Secundus II* were completed.

This concludes the review of the design features of *Nulli Secundus II* except for a few remarks about the weight of various components. The *R.E.C. Extracts* include an interesting weight analysis, which is reproduced in full in Appendix E. The total weight without useful load (crew, fuel and ballast) works out at 3,051 lb (1,400 kg), or about one and one third tons. This, according to the *Extracts*, was about the same weight as *Nulli Secundus I*. To achieve this weight, however, it had been necessary to reduce the fuel-tank capacity from thirty gallons to twelve, giving a range of not much more than 50 miles (80 km).

The lifting capacity is stated to be 3,950 lb (1,800 kg), which allows 900 lb (400 kg) for disposable load, i.e., crew, fuel and ballast. Unfortunately these figures are given without reference to the atmospheric temperature and pressure, and without any mention of the differential pressure inside the envelope. The atmospheric temperature and pressure might conceivably be taken as the standard normal values,* but the differential pressure is uncertain. The *R.E.C. Extracts* also state that the envelope had increased in volume since 1907; but this could simply mean that it had been blown up to a higher pressure.

* Temperature 59°F = 15°C; Barometer 30 inches = 760 millimetres of mercury.

3   Visit of the International Aeronautical Federation
28 May 1908

Although the new airship was not ready until 24 July 1908, a preview was given on 28 May 1908 to the International Aeronautical Federation. This organization, which was usually known for brevity as the F.A.I.,* exercised great influence in the aeronautical world and had close links with the British Aero Club as a constituent member.† The visit to Farnborough was of no little importance to the Balloon Factory.

The visit was part of a three-day meeting (28–30 May), and delegates came from Austria-Hungary, Belgium, France, Germany, Great Britain, Italy, Spain, Sweden, Switzerland, and the United States of America. Rather amusingly, as it must seem today, voting strength of each country within the Federation was assessed by the total amount of gas consumed by its balloons and airships in the previous year. It is interesting to note, therefore, that Britain came third with 238,854 cubic metres, compared with Germany's 492,614 cubic metres and France's 491,300 cubic metres.

The delegates were given a tour of the workshops, skin rooms, and hydrogen plant; but it is clear they were kept well away from most things of military significance, especially work on aeroplanes. Demonstrations were given of balloon filling, but undoubtedly the *tour-de-force* was the new airship. Only the envelope was on show, and such of the understructure and car as may have been completed at this time was kept well out of sight. The envelope was already wearing its new silk cover and, it is interesting to note, was deemed to be 'very much bigger' than its predecessor *Nulli Secundus I*. Once again, therefore, there was demonstrated how large and impressive an airship seems to be when viewed at close-quarters inside her shed; for the envelope, of course, was still the same as before.

The meeting, however, was less significant for its direct aeronautical implications than for the way it revealed Colonel Capper's difficulties with the Press. The episode of the F.A.I. visit was the beginning of an unsatis-

* *Fédération Aéronautique Internationale*. The central authority on international sport in the aeronautical field, founded in 1905.
† The *Aero Club* was the authority in Britain for aeronautical competitions and records. Founded in 1901, it became the *Royal Aero Club* in 1910.

factory relationship that grew steadily worse during the rest of 1908, and did harm to Capper personally as well as to the Balloon Factory.*

The trouble began when a representative of the *Aldershot News* turned up at the Balloon Factory gates with the delegates and was refused admission. He was able to watch the people from other countries pass through while he was rejected; but the bitterest blow came when a reporter from the London *Daily Telegraph* was admitted on the grounds that he was a member of the Aero Club and *ipso facto* a delegate of the F.A.I.

The case for the *Aldershot News*, which for this purpose became symbolic of the whole newspaper world, was as straightforward as it could possibly be. They represented the taxpayer who paid the wages as well as paying for the elaborate items of equipment such as the famous airship. On these grounds, therefore, the public had a right to know what they were getting for their money. It was conceded that military security necessitated a certain amount of secrecy, but it was here that the official case collapsed completely. The visitors were foreigners who not only were not entitled to military secrets, but had no special claim to privileges that were withheld from British nationals. The whole circumstances were rendered more complicated by the side issue of the representative of the *Daily Telegraph* being made an exception and allowed to enter.

Even so, a letter of regret would have done much to smooth things over, but Colonel Capper would not condescend to this. The editor of the *Aldershot News* had sent a letter complaining generally about lack of cooperation and, in reply, Colonel Capper wrote to him on 28 September 1908:

I am of course aware of one instance in which you considered that you had not been properly treated, and that was in connection with the visit of F.A.I., in which case you wrote to the General [Commander-in-Chief, Aldershot] stating that your representative had been debarred entry to the Factory gates, while the representative of the *Daily Telegraph* had been effusively greeted. I sent an explanation, which I hoped had been quite to your satisfaction, that was that no newspaper correspondent as such was admitted on that day, but it was out of my power to prevent any newspaper correspondent, who was entitled as a member of the Aero Club to visit the Factory, from entering.

This, of course, missed the point entirely: the objection was not so much at the *Daily Telegraph* being let in as at the *Aldershot News* being kept out. Clearly Colonel Capper did not want representatives of this or any other newspaper.

* These unsatisfactory relations persisted for several decades, since the mind-your-own-business attitude towards the Press and public was ingrained in the system from Whitehall downwards. It was not until the end of the Second World War that the whole situation was

4   The early flights of *Nulli Secundus II*

24 July 1908

There was plenty of publicity when the completed *Nulli Secundus II* first poked her nose outside her shed on 24 July 1908. The time was shortly after half past five in the evening, and a large crowd had gathered outside the iron railings that separated the Factory proper from the open Common (see Fig. 57).

The day was fine, but no one appears to have taken a barometer reading. The wind was reported to be of strength between eight and twelve miles per hour (13–20 km/hr). The direction of the wind was not put on record, but from what transpired later it is deduced to have been blowing roughly from the south-west. The events which now follow took place in three fairly distinct episodes.

Episode 1

The airship took off from Farnborough Common at approximately 6.0 p.m., with Captain King (Chief Instructor in Ballooning), Captain Carden (Assistant Superintendent of the Balloon Factory), and Lieutenant Westland R.E., on board. Not only was there a dense crowd underneath them, but there was also a complete army encampment with troops undergoing summer training. The impressive scene was captured in a panoramic photograph which is reproduced as Fig. 58.

From the start things went wrong, and differences in recorded evidence are explained to some extent by the tremendous excitement at the time. According to the *R.E.C. Extracts*, the ground-handling crew holding on to the rear ropes got themselves somehow jammed in the crowd and held on too long. In consequence the airship hit the ground with some violence. According to C. M. Waterlow, on the other hand, some of the ropes caught in a marquee and the keel of the airship buckled, though it seems to have miraculously

---

changed through the inspired activity of the Establishment's Director, Sir William Farren, and of his deputy and successor, W. G. Perring. Thereafter the public were treated as partners, if not as employers, and given reasonable access within the bounds of national security and reasonable economy.

straightened itself again. One of the ropes, however, got caught in the port propeller and bent it; but it was taken off and quickly straightened. Seen in retrospect, if there is anything more horrifying than the careless way in which ropes were allowed to become entangled in propellers, it is the casual way in which the bent propellers were hammered straight again.

Episode 2

A second start was made, probably at about 6.10 p.m., the precise time not being recorded. According to *R.E.C. Extracts* a rope caught in a propeller. Waterlow tells a fuller story. The airship did not rise quickly enough, and several ropes that were hanging down failed to clear a clump of trees. The crew of the airship appear to have been as helpless as a fly in a spider's web. The scene was captured by a camera a little later, after she had got clear, and the photograph is reproduced as Fig. 59. The treacherous clump of trees is in the background, and watching it all is S. F. Cody, whose back is seen in the right-hand bottom corner of the picture.

According to Waterlow, the forward rope on the starboard side caught fast in a tree and, swinging backwards, struck the starboard propeller and bent it slightly. The airship eventually broke away and came down on the other side of the trees, and the bent propeller was straightened.

Episode 3

In the meantime a vast crowd had gathered, and the ground-handling crew had some difficulty in holding the people at a safe distance. In Fig. 59 the Royal Engineers are seen to be using a rope as an improvised barrier, but *Nulli Secundus II* is taking to the air again, at 6.20 p.m. approximately.

In accordance with the best practice for an airship trial, *Nulli Secundus II* was flown straight into wind, that is to say, in a south-westerly direction. The photograph reproduced as Fig. 54 was taken a little later just as she was about to pass over the slopes of Farnborough Common.* This is perhaps the best surviving picture of *Nulli Secundus II*, and from the number of bags of ballast still being carried there was plenty of lift that day. Perhaps it would have been better to have jettisoned some of this ballast in order to achieve a quick ascent and get the ropes clear of entanglements. Although none of the ropes caught this time, it is nevertheless incredible that at least eight ropes were allowed to trail along the ground, wriggling hither and thither amongst the crowds of people. Yet so far as is known no person received the slightest injury.

* The sloping terrain in Fig. 54 is believed to be where the terraces were later constructed for the Air Displays of the Society of British Aerospace Companies.

Nulli Secundus II *1908*

Nulli Secundus II turned round at Caesar's Camp, the prominent and historic landmark at the southern end of Long Valley. She came back quickly with the wind, and had practically reached home when the driving belt on the port side came off its pulleys.

For the next part of the story we have Waterlow's own account taken from the actual log of the flight.* As soon as the belt came off, the engine was stopped, and Lieutenant Westland clambered over the outrigger to put it back in place. The airship, however, which had already come down to 400 feet (120 metres) when the belt came off, was descending fairly rapidly owing to release of hydrogen; and before the engine could be restarted the ground was encountered with a bump, fortunately in an open field.

Rebounding upwards, the airship then drifted with the wind, and the stern struck a tree before an effective number of ground-crew could arrive at the scene (see Fig. 60). The starboard rudder was smashed, part of the 'arrow feather' system was damaged, and the silk covering was torn. The photograph reproduced as Fig. 60 shows the smashed starboard rudder; but the rest of the damage, being on the side away from the camera, is not visible. There is to be seen, however, a serious bulge in the bows of the airship, accompanied by distortion of the forward understructure. This could only have been caused by the impact with the ground.

The most disturbing aspect of this incident, however, is the manifestly false account given in the *R.E.C. Extracts*: 'Gas was let out and the balloon was brought down in the field behind the Factory without damage and was towed back.' Throughout the history of *Nulli Secundus I* and *Nulli Secundus II* there are indications of understatement whenever damage to the airship is discussed; but this example goes well beyond the limits of acceptable tolerance for individual variations of opinion.

From this flight the speed of *Nulli Secundus II* was estimated as eighteen miles per hour (29 km/hr). Such an estimate can have little value. According to Waterlow, neither of the two *Nulli Secundus* airships carried an airspeed indicator of any kind, and nothing Colonel Capper ever wrote suggests otherwise. In this particular flight, moreover, not even the total journey was accurately timed. *Nulli Secundus I*, usually considered to have had a speed of about sixteen miles per hour (26 km/hr), was only a little better situated.†

* Waterlow states in his memoirs that a log was kept of the flight trials of *Nulli Secundus II* and that he had access to it.

† The following interview was recorded by the *Daily Chronicle* after the flight round St Paul's on 5 October 1907.

    Question: 'And what was your speed today?'

    Colonel Capper: 'That is mainly guess work, but I should say about fifteen or sixteen miles per hour with no wind.'

Yet Colonel Capper's final report stated positively that the speed of *Nulli Secundus II* showed a considerable increase over *Nulli Secundus I*. The actual words were: 'The method of silk covering over the framework and rigging appears to increase the speed considerably.'

5   The later flights of *Nulli Secundus II*
      August 1908

After the flight of 24 July 1908, the airship was kept in its shed for a few weeks for engine overall and repairs to the damaged structure. According to Waterlow, the car had to be removed entirely for the main structure to be repaired. In the *R.E.C. Extracts*, however, Colonel Capper told a different story: the car was removed because it was too far forward for correct balance and it needed to be suspended further aft. There are no grounds for disbelieving this, but it also provided a convenient explanation for having to remove the car, without prejudicing the official story that no structural damage had been done on the first day out.

Thus it is recorded in the *R.E.C. Extracts*: 'The only change made was the setting of the car further back, and some alteration to the controlling lines.' It would appear that the Royal Engineer Committee were not being told the full story. Possibly Colonel Capper felt vulnerable to criticism for not having used the most experienced crew for the first flight of the new airship. He himself had obviously not realized the extent to which he had impaired Templer's original design by his innovations.

Flight: Friday 14 August 1908
The airship took off between 7.00 p.m. and 7.30 p.m.* Colonel Capper took the helm this time, and had with him Cody and McWade. The time was strangely late, since sunset was at 7.24 p.m. According to the *R.E.C. Extracts* the wind had been blowing earlier at fifteen miles per hour (24 km/hr), and the crew may have been taking advantage of the evening calm. The aeronautical correspondent of the *Automotor Journal* suggested that they may have been trying to avoid the vast crowd that had been such a complication

* *R.E.C. Extracts* give 7.00 p.m. but Waterlow, who is believed to have been quoting the official log, gives 7.30 p.m.

on the previous occasion. If so, they certainly succeeded, since Farnborough people were for once taken by surprise, and there was scarcely anyone there apart from the men on duty.

There was, unfortunately, not much to see. The flight, which consisted of circling around, lasted only for a quarter of an hour. It was hastily terminated when a petrol pipe burst and spewed petrol all over the place; and it was fortunate that the airship did not go up in flames. The engine was stopped promptly, however, and a simple descent made balloon-fashion.

An interesting aspect of this flight was Colonel Capper's comments afterwards about gyroscopic forces interfering with control of the airship. As the airship was turned left or right, the nose of the airship pitched up or down. He attributed this to the gyroscopic action of twin propellers rotating in the same direction, instead of having contra-rotation as on *Nulli Secundus I*. The words actually used in the *R.E.C. Extracts* were:

> Ship behaved well, but the control of the head rudder [forward elevator] was difficult, and the gyroscopic effect was very noticeable in turning, the head mounting or falling very markedly and steering being much harder to one side than the other.

This commentary is absurd: the airship could not possibly turn fast enough to produce such extreme gyroscopic effects on the overall motion of the airship.* The most likely explanation is that there were asymmetric aerodynamic forces acting on a machine that was very unstable in pitch. The various reports, however, do not give enough information for a proper diagnosis. There is no statement, for example, as to the precise relationship between pitching and turning: did the nose tend to go up or down during, say, a left turn?

Flight: Saturday 15 August 1908

The airship went out again with the same crew on the Saturday, starting about noon from Farnborough Common. The weather was squally and provided a very severe test of the now manifestly unstable and almost uncontrollable airship. She pitched and tossed about like some demented creature. Colonel Capper once again complained about his gyroscopic forces, which had now become an obsession with him. Thus he says in the *R.E.C. Extracts*:

> The controls of the head rudder [forward elevator] were bad and the ship pitched very considerably. The gyroscopic action was more violent than before.

The flight did not last long. A water-pipe broke under the severe vibration and the engine had to be stopped. Descent was made by valving the hydro-

---

* It is unlikely that Colonel Capper or anyone else at the Balloon Factory understood the true nature of gyroscopic forces or were able to make the necessary mathematical investigations.

gen balloon-fashion; but when near the ground the airship was struck sideways by a sudden gust of wind. A propeller and the two rudders were damaged, but the crew were unhurt.

According to Waterlow, no entry was made in the log on this occasion. He himself made a note in his diary:

Dirigible came out at 11.15 a.m. for a short run, came down bump and returned to shed.

When the engine was dismantled after this last flight it was found to have run itself almost to death. In the words of the *R.E.C. Extracts* we have:

On examination it was found that the cylinders of the engine had worn so badly that there was no compression. Some of them also leaked, and the crank case was nearly red hot.

The damage could conceivably have been caused by the broken water-pipe. Alternatively, the aeronauts may have been consistently running the engine at too high a power. For reasons not so far discovered, the propellers and transmission system that had done so well in the London flight on 5 October 1907 had been replaced by entirely new designs.

Another possibility is that the engine was suffering from a 'diplomatic' illness. Engine overhaul provided a plausible explanation for keeping the airship inside the shed, which seems to have been the only safe place for her. The envelope was, in fact, deflated permanently on 25 August 1908. As for the engine, this was repaired satisfactorily and then put into 'Cody's aeroplane'.

The story of *Nulli Secundus II* ends with a quotation from the *R.E.C Extracts*, remarkable for its ambiguous naivety:

Owing to other work, the engine was not finished in time to allow of other experiments being made before the end of the year.

This was indeed a tactful way of gently breaking the news that *Nulli Secundus II* would never fly again.

10 Colonel Capper's Baby 1909

I   Planning the future of Farnborough airships
late 1908

The end of *Nulli Secundus II* marked the end of an era for British military airships. The year 1909 was to see many changes. Colonel Capper himself led the revolution by producing an airship that, unlike its predecessors, had a streamline shape and carried a ballonet inside the envelope. Ironically, however, though not without precedent in history, the removal of Colonel Capper himself from the leadership was to become part of the same revolution.

The plan for the future of airship work at the Balloon Factory was prepared by Colonel Capper probably sometime during the summer of 1908. The date is a little indefinite because it matured first in his own mind and then developed in informal discussions with his colleagues at Farnborough and in Whitehall. Eventually, however, it was found convenient to adopt the plan as official War Office Policy. As a plan, it had considerable merit since Colonel Capper was undoubtedly at his best in this no-man's-land of quasi-military, quasi-technical, strategy.

The plan comprehended the construction of three new airships:

1. A re-designed *Nulli Secundus*, which became *Nulli Secundus II*.
2. A new airship with a British car, but with a fabric envelope constructed in France. This became eventually the airship *Gamma*.
3. A small airship to be produced quickly and mainly for research. This became known as *Baby*.

Clarification of this list provides an opportunity for removing once and for all the confusion that has existed in most of the historical records of the early Farnborough airships.

First, there has to be mentioned the inclusion of *Nulli Secundus II*. This is merely an indication of the somewhat retrospective character of the plan as already mentioned. When the plan came to be officially recognized, *Nulli Secundus II* was virtually completed, but her inclusion was clearly essential

234

since she was an integral part of Colonel Capper's original scheme. This airship, it will be noted, had now come to be regarded without question as a re-design, and not as a mere repaired version of *Nulli Secundus I*.

The second airship in the list, which eventually came to be known as *Gamma*, has provided most of the historical difficulties. Owing to her being second in the list she became known officially as *Dirigible No. II*, the presumption being that the original *Nulli Secundus* could be disregarded and the re-designed version (*Nulli Secundus II*) treated as *Dirigible No I*. Unfortunately, however, the name *Dirigible No II* was already being widely used for the airship we now know as *Nulli Secundus II*. Untold misunderstanding has arisen through this dual nomenclature, and it has not been lessened by the fact that when the new airship eventually took to the air she was actually as late as the fifth of the Farnborough airships to be completed.

The anomalous situation was later rectified to some considerable extent by Colonel Capper's successor, Mervyn O'Gorman, who chose Greek letters: Alpha, Beta, Gamma, Delta. *Nulli Secundus* in both versions was to be *Alpha*, but the name did not take root and has practically never been used. The rest followed in order of appearance, the only exception to the rule being airship *Baby*, which was regarded as an immature version of *Beta*. It was this risk of confusion, incidentally, which led to the perpetuation of the name *Nulli Secundus II*, the mild absurdity of which was recognized, especially by the periodical *Punch*, with its humorous remarks about 'Second to none the Second'. Clearly, however, a minor absurdity was preferable to a major misunderstanding.

A good deal of preliminary work was done on the second on the official list – or *Gamma* as we must now call her – during Colonel Capper's term of office as Superintendent, but the main work was done by others later; and she did not fly until late in 1910, about one year after Colonel Capper had ceased to be Superintendent. Airship *Gamma*, therefore, passes out of the present volume.*

Finally, we come to the third on the list: *Baby*. There could hardly have been a more appropriate name; for she was indeed a tiny little thing to have to carry two men. The basic idea was brilliant, however, and one that came to be widely adopted a generation or so later for aeroplanes – to produce something small and cheap both to manufacture and to operate, yet at the

* It might prevent misunderstanding if later events are anticipated in respect of dates: Colonel Capper ceased to be Superintendent of the Balloon Factory on 18 October 1909, but continued as Commandant of the Balloon School until 6 October 1910. The appointment of Mervyn O'Gorman as Superintendent was operative from 19 October 1909, i.e. the day after Colonel Capper surrendered the post.

same time large enough and realistic enough to produce data for later designs that would meet operational needs. She was, moreover, essentially Colonel Capper's airship from start to finish. As Waterlow remarked: 'This ship represented Capper's own ideas in many ways.'

It is appropriate to mention at this stage that the list of projects is taken mainly from the memoirs of Wing Commander Waterlow; and it is a matter for deep regret that this is just about the last thing he dealt with before his tragic death.* A man of acute intelligence, he was becoming increasingly objective and technical as his airship story proceeded. As it is we have to do without him for the story of *Baby*, though grateful to the late Air Commodore E. A. D. Masterman and Lord Ventry for preservation of the earlier testimony.

2 Design and construction of airship *Baby*
Early 1909

Although, like the original *Nulli Secundus*, *Baby* had an envelope made of goldbeater's skin, there were several major differences indicative of a change in design policy. Most noticeable was the new streamline shape, which was intended to be broadly representative of the future designs of Farnborough airships (see Fig. 61).

The principal dimensions of the envelope were:

Length	81 feet	(25 metres)
Maximum width	24 feet	(7·3 metres)
Volume	24,000 cubic feet	(680 cubic metres)

There were nine thicknesses of goldbeater's skin except at the ends, where the number was reduced to seven.

At the rear end of the envelope were two horizontal fins, port and starboard; and in its original form the airship had also a vertical fin above the envelope. These fins were fat and hollow, and blown-up with hydrogen as part of the envelope. The horizontal fins had some additional stiffening to prevent excessive droop, although this varied as different methods of support were tried out experimentally.

Another innovation was an entirely new method of attaching the car.

* See *The Airship*, Vol. 7, No. 3–No. 6, 1948; and also Note 9 of Appendix A to the present History.

236

Previously the connections to the envelope had been through the bands and netting for *Nulli Secundus I*, and through the silk outer cover for *Nulli Secundus II*. In both cases the objective had been to avoid direct attachments to the goldbeater's skin by providing a peripheral harness. Now, for *Baby*, a new technique had been developed for direct connection. A continuous line of loops of silk cord was threaded completely round the envelope, in a horizontal plane somewhat below the central equatorial plane. The lines supporting the car were then attached to these loops by simple toggles. Excessive local stress and risk of tearing in the goldbeater's skin were avoided by dispersing the forces along numerous steel wires embedded between the layers of goldbeater's skin.

Operationally, the most important innovation was the introduction of a ballonet, laid along the inside of the bottom of the envelope. This ballonet would hold three thousand cubic feet (85 cubic metres) of air, which was one eighth of the total volume of the envelope. The air was pumped in by a small fan with a chain drive from the engine.

The controls for hydrogen release followed an obvious pattern. On top of the envelope was a balloon-type valve for manual operation by pull on a line, and this can just be seen in Fig. 62. At the rear end and underneath the envelope was the spring-loaded valve, which released hydrogen automatically if the differential pressure exceeded some prescribed amount. A similar automatic relief valve was provided for the air ballonet, also situated at the bottom of the envelope but more forward and almost directly above the engine.

Simple though these controls appear to be, however, they were to give trouble in flight. This was attributable in principle to there being virtually two separate systems for ensuring the necessary differential pressure for maintaining tautness of the envelope, i.e. the elastically expandable goldbeater's-skin envelope, on the one hand, and the ballonet, on the other. As will be seen, the interaction of these two systems bewildered the operators and produced problems which they were not able to solve.

A silk cover such as that provided for *Nulli Secundus II*, and now no longer required for suspension of the car, was also no longer required for protection of the goldbeater's skin from the rain, for – as mentioned earlier (Chapter 9, Section 2) – it had been discovered that goldbeater's skin would take varnish after all.*

* Wing Commander J. N. Fletcher, who flew both *Beta I* and *Beta II* airships, tells me that Pegamoid varnish was used on these airships as a protection for the goldbeater's skin. He cannot recollect any case of excessive water-absorption by the goldbeater's skin throughout the whole of his long experience.

237

The car was suspended by cables from the silk loops already described, without any intermediate structure. According to Waterlow the original intention had been to use the car of the *Beedle* airship, a private and somewhat unsuccessful design. It was found to be unsuitable, however, and a car had to be designed *ab initio*. As the photograph (Fig. 61) indicates, the car had the appearance of the fuselage of an aeroplane of early vintage. At the rear was a fairly orthodox-looking rudder and elevators projecting on either side of the car. Originally, both rudder and elevators had set-back hinges so as to require only a small effort to move them. There were also two small vertical fins, one above and one below the main car structure, but there were no fixed horizontal planes.

Power was provided in the first instance by two *Buchet* engines connected in line, i.e., co-axially, each being of eight horse-power according to the *R.E.C. Extracts*, although some authorities of the day would have rated them as twelve horse-power. These engines drove a single two-bladed propeller, five feet seven inches (1·7 metres) in diameter.* It was fitted to a shaft situated above the engines. The drive was by a single belt.

The airship could just carry two men when conditions were favourable. The pilot sat in front with the engineer just behind him and in front of the engine.

The new airship was almost completed when Colonel Capper received a remarkable letter from the Director of Fortifications and Works at the War Office, now Colonel Rainsford-Hannay.† The letter, which was dated 26 March 1909, put on record for the Superintendent's benefit the conclusions reached by a special aeronautical sub-committee of the Committee of Imperial Defence.

The main tenor of the sub-committee's conclusions was that airships needed to be developed for both the Navy and the Army. It was considered, in fact, that in the coming estimates for the year 1909/10 the sum of £35,000 should be allocated for a *rigid airship* for the use of the Navy. For the Army, the corresponding estimated requirements were £10,000 for experiments with *non-rigid airships*. Finally, and perhaps most surprisingly, it was firmly recommended that experiments with *aeroplanes* at the Balloon Factory should be abandoned altogether.

These conclusions and recommendations, however, were not quite as

* Colonel Capper appears to have modified his original ideas about gyroscopic forces. A single propeller could not, of course, provide contra-rotation.

† Colonel (temporary Brigadier-General) Frederick Rainsford-Hannay took over from Colonel R. M. Ruck as Director of Fortifications and Works on 1 April 1908.

significant as they might appear to be. The Government subsequently – as governments often are inclined to do – acted just as it thought fit over its airship policy. As for the absurdly sterile policy for aeroplanes, this was soon reversed, mainly as a result of the sensation created when Louis Blériot flew across the English Channel from Calais to Dover on 25 July 1909.

On the whole, the conclusions of the sub-committee, while placing temporarily in jeopardy the Balloon Factory's aeroplane work, would seem to have put Colonel Capper in the strongest possible position for proceeding with new ventures in the airship field.*

3   The flights of *Baby* – an introductory note

1909

The first flights of *Baby* took place in May 1909, but these were only the first stage of a sequence that lasted to the end of the year. The flights were all very much in the nature of pure experiments, with a great variety of control and stabilizing surfaces, and three different types of engine.

There were thirteen flights in all, and they fell naturally into three distinct groups, with the three different types of engine, and several months of separation in time. The overall plan of the tests comprised:

> *1. May Series*
> Engines: two coupled *Buchet* engines of
>   eight horse-power each.†
> Flying dates: 11, 12, 14, 21 and 24 May 1909
>
> *2. August Series*
> Engine: one *R.E.P.* engine of twenty-five
>   horse-power.
> Flying dates: 5 (twice), 10, 13 and
>   16 August 1909
>
> *3. November–December Series*
> Engine: one *Green* engine of thirty-five
>   horse-power
> Flying dates: 23 November; 9 and 10 December 1909.

* The deliberations of the Committee of Imperial Defence and its special aeronautical sub-committee are discussed more fully in Vol. II of the present History.
† As already described in Section 2 of the present chapter.

The thirteen tests were all reported in the *R.E.C. Extracts* (year 1909, Part II, Appendix II), but the reports are in several respects incomplete. There is, however, a limited amount of further information in the Press records and other sources.

For reasons never fully explained, there was some emphasis on secrecy. One consequence of this policy was a tendency to carry out the tests in the early morning, starting perhaps even before the dawn. There were then few people about. The policy was not, however, particularly successful. The paper *Aeronautics* gave quite a lucid description of the original airship, with photographs, in June (1909); and the firm of Gale and Polden published a photograph on a postcard similar to Fig. 61.* Later, the Press showed a declining enthusiasm as interest was transferred from airships to aeroplanes, and there was little need for secrecy.

In all the flights, it is believed, there was a crew of two – a pilot and an engineer – and in most cases this is specifically stated in the *R.E.C. Extracts*. Colonel Capper is taken to be the pilot on all occasions and to be reporting directly on his personal experience. The name of the engineer is not on record but there are indications that, in some flights at least, he was F. McWade, the Works Manager.

Cody had now disappeared from the airship scene having, for all practical purposes, left the Balloon Factory and the Balloon School, and taken to flying his aeroplane on Laffan's Plain. So far as can be judged he was sorely missed: engines were almost invariably unreliable in those days, but Cody seems to have been able to work wonders by way of keeping them going.

In contrast to the disappointing work on the engines of *Baby*, there was superb work on the goldbeater's-skin envelope, and on fabrics and cordage generally. In this respect the best traditions and standards of the Balloon Factory were maintained. As will be seen, however, the tests revealed serious faults in design for both stability and control; and underlying all the troubles was major weakness in the understanding of basic principles.

* I have one of these postcards presented by one of my many contributors. It had gone through the post and the cancellation stamp reads: 'South Farnborough, 31 May 1909.'

48 *top. Nulli Secundus I* in her final form.
The control and stabilizing surfaces of the airship were drastically altered after the
first day out. She is seen here with three men on board on 3 October 1907

49 *bottom.* The first flight of *Nulli Secundus I*, on the morning of 10 September 1907
with three men on board. She had been fitted with wings amidships that could be
raised or lowered, but these were removed permanently after the first flight

50 *above*. The flight round St Paul's Cathedral.

Vast crowds saw an airship for the first time in their lives when *Nulli Secundus I* made a tour of London on Saturday, 5 October 1907, circumnavigating the dome of St Paul's at 12.20 p.m.

51 *left*. *Nulli Secundus I* reconnoitres the Crystal Palace for a landing. Defeated by adverse winds on the way home after his successful journey to London, Colonel Capper decides to land in the grounds of the Crystal Palace

52 *facing top*. The airship in the rain at the Crystal Palace. After her famous flight to London the tethered *Nulli Secundus I* was a great attraction to thousands of sightseers. As the umbrellas show, the steady rain could not keep them away

53 *facing bottom*. The end of *Nulli Secundus I*.

Early on the morning of Thursday, 10 October 1907, the airship became uneasy at her moorings as she was rocked by a gentle breeze. Then the wind increased in strength, and the end came when the airship had to be literally stabbed to death to prevent her escaping altogether

54 *facing (top)*. *Nulli Secundus II* over Farnborough Common on 24 July 1908.
The new airship, a re-designed version of her predecessor *Nulli Secundus I*, is here seen
on her first day out on the way to Caesar's Camp. She has just succeeded in taking off
at the third attempt

55 *facing bottom. An unusual view of* Nulli Secundus II.
This photograph brings out several features in the new airship not possessed by
her predecessor: the powerful front elevator, the 'arrow feathers' at the back, and
the boat-shaped understructure

56 *top left*. Engine and propellers of *Nulli Secundus II*.
Here are to be seen the fat paddle-blades of the propellers, and the heavy single
driving belts on each side, this time without any crossing for contra-rotation. The
'spike' pyramidal landing structure underneath is also clearly revealed

57 *top right*. The *debut* of *Nulli Secundus II* on 24 July 1908

58 *bottom. Nulli Secundus II* over the Army encampment (24 July 1908).
On the first attempt at taking off, a rope was said to have become entangled with
one of the tents

59 *facing top. Nulli Secundus II* tries again for the third time.
On the second attempt at taking off *Nulli Secundus II* was snared by a
clump of trees in which her ropes became entangled. In this picture she has just been
released and is making her third attempt at taking off, this time
successfully (see Fig. 54)

60 *facing bottom.* The injured *Nulli Secundus II.*
The first day's adventures end after the airship has descended with a
heavy bump on her nose; and is then blown hard into the branches of a tree where
further damage is done. The picture shows the injured bows and the wrecked
starboard rudder

61 *above (top). Baby* takes to the air in May 1909.
This tiny airship was the first to have a ballonet as well as a flexible envelope of
goldbeater's skin

62 *above (bottom). Baby* with a sail-fin (May 1909).
The airship was usually almost impossible to steer along a straight course, but
performed best with a fin spread out like a sail at the rear

63 *top*. An early experiment with *Baby* (May 1909). Various arrangements of rudder, fins and elevators were tried in the May tests. The illustration shows the new rudder hinged on its front edge, and the elevators situated amidships

64 *centre*. A later experiment with *Baby* (November 1909).
In the later flight trials of *Baby* still more drastic changes were made, including new types of engine and fantastic arrangements of control surfaces. Note the absence of a vertical fin above the envelope and the presence of the large sail-fin below

65 *bottom*. *Baby* grows up! A real transformation. After the last disappointing flights in December 1909, *Baby* was lengthened and by other drastic alterations turned into one of the most successful of all non-rigid airships – *Beta I*

4   The May flights

May 1909

When *Baby* went out for her first flight on Tuesday 11 May 1909 she was in the condition already described (Section 2 of the present chapter) and as illustrated in Fig. 61. There was, however, an engineer on board as well as the pilot. He sat just behind the pilot and just in front of the two eight horse-power *Buchet* engines. The airship had previously been out on Saturday 4 May 1909 to test buoyancy and overall trim or, in the words of the then new periodical *Flight* (8 May 1909), 'to be given an airing'. According to *Aeronautics* (June 1909) there had been two or three such appearances out-of-doors early in May, one of which had been witnessed by the Prince of Wales.* None of these preliminary ventures amounted to flights, and they were not officially reported.

On 11 May, however, more serious business was intended. The indications are that *Baby* went out at dawn with the air very calm and the temperature just above freezing. Not much flying was done, for the steering was found to be very bad. Colonel Capper attributed this to the trail rope being on the ground.

After this disappointing flight, a most important modification was made. A vertical fin made of a silk sheet was stretched like a sail from the envelope to the rear end of the car, as illustrated in Fig. 62.† This seems to have cured completely all the steering troubles, as was revealed in the next flight on Wednesday 12 May 1909. On this day, weather conditions were much the same as before – calm and cold. The airship was steady enough in pitch, but would not respond to the elevators when the pilot wanted to put the nose up or down.

For the next flight, which took place on Friday 14 May 1909, the elevators were brought forward to a middle position on the car in the hope that this would improve control in pitch. The reasoning behind this change is not understood since in this position the elevators would be almost completely

* Later King George V.
† This illustration is to some extent artificial but it conforms in essentials to one published in *The Aero* for August 1909, and also to others that are too imperfect for successful reproduction.

ineffective, having virtually no tilting action on the airship. The steering control and stability remained good, but the *R.E.C. Extracts* give no clue as to the resulting control in pitch. Perhaps this was not thoroughly tested, since the engines gave so much trouble that further flying was considered not worth-while.

On the following Tuesday, 18 May 1909, King Edward VII visited the Balloon Factory once again. He was not able to see *Baby* fly, however, probably because the airship was undergoing fairly major alterations; but he was able to watch her being re-inflated.*

When *Baby* flew again on the following Friday, 21 May 1909, some fairly radical changes had been made. The rudder had been reduced in size; and the hinge moved to the front edge, which must have rendered it more difficult for the pilot to operate. In addition, the lower vertical fin at the rear end of the car had been removed. Finally, the sail-fin that had previously been suspended between the envelope and the rear of the car had also been taken away. These changes are illustrated in Fig. 63, which is taken from the actual report in the *R.E.C. Extracts.*

So many changes being made at the same time rendered it impossible to judge the individual effects of each, and transgressed an obvious and fundamental rule of scientific experiment. Furthermore, removal of the sail-fin was in itself a retrograde step, since the earlier tests had established that the sail-fin was ensuring reasonable steering control and directional stability. As things turned out, *Baby*, bereft of so much vertical fin-power in the rear, would not even fly straight, and gyrated over Farnborough and Cove Commons like a drunken man.

What seems to have happened next in this flight when a descent was negotiated is so incredible that a reader may well doubt the interpretation placed upon the *R.E.C. Extracts*: yet the circumstantial evidence is too substantial for doubts to survive. An attempt was made to descend from a height of about five hundred feet (150 metres) by pumping air into the ballonet in order to force hydrogen out of the automatic release valve.

What should be expected in such circumstances can readily be worked out. The automatic valve was spring-operated and until the prescribed differential pressure was reached no hydrogen would be released. As the pressure was increased beyond this value the valve would begin to open, but only a little at first, and an appreciable increase of pressure would be necessary to produce a noticeable effect in reasonable time for control of the airship's descent. The extra pressure however, would inevitably be accompanied by

* See *The Graphic,* 22 May 1909.

expansion of the goldbeater's-skin envelope. In consequence, if the extra pressure in the hydrogen was produced by pumping air into the ballonet then a considerable proportion of the effort expended – perhaps as low as four-fifths, perhaps as high as nine-tenths – would be used merely in blowing out the expandable envelope. The effect would be an apparent absence of response initially, with a noticeably delayed response later. In such circumstances an attempt would in all likelihood be made to continue and, if possible, to intensify, the pumping of air into the ballonet. Benefit would seem thereby to be obtained but, as will be seen, only at the price of more serious trouble later.

With this argument in mind there is no surprise when we read in the *R.E.C. Extracts*:

Apparently she would not come down at all, so had to let a good deal of gas out of the automatic valve and worked the fan to pump air into the ballonet.

So far we have been considering only what may be regarded as the first stage in a rather complicated phenomenon, with consequences no more serious than delay in initiating descent. With the second stage, however, serious trouble is liable to occur in a way that is predictable. When the desired state of equilibrium or rate of descent has been reached, pumping of air into the ballonet will naturally be stopped, but hydrogen-release will still continue for an appreciable time, automatically. The stretched envelope contracts in its own time and of its own accord; and eventually subsides like the final wail of a bagpipe when the piper has stopped blowing, though in the case of the airship the process will end when the prescribed pressure for closing the automatic valve is reached. The overall effect, of course, is an unwanted descent of increasing rapidity unless this can be arrested by discharge of ballast.

We now pass again to the reality as reported in the *R.E.C. Extracts*. Unfortunately, at the critical stage of descent-control a situation even more critical developed. The petrol tank suddenly began to leak and petrol poured over the hot exhaust pipes, so that the engine had to be stopped instantly. This did not affect the almost uncontrolled descent as already predicted, however, for we read:

As soon as the engine stopped the balloon began to descend rapidly and all available ballast was thrown overboard.

It has already been suggested that the trials of both versions of *Nulli Secundus* indicated that neither Colonel Capper nor his men understood the basic principles of the expandable envelope. This being so, it is not surprising that the introduction of the ballonet led to interactions that completely bewildered them.*

The last flight of the May series, made on Monday 24 May 1909, was very much a repetition of the previous flight, though without the petrol leakage. The airship was towed to the middle of Cove Common, and although a height of eight hundred feet (250 metres) was reached she would not pursue a straight course.

The same trouble was experienced as before in initiating descent, despite help from the engine. Thus the *R.E.C. Extracts* read:

> The engines were kept going and the planes depressed in order to bring the balloon down on Laffan's Plain. At the same time gas was let out of the Mallet [automatic] valve and air was pumped into the ballonet, but this had little effect. The balloon was checked from rising but could not be brought down.

Later, it is stated, an excessive rate of descent occurred and had to be arrested by throwing out ballast. This was only partially successful, however, and *Baby* landed with a bump on Laffan's Plain, one of the skids under the car being damaged. The airship was then blown against a tree before the ground-handling party could reach the scene. Tubes of hydrogen had to be sent for in order to replenish what had been lost, and then *Baby* was ignominiously towed back home by man-power.

5   The Advisory Committee for Aeronautics
     and The National Physical Laboratory

     Mid-1909

After the tests in May 1909, no further flying took place until the following August. Much of the time was spent in re-design and new construction yet to be described, but meanwhile there are events to be considered for this interim period that have an even wider scientific import.

* Despite the apparent incompatibility of expandable goldbeater's-skin and use of a ballonet, proper buoyancy control was possible. It was necessary to have a drill, however, based upon an understanding of the underlying scientific principles, without which chaos could result. The later airship *Beta I*, and her successor *Beta II*, had goldbeater's-skin envelopes as well as ballonets, yet both gave remarkably good service. For this much credit should go to Mervyn O'Gorman, Colonel Capper's successor as Superintendent.

On 5 July 1909 history was made when the Balloon Factory was visited by the recently created Advisory Committee for Aeronautics. From letters exchanged between the Secretary of the Committee, F. J. Selby, and Colonel Capper the whole affair was most successful. Precisely what the Committee saw is not on record and is not important. Significance lies in the vital part the Committee was to play in the future of British aeronautics, and in the fact that contact with the Balloon Factory was regarded as one of its first duties.*

It was on 30 April 1909 that a letter was sent out from 10 Downing Street, the home of Prime Minister H. H. Asquith, addressed to several leading scientists. The letter proposed that a committee of scientists should be formed to advise the government on aeronautical matters. Action followed immediately with the creation of a committee under Lord Rayleigh, comprising:

> Lord Rayleigh (President)
> Mr Horace Darwin
> Dr R. T. Glazebrook
> Sir A. G. Greenhill
> Mr F. W. Lanchester
> Mr H. R. A. Mallock
> Prof. J. E. Petavel
> Dr W. N. Shaw
> Captain R. H. Bacon R.N.
> Major-General Sir Charles F. Hadden
> Mr F. J. Selby (Secretary)

The appointment of Lord Rayleigh as President gave the new Committee a status in the scientific world that could scarcely have been attained in any other way. He was recognized throughout the world as one of the greatest mathematical and experimental physicists, and one of the most successful in the way of original achievement.†

Lord Rayleigh had on his committee a representative of the Navy in the

* The *Advisory Committee for Aeronautics* became the *Aeronautical Research Committee* in 1920, when Mr. J. L. Nayler was made Secretary; and it is to him that I am indebted for much of the information on the early history of the original body. In 1945 the Committee became the *Aeronautical Research Council* with control over subordinate committees in the now many specialized branches of aeronautical activity.

† Lord Rayleigh (1842–1919), 3rd Baron, received many distinctions, which included the Order of Merit and the Nobel Prize for Physics. He was Professor of Experimental Physics at Cambridge from 1879 to 1884, and became Secretary and President of the Royal Society. With Sir William Ramsay he shared the credit for the discovery in the atmosphere of the previously unknown element, argon.

person of Captain R. H. Bacon R.N.,* Director of Naval Ordnance and Torpedoes at the Admiralty; and a representative of the Army in Major-General Sir Charles Hadden, Master-General of the Ordnance at the War Office. The secretary, F. J. Selby, was also Secretary of the National Physical Laboratory at Teddington.

The rest of the list contains several great names in science and aeronautics, but for the immediate purpose it is sufficient to consider only Dr Glazebrook,† though later F. W. Lanchester also comes up for special consideration. At that time Dr Glazebrook, who was a very active member of the Committee, was Director of the National Physical Laboratory at Teddington. It is in this context that he again enters R.A.E. history, for it was the N.P.L. – to use the well-established abbreviation for the National Physical Laboratory – that carried out tests on airship models for the Balloon Factory.

Some correspondence has survived, among the few Balloon Factory papers for this period, between Colonel Capper and Dr Glazebrook; and there is also some between Captain A. D. Carden, Assistant-Superintendent of the Balloon Factory, and Thomas Stanton, who was in charge of aerodynamic work at the N.P.L.‡ Airship models were sent by the Balloon Factory to the N.P.L. for testing in the Laboratory's special water channel.

This water channel was twelve inches (30 cm) wide and seven inches (18 cm) deep, and the water flowed along at a speed between one and two feet per second (30–60 cm/sec). The airship models were suitably suspended in the flowing water, and the forces upon them were measured. The Balloon Factory's airship models were about six inches (15 cm) long and made of vulcanite. As a general rule they were fabricated in the Balloon Factory's own workshops. Despite the relative crudeness and simplicity of the apparatus it gave useful *comparative* figures for resistance to motion in an age when aerodynamic data were very difficult to obtain. The main objections were the small scale and low speed, but the use of water instead of air partly compensated for these limitations.

Most of the models took general forms, as though part of an investigation

---

* Later, Admiral Sir Reginald Bacon. He has already appeared in this History in connection with Cody kites: see Chapter 6, Section 6.

† R. T. Glazebrook (1854–1935), who later became Sir Richard Glazebrook, was another distinguished mathematician and physicist. He was Director of the National Physical Laboratory from 1899 to 1919, and Professor of Aviation at the Imperial College, London, from 1920 to 1923. He became Chairman of the Advisory Committee for Aeronautics, under Lord Rayleigh's Presidency, in 1912. When Lord Rayleight died in 1919, the post of President was abandoned and Sir Richard became titular Head, and he continued as Chairman until 1933.

‡ Thomas Stanton (1865–1931) later became Superintendent of the Engineering Department at the National Physical Laboratory. He received a knighthood in 1928.

in search of the best design. This was probably in anticipation of the proposed new airship officially known as *Dirigible No. II*, and now known as *Gamma*. In all likelihood it was getting rather too late to do very much for *Baby*, though at least one model of this airship is mentioned in surviving correspondence. Only determination of resistance was called for in the first instance, but later some help was requested in the field of stability. In a letter to Dr Glazebrook, dated 9 July 1909, Colonel Capper wrote: 'I do not know if you could also obtain information about stability.'

It is doubtful whether anything of immediate value came of this request, at least so far as regards *Baby*, but the approach led to some interesting comment by Colonel Capper on his practical experience with *Baby*. It would appear that Colonel Capper now realized that the only occasion when he had achieved proper steering control and stability was when he had the sail-like fin at the back. Thus he wrote to Dr Glazebrook on 5 August 1909:

> From experiments we have made with the 'Baby' balloon I am rather of the opinion that it will not be necessary to put stabilizators [sic] either on top or bottom, but it will be necessary to put a plane, which may take the form of a simple stretched sail, as a sort of keel aft of the centre line.

As things turned out, the actual work done on model airships in 1909 was less important than the creation of a working relationship between the two Establishments: the one concerned almost exclusively with aeronautics; the other also concerned, but only as part of the wider scientific field. Possibly the outcome of the liaison was not quite what Colonel Capper intended. Access to the scientific knowledge of the N.P.L. was indeed precious, but it could never be a substitute for scientific knowledge inside the Balloon Factory itself. This was a matter, however, soon to be put right, as discussed a little later in this History, and at this stage there only remains to be recorded – what many people already know – that the association between the Royal Aircraft Establishment (under its various names) and the National Physical Laboratory has continued to the present day.

6   The August flights

August 1909

We now return to *Baby*'s flying activities. It is August (1909), and in the two or three months that have elapsed since the May flights some drastic alterations have been made to the airship. Conspicuous among these is the new engine, the *R.E.P.* of twenty-five horse-power.* In the May tests the two *Buchet* engines had continuously given trouble, though how much was attributable to intrinsic defects in the engines and how much to inadequate care and maintenance is uncertain since, as will be seen, the new single engine gave even more trouble than the two original ones.

With the new engine came an entirely different method of installation. Two propellers were used with shafts on port and starboard outriggers, arranged on much the same lines as previously for *Nulli Secundus*. The propellers were driven by chains, however, one being crossed to give contra-rotation.

A change in the entire seating arrangements appears to have accompanied the changes in the engine system. The engineer sat just behind his engine, which does not seem inappropriate; but for some unexplained though not necessarily insubstantial reason the pilot – or steerer as he was usually called – was placed behind the engineer.

Several changes had been made to the control and stabilizing system. For reasons not at all clear, the blown-up vertical fin on top of the envelope had been removed, as illustrated for the later November version in Fig. 64. A sail-fin, however, was now fitted once again between the underside of the envelope and the rear end of the car. This was to have been expected after the May flights and Capper's conclusion that such a device was necessary for steering control and stability. Unfortunately photographs have not survived for the August flights, but the sail-fin was more likely to have been similar to that shown for the November-December flights in Fig. 64, than to the smaller version for the May flights illustrated in Fig. 62.

A minor change was removal of all silk covering from the car structure, although no reasons are given for this. More significant was the installation of the elevators in the front of the car. Colonel Capper, it will be remembered, had always been in favour of a forward elevator system, which he regarded as a more effective method of controlling pitch.

In this condition the August version of *Baby* began her most depressing flight career. On Thursday 5 August 1909 she first took off, with the air warm and still. Just enough flying was done to establish that steering control and stability were satisfactory, but nothing would induce *Baby* to raise her bows and climb. Thus the *R.E.C. Extracts* record:

Directly the propellers started the balloon dipped. She steered well and went with a fair pace, but could not be induced to rise. Only in the air a few minutes.

* R.E.P. are the initials of the French aviation pioneer Robert Esnault-Pelterie who produced this engine.

The pilot's seat was moved further back with a view to altering the trim of the airship and raising the nose, and a second flight made the same day. But *Baby* still refused to climb!

The horizontal blown-up fins on the airship envelope were thereupon fitted with bracing wires, attached to the top of the envelope. This was done in case the climbing difficulty had been caused by the fins drooping excessively, or in other ways distorting. The flight which followed this change, made on Tuesday 10 August 1909, did actually show some improvement, and three runs of about three miles (5 km) each were accomplished. Unfortunately, the basic performance of the airship could not be assessed owing to continuous mal-functioning of the engine, and the test was terminated summarily when the engine stopped altogether.

The two final tests made on Friday 13 August 1909 and on Monday 16 August were exceptionally brief. On the first of these two days the airship had scarcely got into the air when the engine seized and rendered further flying impossible. On the second of these two days, conditions were a little better, but the engine gave trouble throughout the flight. The only outcome was a decision to try another type of engine, and not to fly again until it had been installed.

7   *Baby's* last flights

November–December 1909

In order to complete the story of *Baby*'s flights we have to depart a little from strict chronology of important events. It is now November and since the August flying there have been important changes in the organization of the Balloon Factory. Colonel Capper is no longer Superintendent, but has been replaced by Mervyn O'Gorman – a story that is told in the Epilogue to this Volume.

Colonel Capper did indeed continue to fly airships for some time after he had left the Balloon Factory, but normally in the capacity of master test-pilot and Commandant of the Balloon School. It was scarcely in these more restricted roles, however, that the last flights of *Baby* were undertaken by him, but rather as a carry-over from the previous regime, and as completion of a task already far advanced and near its end.

The old and the new superintendents were never at loggerheads, and the changeover was by all accounts effected reasonably and smoothly. It is a reasonable assumption, therefore, that the new superintendent encouraged Colonel Capper to finish the work he had begun, and to bring the final tests of *Baby* to a conclusion on lines that had already been planned, without intervention on his part.

Accounts of the flights in November and December of the year 1909 are to be found in the *R.E.C. Extracts*, but there seem to be only traces elsewhere. Even the early historians such as Lieutenant Crosson* and Observer Officer Insoll seem to have been unaware that *Baby* ever existed in her final form with a *Green* engine installed, although this engine is remarked upon by them later when *Baby* had been converted into the later airship known as *Beta I*. The *R.A.E. Chronicles*, however, do mention the *Green* engine, though vaguely under the year 1909, with no precise date:

An order was placed with Astra Engineering Company for a 'Green' engine to replace the Esnault-Pelterie [i.e. *R.E.P.*] in 'Baby'. The new motor was guaranteed to develop 35 H.P. with weight not exceeding 8 lb per brake horse-power.

Unfortunately, there is no further reference in the *Chronicles* to the *Green* engine being installed nor, in fact, any further reference to *Baby* at all.

The dearth of information about these last flights is probably attributable less to intentional secrecy than to declining interest and counter attractions. Inside the Balloon Factory there had just been the revolutionary change of superintendents and all that this entailed. In the country at large, aeroplanes were now completely in the news. Since the August flights of *Baby* there had been the most sensational aviation meeting ever experienced – at Reims on 22–29 August 1909 – and this followed close upon Louis Blériot's Channel crossing on 25 July 1909. Perhaps even more significant from the British standpoint was the growing trend towards holding aeroplane exhibitions and competitions in Britain, such as the Doncaster Aviation Meeting held on 15–23 October 1909.

In the circumstances, it is unfortunate that the *R.E.C. Extracts* give for the last three flights of *Baby* little more than a collection of rough and random notes,† although a photograph, reproduced here as Fig. 64, gives

* Previously referred to as Mr Percy E. Crosson. It was, however, as a temporary Lieutenant of the First World War that he made his original *written* contribution to airship history. See Note 7 of Appendix A. Observer Officer Insoll is also discussed in Note 8 of the same appendix.
† It is remarkable, however, how much can be deduced from a seemingly casual or irrelevant remark. Thus for the test on 21 December 1909 it is stated that 'the crossed chain broke and a new link had to be put in.' This, however, is the first intimation we are given, not only that one chain was crossed – to produce contra-rotation – but also that there was a chain-drive at all.

some idea of the appearance of the airship in its new form. The car has clearly been altered since August, and most conspicuous are the seemingly absurdly large fin and rudder at the back of the car. There is also an enlarged version of the earlier sail-fin stretched between the envelope and the rudder post. As in the August tests there is no vertical fin on top of the envelope, and the car skeleton structure is still uncovered.

In many ways, however, the most significant change was the new engine – the thirty-five horse-power *Green*. This gave nominally ten horse-power more than the previous *R.E.P.* engine; and the difference may have been even greater, since the *Green* engine had a better reputation for achieving what was claimed for it than the *R.E.P.* had. There was the further advantage that the *Green* engine was of British design and manufacture, a most important consideration in a British military aircraft. Above all – at least so far as tests with *Baby* were concerned – the *Green* engine seems to have been reasonably reliable, which is more than can be said of either the *R.E.P.* or the two *Buchets.**

The installation of the *Green* engine followed much the same pattern as the previous *R.E.P.* engine. Twin outrigger propellers were chain driven, with one chain crossed to give contra-rotation. There was, however, one unusual feature that is difficult to explain: the propellers were geared down to run at roughly two-thirds engine speed but the precise speeds were slightly different from each other.

The first flight, on Tuesday 23 November 1909, produced minor troubles. Some front handling ropes that were supposed to be held by clips broke loose and fouled a propeller. In addition, there was trouble with the fan that was used to blow up the ballonet. The driving chain coupling it to the engine came off, and it was not possible to put it back again during the flight. In consequence the crew decided to be content with a short flight.

Steering was again reported as being difficult, and in the account given there is a strong suspicion of some directional instability. In the *R.E.C. Extracts*, however, it is naïvely suggested that the steering difficulties were probably caused by the propellers revolving at different speeds. No reason is given why they were designed to do so!

---

* Gustavus Green (1865–1964) was the first successful aero-engine designer in Great Britain, and in course of time his Company built several designs covering a wide range of power. In 1912 a sixty horse-power Green engine won the British Government's aero-engine competition. Despite their relative success, however, the Green engines were often adversely criticized for aeronautical work, and probably did best at propelling Royal Navy motor boats. Gustavus Green was made an Honorary Companion of the Royal Aeronautical Society in 1959. He died within less than three months of his century.

The elevators were now at the front end of the car and appear to have been reasonably effective. It was reported, however, that there was a pronounced tendency for the nose of the airship to rise unduly.

In view of what had happened on some of the previous flights, the final descent achieved by hydrogen release is especially interesting. It was clearly no longer possible to make the mistake of forcing hydrogen out of the automatic relief valve by pumping up the ballonet, since the ballonet was not operative owing to the fan driving-belt having come off. Instead, hydrogen was released by the manually-controlled valve at the top of the airship. Descent seems to have been made in good order, but there was insufficient differential pressure entirely to compensate for the hydrogen loss, and the envelope became rather flabby.

For the second flight, made on Thursday 9 December 1909, wooden propellers were fitted for the first time ever on a Farnborough airship. If properly designed they should have produced a worth-while improvement in propulsive efficiency equivalent to an increase in engine power, but regrettably there is no information on how they were made or how they came to be used.

The top bracing wires for the horizontal blown-up fins on the envelope were removed for this flight, so that the fins drooped slightly. In addition some of the vertical fin area was removed, but it is not clear exactly what this was.

In flight, the airship rose to a considerable height, but *Baby* was very unstable and almost uncontrollable. For the first time it is suggested in the *R.E.C. Extracts* that the envelope was too short and stumpy.

The final descent is again of special interest. The hydrogen release was accomplished – this time intentionally – by direct operation of the manually-operated valve, and not by forcing hydrogen through the automatic valve. It seems likely that this technique was first thought of as a result of the previous flight when the ballonet could not be used at all. The description of what happened is far from clear, probably because no one really knew, but there is one remark that seems significant: 'Had to valve to come down. The ballonet does not compensate for loss of gas in valving.'

This is clearly a case of the old misunderstanding in another form. The ballonet was now being used simply to restore pressure lost as hydrogen was forced out through the open valve by the elasticity of the contracting envelope. It does not appear to have been realized how rapid and effective this 'elastic' method of hydrogen release really was, or that hydrogen could be discharged much faster than air could be pumped into the ballonet for compensation.

The last flight, made on Tuesday 21 December 1909, was completely unsuccessful. First of all the crossed chain broke and a new link had to be fitted. The airship then ascended gently to about one hundred feet (30 metres). The engine was then speeded up, whereupon the airship dived fiercely. She hit the ground with some violence and the structure of the car was damaged. She then rose even more fiercely on the rebound, tearing out the grapnel which had been hastily thrown out and had held on to something. Descent was eventually achieved by release of hydrogen.

The probable cause of this misadventure was the removal of all the external supporting wires for the horizontal fins on the envelope, and relying entirely on the internal bracing by canes. Examination showed that the starboard fin had partly broken away from the envelope, and had distorted in a way that rendered the airship dangerously uncontrollable when proceeding under engine power.

This was the end: so far as records go the airship never flew again in the form known as *Baby*.

Colonel Capper's last recommendation when handing *Baby* over to his successor was that she should be lengthened by insertion of a cylindrical portion of envelope amidships. This was readily agreed by the new Superintendent, and a length of about twenty-four feet was in due course inserted. Many other alterations were made to produce the new airship *Beta I*. The hollow blown-up fins at the rear of the envelope were replaced by large and more efficient thin ones; and behind the large vertical fin was installed a powerful rudder, to produce a really effective steering device. Adequate control in pitch was ensured by forward elevators, placed well forward on a lengthened control car. Finally, the engine performance was greatly improved by experienced men, and the ancillaries such as pipe lines, transmission belts, cooling systems and fuel tanks were rendered infinitely more reliable.

Beta I, shown in Fig. 65, was one of the most successful airships of her day and age, and she did useful work in military manoeuvres for several years. She was always recognizable by what looked like a bandage amidships, this being, of course, the extension piece by which she grew out of *Baby*.

Epilogue

The New Dawn 1909–10

Re-organization of the Balloon Factory became almost a foregone conclusion with the creation of the Advisory Committee of Aeronautics under Lord Rayleigh. At that time, the Balloon Factory must have been the Committee's main concern. To Lord Rayleigh, to Dr Glazebrook and, indeed, to all the scientific members of the Committee, reconstitution of the Balloon Factory on more scientific lines must have appeared a prime necessity.

There was, however, another brain behind the changes that took place – that of R. B. Haldane, the Secretary of State for War. Naturally, he was responsible for all the overt action necessary to reform the old Balloon Factory; but to understand all that took place it is necessary to probe deeper than this and reflect upon Haldane the scholar and thinker. Haldane has been described as a statesman, lawyer and philosopher, and he was undoubtedly one of the most brilliant men who ever became a member of a British Government; and as a Secretary of State for War he was unique. Intellectually, therefore, he could parley on equal terms with Lord Rayleigh and the rest of the Advisory team. He would not, of course, have claimed to be a scientist, but as a man fully-qualified in philosophy he came much nearer to being one than most intellectuals, and his mathematics was exceptional.*

Haldane's actions behind the scenes may never be known with certainty, since there were too many things against their going on record. He was a politician, and one who in his Parliamentary statements often carried discretion to the point of meaningless obscurity. Had he shown, in fact, less of

* Richard Burdon Haldane (1856–1928) was created Viscount Haldane in 1911. He was educated at Edinburgh and Göttingen Universities, and among a host of academic distinctions was Fellowship of the Royal Society. He served as Secretary of State for War from 1905 to 1912, when he became Lord Chancellor. An authority on pre-war Germany before 1914, he came to be regarded – quite wrongly – as pro-German, and acquired much undeserved unpopularity. King George V, however, who would not accept the conventional view, awarded him the Order of Merit.

254

the caution of the lawyer and more of the outspokenness of a philosopher he might have achieved more, not only for British aeronautics, but also for his own political career as well.

It has to be remembered, moreover, that officially he was head of the British Army, but no more. The Advisory Committee for Aeronautics was a national institution, and so whatever he did to sponsor it in a quiet way behind the scenes, he could not afford to prejudice its all-embracing interest: its concern with aeronautical science in the universities, with enterprise in industry and, so far as the Services were concerned, with the Navy as much as with the Army.

The official actions of Haldane as Secretary of State for War are, of course, all on record, and the foregoing remarks are merely to remind ourselves that, where the Balloon Factory was concerned, these actions were almost certainly the product of deep thought and of consultation with men like Lord Rayleigh. The single action that inaugurated the revolution in Balloon Factory affairs was the appointment, on 19 October 1909, of Mervyn O'Gorman to be Superintendent of the Balloon Factory, and to make him directly responsible to the Master-General of Ordnance at the War Office.*

Mervyn Joseph Pius O'Gorman (1871–1958) was at the time of his appointment a consulting engineer in London, and working mainly in the field of automobile engineering. He was a professional engineer with a good scientific and general educational background. In three years at University College, Dublin (1900–1902), he had obtained qualifications in French and Engineering. He had then spent two years at the City and Guilds Institute, London, for which he received a diploma in Engineering and Physics. This was followed by work in the engineering industry in both France and Britain.

At the time of his appointment, O'Gorman was doing quite well as a consulting engineer. He was, moreover, a prolific and useful writer, with a colloquial style that appealed to practical engineers. Curiously, although his appointment was for seven years, it was initially for only three days per week. It is not clear whether this was a case of War Office economy or a desire on the part of Haldane that the new Superintendent should maintain his valuable engineering contacts with the world at large. Later, the number of days was increased, and eventually the appointment became a full-time one.

O'Gorman was what would now be described as an 'engineer-scientist', and on this ground alone his appointment had a revolutionary effect upon the

* Then Major-General Sir Charles F. Hadden, a member of the Army Council and, as already mentioned, a member of the Advisory Committee for Aeronautics. He was a man for whom the new Superintendent came to have the highest respect.

previously military-controlled Balloon Factory. O'Gorman, however, had two other qualities: abounding energy and a gift for choosing good men and gaining their loyalty. His energy was essential to produce the necessary changes quickly, but it is his choice of men that has left a permanent mark on British aeronautical history.

His first concern was to select a Chief Engineer, and in this he sought the aid of F. W. Lanchester who was, it will be remembered, a founder-member of Lord Rayleigh's Committee.* By posterity Lanchester has come to be permanently acclaimed for his contributions to aeronautical theory and other erudite scientific accomplishments, but at the time in question he was a most distinguished practical engineer, working mainly in the automobile field. He is said to have made the first British automobile propelled by an internal combustion engine, and he founded the Lanchester Motor Company in 1899.

Lanchester's choice was F. M. Green, who was then employed by the Daimler Company. At that time Lanchester appears to have had connections and influence with practically every motor-manufacturing concern in Britain, and he seems to have had no difficulty in arranging Green's transfer in the national interest. Accordingly the new Chief Engineer took up his new duties at Farnborough in January 1910.†

The impact of O'Gorman upon the Balloon Factory, and later upon British aviation generally, was so great that history has not done justice to the contribution of his lieutenant. In the latter years of the last century the Balloon Factory's workshops – primitive and ill-equipped though they may have been by modern standards – had been Colonel Templer's pride and joy. So much was this so that with almost unanimous approval at the time he provided an engineering repair-and-maintenance service for practically the

---

* Frederick William Lanchester (1868–1946) was a member of the Advisory Committee for Aeronautics from 1909 to 1920. He shares with Professor Ludwig Prandtl (1875–1953) of Göttingen the credit for independent discovery of the theory of circulation, which is the basis of all later work on the lift of an aeroplane wing. In addition to his practical contributions to automobile engineering, he found time to write numerous books and papers on engineering, mathematics, warfare and aviation theory, all being subjects he treated with great originality and, some would say, almost to the point of eccentricity.

† The official title of F. M. Green was 'Engineer in charge of Design'; but in referring to him as 'Chief Engineer' I have used the most realistic modern equivalent.

Frederick Michael Green (b. 1882), or Major F. M. Green as he later came to be widely known, had already had a good engineering training when he joined the Daimler Company in 1904. In 1917, after seven years at Farnborough, he became Chief Engineer to Armstrong-Siddeley Motors and later also to Sir W. G. Armstrong Whitworth Aircraft Ltd. Major F. M. Green must not be confused with Gustavus Green mentioned earlier (Chapter 10, Section 7).

whole of Aldershot Command.* In the few years preceding 1909, however, the engineering standards had declined considerably, and by 1909, according to some accounts, the workshops had been reduced almost to a shambles. In token of this, it is only necessary to reflect upon the chronic unserviceability of the various airship engines as already recounted, and even more upon the unreliability of petrol pipes, tanks, driving belts, and all the paraphernalia that goes with any mechanical system.

F. M. Green changed all this. How he did so has never been clearly stated, and he has made few, if any, claims on his own behalf. What is certain is that his authority was accepted without question by all who worked under him, and in some almost mystical way he provided an inspiration for good work that was rivalled only by that of his chief. Curious though it may seem, O'Gorman never paid much open tribute to his Chief Engineer. Papers written in his old age, however, have come to light in which O'Gorman acknowledges his debt to F. M. Green and reveals a kind of nostalgic regret that he did not do more for him.†

O'Gorman's entry into the more scientific aspects of aeronautics was a more gradual process so far as recruitment was concerned than that for specialized engineering. For a time, perhaps, he himself met much of the demand for scientific knowledge; and, although there was at all times a steady improvement in scientific strength within the Establishment, he did not fully attain his objective until war came in 1914. Then, as is well-known, he built up an organization of brilliant young scientists that was to prove itself unique in history.

One of O'Gorman's earliest ventures in enlightened recruitment was of a somewhat different kind to those just discussed, and for those times quite revolutionary. On Green's advice, O'Gorman engaged a young pioneer aviator, Geoffrey de Havilland,‡ who had already made a somewhat imperfect but promising aeroplane to his own design. Green had known de Havilland when he was a student-apprentice at the engineering firm Willans and Robin-

---

* For this good service, it will be remembered (see Chapter 3: 'The last years of Colonel Templer'), Colonel Templer was virtually reprimanded and instructed to confine his mechanical interests to balloons.

† O'Gorman was a forthright generous person, and there is no doubt that concern with his own tempestuous affairs was the cause of any reticence on his part. The full story of O'Gorman and the Royal Aircraft Factory – as the Balloon Factory came to be called – has yet to be written, and only sufficient is given here to show the general trend of history and to round-off the present Volume.

‡ Geoffrey de Havilland (1882–1966) later became Sir Geoffrey de Havilland, and was perhaps best known as the founder and President of the de Havilland Aircraft Company. See also his autobiography *Sky Fever* (1961), and *D.H.* by C. Martin Sharpe (1960).

son of Rugby, and so could speak with first-hand knowledge of the new recruit. The engagement was officially authorized, so far as can be judged, in December 1910, and with the authority came also permission to purchase de Havilland's aeroplane for £400.*

The appointment of de Havilland was symbolic; for he was an aeroplane man from the beginning and never seems to have been interested in lighter-than-air machines. It is indeed one of the paradoxes of history that the original plans for the Advisory Committee for Aeronautics, as well as those for re-organization of the Balloon Factory, were prepared when the airship was officially and generally regarded as the aerial weapon of the future. Yet the implementation of these plans took place in what was manifestly the age of the aeroplane, the cuckoo bird which was soon to throw its rival right out of the nest.

O'Gorman was keen on aeroplanes from the beginning of his reign at Farnborough; and, although the Balloon Factory continued to design and manufacture airships until the Royal Navy took over the airship work in 1914, it is the aeroplane work that is now remembered. For the early story of aeroplanes at Farnborough, which is the subject of Volume II of this History, we have to go back to 17 December 1903, when the Wright Brothers made the world's first powered heavier-than-air flights. This is the starting point for the Farnborough aeroplane story, for it was Colonel Capper's friendship with the Wright Brothers and his study of their work that led to the first successful aeroplane flight in Britain, made by S. F. Cody on Farnborough Common on 16 October 1908.

On Mervyn O'Gorman's appointment as Superintendent, Colonel Capper reverted to his single post as Commandant of the Balloon School, and continued to fly airships for a time. After about a year, however, he decided to accept promotion to substantive Colonel, which necessitated his leaving his Farnborough post. He thereafter had a distinguished career as a soldier, without any aeronautical complications, and became a Major-General in the First World War. He did not lose his interest in ballooning, however, and the story is told of how he watched his Division attack in the Battle of the Somme from the basket of a captive balloon. His pioneer work as an airship pilot did not remain unrecognized, moreover, for when pilots' certificates were first issued by the British Aero Club in 1911, Colonel Capper was awarded Airship Pilot's Licence No. 1.

* This information is from Sir Geoffrey himself in 1943. The precise date of engagement seems a little uncertain. Young men of de Havilland's stamp were too busy making history to be concerned with the writing of it.

Appendix A

Special notes on some auxiliary historical sources

So far as is practicable the present History is derived directly from original documents, that is to say, contemporary reports, correspondence and official minutes, but also including Press reports and published work written at or close to the time of occurrence of the events described. This appendix deals primarily with other potential sources of information that for one reason or another call for special comment. With the possible exception of the *R.E.C. Extracts,* none of the items discussed below is a primary source that falls strictly within any of the categories enunciated above.

I. THE R.A.E. CHRONICLES

What I have for convenience of reference called *The R.A.E. Chronicles* comprise a brief synopsis of early R.A.E. history that was once included in an Air Ministry file numbered RU 9089. Only a *copy* has survived intact, having been preserved by R.A.E. Library.

Authorship is attributed to one Halcott Glover, about whom little is known. He accomplished the work in 1918 and 1919 while employed in the Establishment, specifically for the use of Sir Walter Raleigh in the preparation of Vol. I of *The War in the Air,* which was published in 1922.

Glover's work has the great advantage that it was prepared from actual documents found in official files, without any reliance having to be placed on peoples' memories. Glover shows, moreover, a praiseworthy respect for precise dates and rarely tries to improve upon the available evidence by his own surmising.

Although full use is made of the *Chronicles* in the present History, considerable caution has been necessary in deciding what to accept as positive truth. Glover was handicapped by a somewhat limited knowledge of the subjects he was treating. He was restricted, moreover, to those documents which had remained in R.A.E.'s possession, and since his time a great many other documents have been discovered which he had never seen. Finally, the synopsis was intended to be read with the parent documents close at

259

hand for reference when required. These were sent along as appendices to the synopsis, but most of them have disappeared, and have almost certainly been destroyed. It is ironical that the mere mention of a document in the *Chronicles* is virtually a certificate of destruction, while anything Glover happened to miss is likely to have survived.

2. R.E.C. EXTRACTS

The full title of these is *Extracts from the Proceedings of the Royal Engineer Committee*. They are treated for the purpose of the present History as authentic contemporary documents, and cover the aeronautical activities of the Royal Engineers from 1871 to 1909. The extracts were issued by the School of Military Engineering, Chatham; originally for 'Official use only'.

3. PROFESSIONAL PAPER – *Sir Charles M. Watson*

The full title of this paper is 'Military Ballooning in the British Army'. It was a contribution to Volume 28 of a series of volumes published by the Royal Engineers Institute under the general title *Professional Papers of the Royal Engineers*, and this particular volume appeared in 1902. Sir Charles Watson's paper provides the most authentic and most complete account of British military ballooning up to the beginning of the South African war. Sir Charles wrote with first-hand aeronautical experience, having been for a period in full command of all military ballooning in Britain. Owing to the date on which it was written, however, this *Professional Paper* provides only introductory material for the present History.

4. R.A.E. HISTORICAL SUMMARY

This is an official publication issued in 1947 under the title *A Historical Summary of the Royal Aircraft Factory and its Antecedents: 1878–1918*. The authors are given as S. Child and C. F. Caunter, and the publication is registered as R.A.E. Report No. Aero 2150. I have not made use of this paper since it conflicts with many of my own findings derived from authentic original documents. Reference is made to it on occasion, however, owing to the influence it has had on a number of published histories.

5. EARLY MILITARY AERONAUTICS – P. W. L. Broke-Smith

This work by the late Brigadier P. W. L. Broke-Smith, under its full title 'The History of Early British Military Aeronautics', has come to be regarded as the classic work on the more military aspects of early Farnborough history. It was published in instalments in *The Royal Engineers Journal* for March, June and September 1952.

Brigadier Broke-Smith had special knowledge of balloons in South Africa through his personal acquaintance with most of the British commanders, and he also had special knowledge of man-lifting kites through operating them in 1905 with the Balloon Sections, though his technical understanding seems to have been rudimentary for a professional Royal Engineer. Apart from such special knowledge, he is not used as a primary source of factual information, since this is now available in original documents to which the Brigadier does not appear to have had access. Perhaps his most valuable contribution to aeronautical history is to be found in his commentaries on policy and general trends.

6. OFFICIAL R.E. HISTORY

The full title of this important work is *The History of the Corps of Royal Engineers*. New volumes of this are produced at long intervals by different authors. Those of present interest are:

> Volume II (1888), by Major-General Whitworth Porter.
> Volume III (1915), by Colonel Sir Charles M. Watson.
> Volume IV (1952), by Brigadier-General W. Baker Brown.

These volumes are not, in general, used as a source of aeronautical history, but for the accounts given of the constitution of the British Army and the special responsibilities of the Royal Engineers.

7. NOTES ON AIRSHIPS – Lieutenant P. E. Crosson

Mr P. E. Crosson joined the Balloon Factory, then at Aldershot, in 1896 and stayed until he retired as Workshop Superintendent at the R.A.E. in 1950. As Lieutenant Crosson he compiled in 1919 some notes on the Farnborough airships. These were, it is believed, intended for the Air Historical Branch of the Air Ministry.

The notes indicate that a tremendous amount of original work was accomplished by Colonel Templer and his team which was never properly recorded. Unfortunately, Lieutenant Crosson appears to have relied largely upon memory and there are indications in places of conflict with documentary records. The testimony is used mainly to provide realistic detail within a framework of history established elsewhere.

I am indebted to Mr Crosson for letting me have his 1919 writings, as well as personal consultations.

8. LIGHTER-THAN-AIR – A. F. Insoll

Not much is known about A. F. Insoll beyond his having been an Observer-Officer during the 1914–18 war. In 1919, or thereabouts, he was commis-

sioned to collect information about Farnborough airships for the Air Historical Branch. His findings were submitted in a carefully-written document
entitled *Lighter-than-Air*.

There is much useful material in this work, which needs, however, to be
checked against other sources whenever possible since there are a few
indisputable errors. He says, for example, that *Nulli Secundus I* was fitted
with ballonets – which is absurd – and then contradicts himself in a tabular
summary by saying that the airship had no ballonet at all.

I am indebted to Mr L. G. Seed and the Public Record Office for discovery
of the Insoll papers.

9. MEMOIRS (AIRSHIPS) – Wing Commander C. M. Waterlow R.N.

C. M. Waterlow was posted as a Second Lieutenant to the Balloon School at
Farnborough on 18 October 1906, and thereafter his life was dedicated to
airships until he was killed at Cranwell on 25 July 1917 through being yanked
into the air by an airship that he was handling from below. While at Farnborough he acquired first-hand experience of the early military airships, and
was seconded to the Royal Naval Air Service for airship work on 1 July 1914,
reaching the rank of Wing Commander R.N. in August 1916.

It was in 1916 that he began work on a history of British military airships,
but he had not got much further than *Nulli Secundus II* when he was killed.
Thirty years or so later his notes were collected and edited by Air Commodore E. D. Masterman and published in 1948 in *The Airship*, Vol. 7,
Nos. 3–6. Waterlow's *Memoirs* have special value because he did not rely
upon memory but had available notes that he had made at the time events
occurred. He also had access to the log books for *Nulli Secundus II* and later
airships.

I am indebted to Lord Ventry for letting me have the Waterlow papers,
and to Mr D. W. King for particulars of Waterlow's service career.

Appendix B

S. F. Cody's inability to read or write

A detailed study of Cody's life and work leads to the firm conclusion that he was unable to read or write. When this conclusion is reached, in fact, a host of anomalies and misunderstandings immediately become comprehensible. At once there is explained why he did not so readily contradict inaccurate stories written about him, and why he kept no exact records of dates that have since become controversial. There is also explained the different hand-writings of his correspondence, and the variety of 'signatures', from a mere typewritten 'S. F. Cody' on an official letter to an expenses claim signed on his behalf by Colonel Capper; and, above all, there is the genuine signature that, through sheer determination, he ultimately accomplished – an enormous 'S. F. Cody', sprawling across the page.

Nevertheless, the fact of his illiteracy appears to have been a strain on many peoples' credibility; and from some points of view this is understandable. Not only was Cody extraordinarily intelligent in his own particular way, but he had a fine colourful style of composition – using an amanuensis – that was almost biblical in its directness and simplicity. Furthermore, there is to be taken into account his success as a playwright, with *Klondyke Nugget* (see Appendix C), not a mere flash in the pan, but one – albeit the best – of a lengthy series.

In these circumstances it has seemed worthwhile to seek fresh evidence by interviewing people who knew Cody intimately. The first man I interviewed was Mr P. E. Crosson, who was employed at the Balloon Factory throughout the entire period of Cody's aeronautical activities, and served for at least a year as an assistant to Cody. He was unshakeable in his testimony that Cody could not read or write, and seemed surprised that I should even question this. Mr Crosson also gave a lucid description of how Cody produced his egregious signature, holding his pen as one would hold a trowel.

Mr R. B. Tudgey was the son of the owner of a local nursery and in later years became a familiar figure as an R.A.E. driver. He described himself as

263

a close friend of Cody, who used to help him with his aeroplane construction work on Laffan's Plain, from 1909 until Cody's death in 1913. When interviewed, Mr Tudgey testified that Cody could not read or write, and later confirmed this in a letter. He also seemed surprised that this had ever been questioned, and described how Cody would bring along a letter or newspaper article and ask to have it read to him.

Mr W. F. Coleman was engaged by Colonel Capper in 1907, and later became principal foreman of woodworkers. He was employed for two years as Cody's assistant, and was lent to Cody for a time after Cody had left the Service. Mr Coleman's testimony was convincing in its simplicity: there was nothing to argue about – Cody was entirely unable to read or write.

Wing Commander J. N. Fletcher was unique as a witness, being the only man whom Cody ever taught to fly. In 1912 it was necessary to have a flying certificate before being accepted into the Royal Flying Corps, though on acceptance the Service paid £75 retrospectively towards the cost of training. Wing Commander Fletcher made a bargain with Cody that, if he passed the test as a result of Cody's tuition, then Cody could have the £75. The Wing Commander, in his testimony, agreed that Cody could not read or write, and described the indelible mental picture he had retained of Cody struggling with his signature to the receipt for the £75, to which he became entitled when his pupil was awarded Aviation Certificate No. 229 on 4 June 1912.

Appendix C

First performance of *The Klondyke Nugget*

The following advertisement appeared in the *Walsall Observer* for 3 December 1898:

ST GEORGE'S THEATRE,

WALSALL.

MONDAY, December 5th, 1898, the World-Renowned

S. F. CODY

in

'THE KLONDYKE NUGGET'

A critical review appeared in the *Walsall Observer* for 10 December 1898:

On Monday evening last was produced, at St George's Theatre, a new spectacular drama, in five acts, entitled, *The Klondyke Nugget*, written by S. F. Cody, the following being the cast:

Sam Deats, alias Geo. Exelby	*Jim Wilson* Mr Cecil Wallis
Mr S. F. Cody	*Judge Matherson* Mr Arthur Moreton
Joe Smith Mr Duncan McRae	*Steve Grey* Mr Walter H. Clacton
Waco Mr Edward Leroy	*Captain of Emigrant Train*
Bill Sykes Mr Fred Arnold	Mr Geo. Leigh
Tom Lee Mr Fred F. Allen	*Raven* Mr Harry Brighter
Ted Lee Mr Leon Cody	*Usher* Mr Ben Hart
Vivian Lee Mr Vivian Cody	*Henri* Mr Albert Freeman
Dr O'Donohue Mr Charles Mawson	*Nigger Beggar* Mr Albert Blackmore
Nellie Miss Florrie Archer	*Rosie* Mrs Lela Cody

The play purports to be a realistic presentment of life in the Klondyke gold regions, of which district the author has had some personal experience. The drama is full of highly sensational incidents, and affords opportunities for the introduction of some very effective scenery and for the Messrs Cody to exhibit their skill as crack shots; while the performances of some trained horses lend further aid to the exciting situations of the play. The story deals with the love affairs of Joe Smith and Rosie Lee and the machinations of the arch-villain, Sam Deats, who, inspired by jealousy, executes various evil plots for the destruction and ruin of the hero and heroine. Needless to say, these plots are all frustrated and the play ends happily by the union of the lovers and the death of Sam. As Sam Deats Mr S. F. Cody plays with much force, and gives a picturesque personality to the part. Mr Duncan McRae makes a capital Joe Smith, and Mrs Lela Cody is well placed as Rosie. Messrs Edward Leroy, Fred Arnold, Leon and Vivian Cody, and Chas Mawson also contribute good work; while the other members of the company are sufficiently capable. Altogether the play forms an acceptable addition to the list of sensational American dramas.

Note: I am indebted to the Borough Librarian of Walsall for the discovery of these notices.

Appendix D

The first Farnborough wind-tunnel

According to the *R.E.C. Extracts*, the Royal Engineer Committee, on 6 June 1906, allotted to Colonel Capper the sum of £50 for building a wind-tunnel, referred to as 'apparatus for testing air resistances'. By 12 December 1906, Colonel Capper was able to report completion of the construction.

The following is the full description of the wind-tunnel as submitted by Colonel Capper to the Committee.

DESCRIPTION OF AIR TUNNEL – BALLOON FACTORY

This air tunnel was constructed for testing fans [propellers] in still air and in an air blast, and also for testing air resistance.

It consists of a light timber framework, rectangular in section, 6 ft. 6 in. by 6 ft. 6 in. inside measurement, and 55 ft. long; the inside of the walls and roof are covered with canvas to which glazed paper is pasted so as to form a smooth surface offering least resistance to the wind: the floor is planked. The nose of the tunnel is contracted to a circular opening, 4 ft. in diameter, a 4 ft. Blackman Air Propeller Ventilating Fan, driven by an electric motor, is fixed in this opening: a wire screen for breaking up the blast is fixed 4 ft. in front of the fan.

The tunnel is entered through a glazed door about the middle. A continuous glazed window runs the whole length of the tunnel, so that experiments can be watched from the outside.

An apparatus, which can easily be removed, for testing the thrust of fans [propellers] has been erected in the tunnel; the fan [propeller] shaft is driven by an electric motor placed outside the tunnel: the revolutions can be read through a glazed window. A switchboard with voltmeter, ammeter, resistances, etc. controls the speed of the fan shaft.

A diagram of the interior of the tunnel, looking towards the nose, is on Plate XI [i.e. Fig. H, page 186]: the fan testing apparatus is shown in the foreground.

Appendix E

Weight analysis for *Nulli Secundus II*

Taken from *R.E.C. Extracts*, Appendix I to the Year 1908, Part 2.

	lbs	kilograms
Envelope and valves	1,221	555
Small balloon	33	15
Silk cover [main]	332	151
Silk cover connecting envelope to understructure	35	16
Rigging frame to envelope	34	15
Guy ropes	73	33
Girder with rudder planes etc.	277	126
Front plane and supports	48	22
Engine frame, car, radiators, propellers, etc.	944	429
Rigging to car	30	14
Petrol tanks	24	11
	3,051	1,387

Notes from *R.E.C. Extracts*:

(a) The total tare weight given above was practically the same as in 1907.

(b) The envelope had stretched a little and with the small balloon the total lifting capacity amounted to 3,950 lbs (1,800 kg).

(c) The petrol tanks were smaller [i.e. than for *Nulli Secundus I*] and allowed a total of 12 gallons (55 litres) being carried, or sufficient for $3\frac{1}{2}$ to 4 hours run.

Appendix F

Glossary

SOME AERONAUTICAL TERMS USED IN THE FIRST DECADE OF THE TWENTIETH CENTURY

In the early years of the present century the language of aeronautics was developing in parallel with the actual aerial objects themselves, and not all the terms used have retained their earlier meanings. As a general rule the meaning of each word used in this Volume is made clear in the text; but the following brief glossary may at times prove useful. Words in italics are to be taken in their earlier sense, while modern usage is denoted by roman print.

Aeroplane	1 Aeroplane or airplane 2 Cody kite (used mainly by Cody) 3 Any aerodynamic lifting surface
Aileron	Aileron; a small 'winglet' or extension of a main wing used for controlling roll; roll-control device distinct from wing-warping (*q.v.*). Note: the word 'aileron' was not much used in Britain in the early years
Airship or *air-ship*	1 Airship (see also Balloon) 2 Any self-propelled aircraft; airship *or* aeroplane; aerial vehicle
Balloon	1 Balloon 2 Balloon *or* airship; any lighter-than-air aircraft 3 Envelope of a balloon or airship
Dirigible Balloon	Airship
Elongated Balloon	1 Balloon of ovoid or near-cylindrical shape instead of spherical 2 Kite-balloon 3 Airship
Navigable Balloon	Airship
Steerable Balloon	Airship

Appendices

Dirigible	Airship. Note: some people still speak of a dirigible, meaning an airship
Fan	Propeller; airscrew
Flyer	Aeroplane or airplane. (Used frequently by Wright Brothers and several other pioneers, and occasionally used by Cody)
Kite	1 Kite 2 Aeroplane or airplane (colloquial usage in later years)
Power Kite	Aeroplane or airplane (used by Cody and others)
Plane	1 Plane; pair of opposed wings, port and starboard 2 Any more-or-less flat aerodynamic lifting surface
Balancing Plane	Aileron; separate aerodynamic surface for control of roll
Steering Plane	Aileron; separate aerodynamic surface for control of roll. Note: this was a misused and misleading term
Rudder	1 Rudder *or* elevator, i.e. device for steering an airship or aeroplane either up-and-down or right-and-left 2 Rudder, i.e. device specifically for steering horizontally (later meaning)
Head rudder	Forward elevator, i.e. pitch controller placed ahead of main wings of an aeroplane or at the front of an airship
Wing-warping	Opposed twisting of opposite wings to control roll of an aeroplane

270

Index

Military rank or civilian status is quoted as most appropriate to the period under consideration. Later distinctions are given in parenthesis when they might assist identification or have historic interest.

The following well-recognized abbreviations are used freely:

R.A.E. : Royal Aircraft Establishment
R.A.F. : Royal Air Force
R.N. : Royal Navy
R.E. : Royal Engineer(s)

The following abbreviations are sometimes used when the meaning is clear from the context:

R.E.C. : Royal Engineer Committee
S.A.W. : South African War
N.P.L. : National Physical Laboratory

Numbers refer to pages, and direct references to footnotes are indicated by the appropriate footnote symbol.

Index

Index

Index